THE X FILES™

THE AGENTS,
THE BUREAU AND THE SYNDICATE
VOLUME 1

TITAN

WWW.TITAN-COMICS.COM

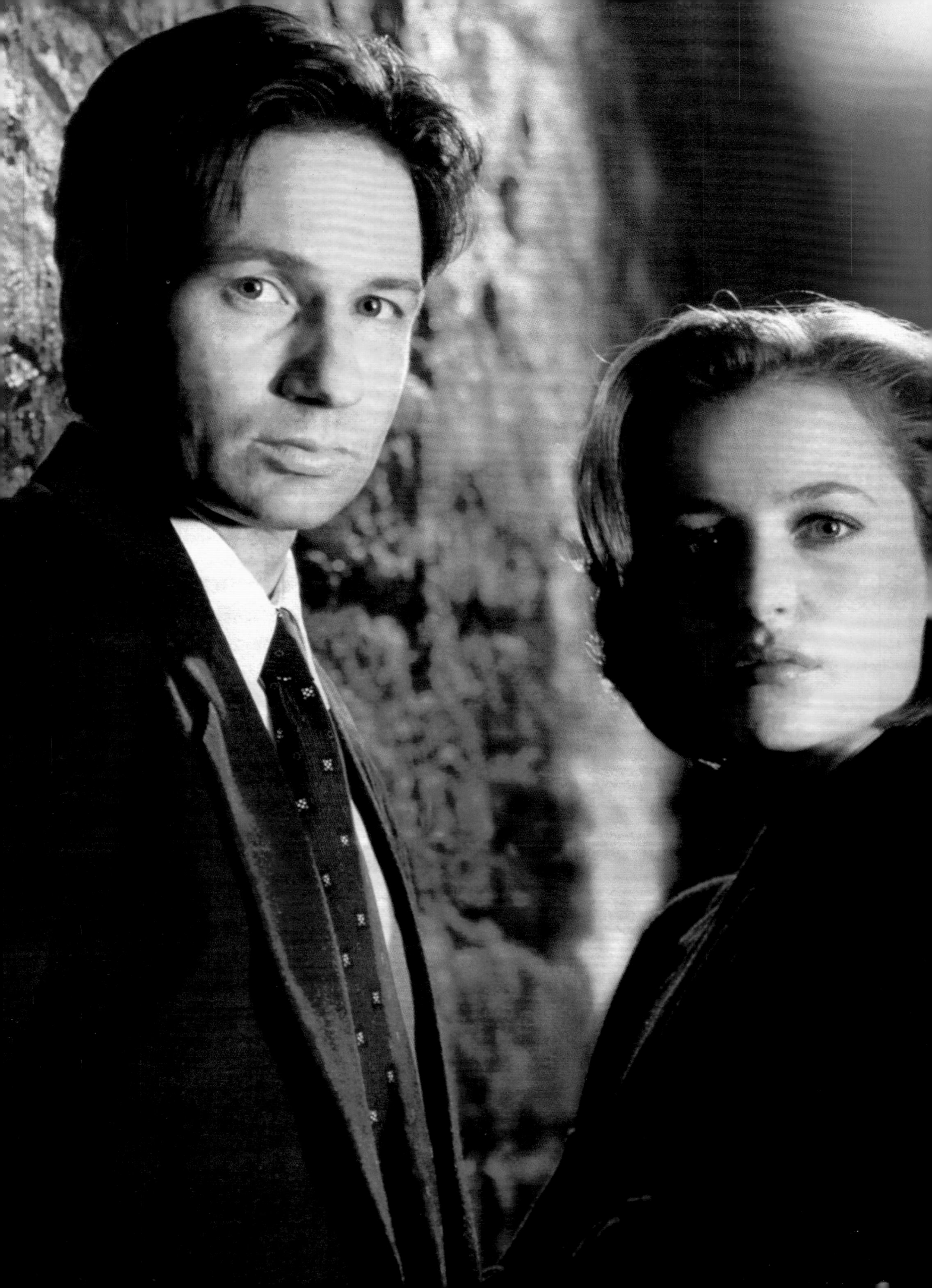

THE (X) FILES

MULDER: "SORRY, NOBODY DOWN HERE BUT THE FBI'S MOST UNWANTED."
SCULLY: "AGENT MULDER, I'M DANA SCULLY. I'VE BEEN ASSIGNED TO WORK WITH YOU."
MULDER: "OH, REALLY… I WAS UNDER THE IMPRESSION YOU WERE SENT TO SPY ON ME."

WITH THESE FATEFUL WORDS, ONE OF THE MOST ICONIC PARTNERSHIPS IN GENRE TV MET FOR THE FIRST TIME. TWO AGENTS, DEDICATED TO THE PURSUIT OF THE TRUTH, BUT FROM DIFFERENT PERSPECTIVES: MULDER, THE ULTIMATE OPTIMIST — ALWAYS WANTING TO BELIEVE IN THE SUPERNATURAL AND EXTRATERRESTRIAL, AND SCULLY, THE ULTIMATE SKEPTIC (AT LEAST TO BEGIN) — CONVINCED THAT EVERYTHING COULD BE EXPLAINED BY SCIENCE. PUT THE TWO TOGETHER AND THE RESULT WAS A DYNAMIC, ENTERTAINING PARTNERSHIP — WHOSE EPIC QUEST FOR THE TRUTH KEPT VIEWERS ENTHRALLED FOR NINE YEARS.

NOW, IN THIS FIRST SPECIAL COLLECTION CELEBRATING ONE OF THE MOST INFLUENTIAL SHOWS OF THE NINETIES, THE BEST FEATURES, INTERVIEWS AND PROFILES FROM *THE OFFICIAL X-FILES MAGAZINE* SHINE A FLASHLIGHT INTO THE DARKEST CORNERS OF THE FBI ONCE AGAIN. REVISIT THE PLETHORA OF AGENTS WHO HAVE HELPED (AND HINDERED) MULDER AND SCULLY OVER THE YEARS; WALK THE CORRIDORS OF POWER TO WITNESS THE INNER WORKINGS OF THE FBI; AND MEET THE SHADOWY SYNDICATE, INTENT ON CONCEALING THE TRUTH OF THEIR GLOBAL CONSPIRACY AT ALL COSTS.

THE X-FILES
THE OFFICIAL COLLECTION
VOLUME ONE
ISBN: 9781782763710

PUBLISHED BY TITAN
A DIVISION OF TITAN
PUBLISHING GROUP LTD.,
144 SOUTHWARK STREET,
LONDON SE1 0UP.

THE OFFICIAL X-FILES
MAGAZINE
1993-2002.

NO PART OF THIS PUBLICATION
MAY BE REPRODUCED, STORED
IN A RETRIEVAL SYSTEM, OR
TRANSMITTED, IN ANY FORM OR
BY ANY MEANS, WITHOUT THE
PRIOR WRITTEN PERMISSION OF
THE PUBLISHER.

A CIP CATALOGUE RECORD FOR
THIS TITLE IS AVAILABLE FROM
THE BRITISH LIBRARY.

FIRST EDITION JANUARY 2016
10 9 8 7 6 5 4 3 2 1

PRINTED IN CHINA.
TITAN.

Editor
Natalie Clubb

Senior Art Editor
Rob Farmer

Contributing Editor
Martin Eden

Art Director
Oz Browne

Acting Studio Manager
Selina Juneja

Publishing Manager
Darryl Tothill

Publishing Director
Chris Teather

Operations Director
Leigh Baulch

Executive Director
Vivian Cheung

Publisher
Nick Landau

ACKNOWLEDGMENTS
Titan Would Like to Thank...

The cast and crew of *The X-Files* for giving up their time to be interviewed, and Josh Izzo and Nicole Spiegel at Fox for all their help in putting this volume together.

THE AGENTS

16

CONTENTS

C O N T

36

66

THE BUREAU

100

THE SYNDICATE

THE SHOW

E N T S

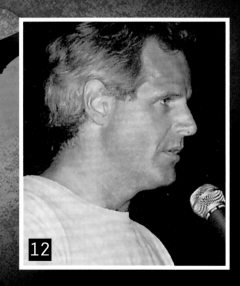

12

114

CONTENTS

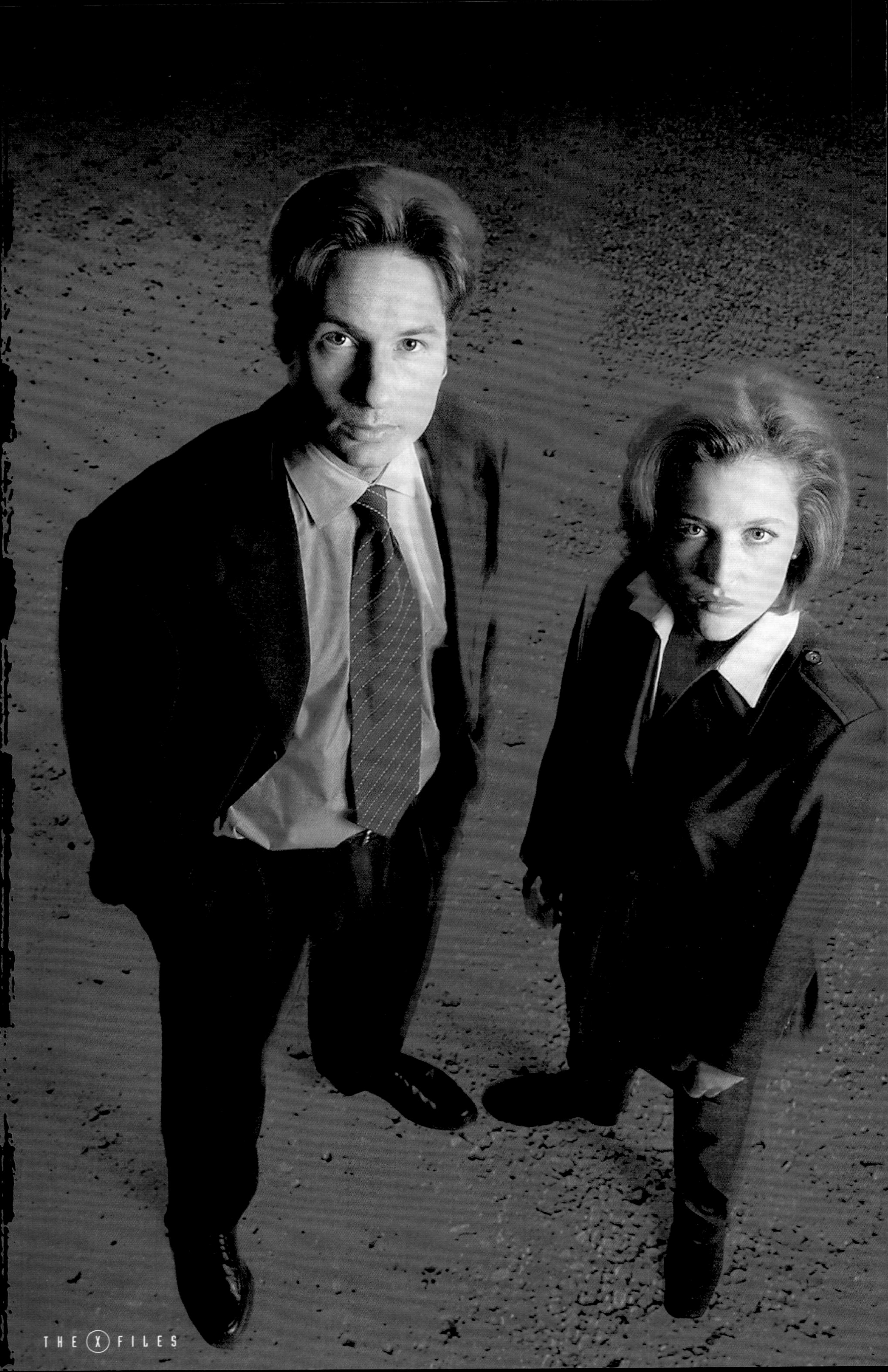

Deep Impact

FROM ITS POLISHED, MOVIE-LIKE PILOT TO WORLD-WIDE HIT, OVER THE COURSE OF THE LAST DECADE, THE X-FILES HAS UNDENIABLY CHANGED THE FACE OF TV. KATE ANDERSON EXPLORES THE PHENOMENON

We knew the day would come. It was inevitable. And now, after the series finale on 19 May 2002, *The X-Files* TV series is no more. After nine seasons and 202 episodes, *The X-Files* has reached the end. And while Mulder and Scully's alter egos, David Duchovny and Gillian Anderson seem certain to continue their careers on the big screen, *The X-Files* will go down in TV history as a show that popularized the science fiction genre; no longer was sci-fi perceived as 'nerd TV'; *The X-Files* made sci-fi cool.

Of course, no one knew whether the show would even last a season, yet alone nine years. In those early days, even David Duchovny doubted the show's longevity. After all, who'd have thought a show about two F.B.I. agents chasing U.F.O.s and government cover-ups, week in, week out, had staying power. If the truth be told, it was only mainly word-of-mouth and positive critical response that kept the show alive and convinced Fox to pick up the series for a second season. More often than not, similar themed shows counted their blessings if they survived a whole season.

But right from the pilot episode, it

was clear that there was so much more to *The X-Files* than just flying saucers and little green men. Here we had an episode that looked and played more like a feature film than the pilot of a TV show. Visually stunning and tightly written with a moody style to complement its dark nature, as pilot episodes go it was in a league of its own. From the teaser sequence depicting an alien abduction to the closing moments in

the Pentagon vault, we were privy to the origin of a show that would inspire a generation and spawn more than its fair share of wannabes (see boxout). Two other factors in the Pilot would prove to be an integral part of turning *The X-Files* into a TV phenomenon – one Fox William Mulder and Dana Katherine Scully.

Here we had two of the youngest – not to mention sexiest – F.B.I. agents ever seen on TV. No, scratch that; ever seen, period. Who can forget the moment in the pilot when a scantily-clad Scully asked Mulder to examine some strange marks on her back? Okay, so they turned out to be nothing more than mosquito bites. But the fact of the matter is, in that instance, so began the longest flirtation in TV history; a flirtation that the show used to keep the series fresh, exciting and always one step ahead of the competition. Their will-they-won't-they relationship captured the hearts and imagination of millions of viewers across the globe.

As we know now, the fact that Mulder and Scully didn't end up in a passionate clinch in the Pilot was essential to the plot and essential to the establishment of Mulder and Scully's relationship. Series creator Chris

CLONING THE X-FILES

THE POPULARITY OF *THE X-FILES* PROMPTED A PLETHORA OF SCI-FI AND SUPERNATURAL SHOWS, ALL HOPING TO COPY ITS SUCCESS. SOME WERE PRETTY GOOD IN THEIR OWN RIGHT; OTHERS STARTED OFF POORLY BUT EVENTUALLY FOUND THEIR OWN VOICE. AND THEN THERE WERE THOSE THAT JUST SEEMED TO RIDE ON THE COAT TAILS OF *THE X-FILES'* SUCCESS AND THE CURRENT INTEREST IN ALL THINGS PARANORMAL...

BAYWATCH NIGHTS — A SPIN-OFF OF THE BEACH-BASED SERIES CHANGED ITS FOCUS AND SAW DAVID HASSELHOFF AND CO. INVESTIGATING CASES WITH A FLAVOR OF THE PARANORMAL.

CHARMED — THREE SISTERS WITH A SECRET; THEY ARE POWERFUL BUT GOOD WITCHES WHO BAND TOGETHER TO FULFIL AN ANCIENT WITCHCRAFT PROPHECY.

DARK SKIES — THIS 1960s CONSPIRACY-BASED DRAMA FOLLOWED THE EXPLOITS OF A YOUNG IDEALISTIC KENNEDY-ERA POLITICAL AIDE.

FIRST WAVE — ONE MAN ALONE CAN SAVE THE EARTH FROM A HOSTILE TAKE-OVER BY ALIENS.

FREAKYLINKS — STRANGE PHENOMENA ARE IDENTIFIED AND SOLVED BY INTERNET-SAVVY INVESTIGATORS

MILLENNIUM — DARKER, CREEPIER SISTER SHOW OF *THE X-FILES*.

NOWHERE MAN — A MAN WHO HAS HIS IDENTITY ERASED BY A SECRET ORGANISATION SEEKS TO DISCOVER THE TRUTH AND FIND THOSE RESPONSIBLE FOR HIS PREDICAMENT.

THE OTHERS — A GROUP OF SIX PSYCHIC INDIVIDUALS WHO HAVE THE ABILITY TO SEE THE OTHER SIDE, TOGETHER WITH A PROFESSOR OF MYTHOLOGY AND FOLKLORE, MEET TO DISCUSS THEIR PARANORMAL ADVENTURES AND FIGURE OUT HOW THEY CAN USE THEIR GIFTS TO HELP PEOPLE.

POLTERGEIST: THE LEGACY — A SECRET AND ANCIENT SOCIETY LEADS THE BATTLE AGAINST EVIL FORCES.

THE PRETENDER — FOLLOWS THE EXPLOITS OF A MAN WHO HAS THE ABILITY TO BECOME ANYONE HE WANTS TO BE, ON THE RUN FROM THE NEFARIOUS THINK TANK THAT RAISED HIM.

PROFILER — SAM WATERS, A FORENSIC PSYCHOLOGIST WITH THE F.B.I. VIOLENT CRIMES TASK FORCE, HAS AN UNCANNY ABILITY TO GET INTO THE MIND OF THE KILLER; TO SEE THINGS THROUGH THEIR EYES.

ROSWELL — TEENAGERS FROM OUTER SPACE ATTEMPT TO KEEP THEIR REAL IDENTITIES HIDDEN FROM THE AUTHORITIES

SLEEPWALKERS — A TEAM OF RESEARCHERS INVESTIGATE PEOPLE'S NIGHTMARES BY GOING INTO THEIR DREAM STATE THROUGH CUTTING EDGE TECHNOLOGY.

STRANGE LUCK — THE PROTAGONIST IS CURSED WITH HAVING BOTH LUCKY AND UNLUCKY THINGS HAPPEN TO HIM.

THE VISITOR — ROLAND EMMERICH AND DEAN DEVLIN (THE BRAINS BEHIND *INDEPENDENCE DAY*) MADE THIS SHORT-LIVED SERIES ABOUT A MAN WHO MYSTERIOUSLY DISAPPEARED IN THE BERMUDA TRIANGLE SOME 50 YEARS PREVIOUSLY, TO RE-EMERGE WITH NEW AND ENHANCED SKILLS.

7 DAYS — A TIME-TRAVELING SERIES ABOUT A GOVERNMENT AGENT WHO USES A TIME MACHINE MADE FROM TECHNOLOGY RECOVERED FROM ROSWELL TO JOURNEY BACK IN TIME UP TO SEVEN DAYS.

Carter was adamant that the agents would never consummate their attraction; he knew that the show would die a slow death if he gave in to temptation – and the wishes of network execs. The nature of Duchovny and Anderson's relationship was central to whether the show would work – and the nature of Mulder and Scully's relationship was central to whether people would keep on watching. And the rest of course is history. Mulder and Scully topped poll after poll as the sexiest couple on TV. Internet chat rooms were swamped with fans dissecting Mulder and Scully's relationship. And magazine after magazine ran exclusive photos of the two stars in various states of undress – who could forget that infamous

Rolling Stone 'in bed' cover? And X-philes couldn't get enough.

At the height of the show's popularity, it seemed as though you couldn't go anywhere without seeing Anderson and Duchovny's faces plastered somewhere. Posters, T-shirts, books and magazine covers... *The X-Files* was everywhere. The show had taken on a life of its own. It became more than just a TV show. It became a worldwide phenomenon turning its stars into global icons no less. Mulder and Scully even appeared on an episode of *The Simpsons*!

There's no doubt that the casting of Anderson and Duchovny was the coup of the 1990s and *The X-Files* created interest in the most asexual sexual relationship on TV. But it wasn't just Duchovny and Anderson's onscreen chemistry that made *The X-Files* so popular and successful. In fact, if it hadn't been for the creative genius of Chris Carter, neither Mulder nor Scully would exist.

In 1992, former surfing magazine writer/editor and sitcom writer/producer Carter signed a development deal with Twentieth Century Fox television. Carter had been captivated and scared by the 1971 made-for-TV movie *The Night Stalker* – which spawned a sequel and a TV series – and he wanted to create a series that would evoke a similar reaction in a new generation. And so *The X-Files* was born. And over the past nine years, Carter and his team of writers, directors and producers have delivered some groundbreaking TV. Who can forget the infamous "Home," the first episode (although not the last) to broadcast a warning (on US television, at least) about the show's graphic content before its broadcast? Or the Scully abduction storyline comprising "Duane Barry," "Ascension" and "One Breath"? (Of course, it was Gillian Anderson's real-life pregnancy that provided the need to separate Mulder and Scully. One can only wonder as to what direction the show would have taken if that situation hadn't arisen).

Then there was the exquisitely executed "Memento Mori"; the split-screen "Triangle" (notable for being filmed in letterbox format); the black and white "Post-Modern Prometheus" and *The X-Files*' first real attempt at full-on comedy, "Humbug." But more about that in a moment.

It's thanks to Carter and Co. that we were introduced to some of television's most memorable characters; like the Cigarette-Smoking Man, Pusher and Eugene Victor Tooms. *The X-Files* may have started life as a scary science fiction show, but it soon became apparent

that to label the series as purely science fiction was to not do it justice. In fact, by the end of the third season, *The X-Files* was displaying a talent for all things comedy! And that was largely thanks to the success of Season Two's "Humbug." When the episode was first broadcast in the US back in March 1995, almost 10 million homes tuned in; "Humbug" was a hit with fans and so began *The X-Files*' love affair with comedy. Some of the most rewarding episodes have had their roots in comedy, most notably "War of the Coprophages" and "Jose Chung's 'From Outer Space.'" One thing's for certain, Mulder and Scully knew how to wield a sharp one-liner as good as *Seinfeld* and *Frasier et al.*

By the time Season Three aired, *The X-Files* was well into its stride and Season Four saw the show at the top of its game, producing perhaps the series finest episode, ever – "Memento Mori." By the end of Season Five, production in Vancouver was to switch to Southern California.

The hiatus between Seasons Five and Six also saw *The X-Files* up the ante on the big screen. But success usually carries its own seeds of destruction and by this stage the show that had started out as a cult hit, only

to go mainstream in a big way, was starting to show signs of slowing down and becoming a cult again.

By the time Season Eight came to fruition, David Duchovny had left (albeit making sporadic appearances as Fox Mulder) and the show saw the introduction of a new lead, played by Robert Patrick.

They say you must come full circle to find the truth. And with 19 May, as Season Nine culminated in a two-hour special, that truth was revealed. At time of writing, it's not known whether the finale will tie up all the loose ends – whether it will be a satisfactory conclusion to nine years' worth of exceptional TV – only time will tell. But one thing's for certain, over the course of nine seasons, it's been a rollercoaster of a ride.

The X-Files was without doubt the show of the 1990s. Now we're into a new decade and numerous pretenders for the throne will surely come and go. But it's safe to say that it'll be quite some time before a show comes along that deserves to wear the crown. None of us really want the show to end. Nothing will ever be the same ever again. But all good things *must* come to an end. We should let the show bow out with some grace. We owe it that at least. ●

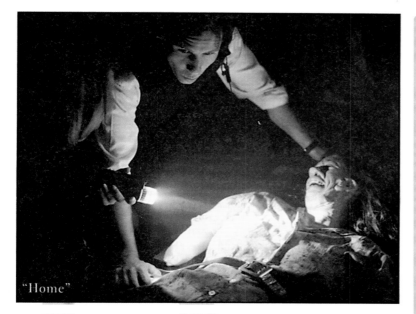

"Home"

"Humbug"

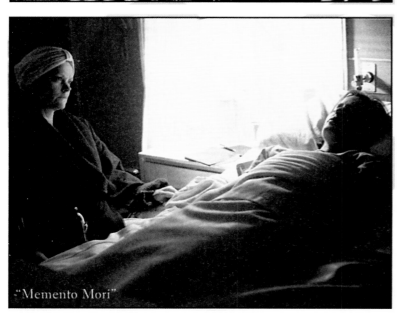

"Memento Mori"

10 REASONS WHY *THE X-FILES* WAS THE GREATEST TV SERIES OF THE 90S

1. CHRIS CARTER – THE GENIUS BEHIND *THE X-FILES* EVOLUTION.

2. TIMING – IN TERMS OF SOCIETY'S GENERAL MISTRUST OF THE GOVERNMENT, *THE X-FILES* COULDN'T HAVE COME ALONG AT A MORE APPROPRIATE TIME.

3. THE SUBTEXT – MULDER AND SCULLY'S WILL-THEY-WON'T-THEY RELATIONSHIP IN MANY WAYS ECLIPSED THE SHOW'S PARANORMAL THEME.

4. DAVID DUCHOVNY AND GILLIAN ANDERSON – THEIR ONSCREEN CHEMISTRY WAS THE MOST TALKED ABOUT OF THE DECADE TURNING THEIR CHARACTERS INTO GLOBAL ICONS.

5. BEHIND THE SCENES – A POOL OF TALENTED WRITERS, DIRECTORS AND PRODUCERS ENSURED THE HIGHEST OF STANDARDS EVER SEEN FOR A WEEKLY TV SERIES. EVERY EPISODE LOOKED AND PLAYED LIKE A MINI FEATURE FILM.

6. BREAKING NEW GROUNDS – *THE X-FILES* WAS RESPONSIBLE FOR CHALLENGING OUR EXPECTATIONS WEEK IN WEEK OUT. ITS INNOVATIVE STORYTELLING METHODS BROUGHT US EPISODES LIKE "HOME," "THE POST-MODERN PROMETHEUS" AND "MEMENTO MORI."

7. DARIN MORGAN – WITH ONE INVENTIVE AND HUGELY FUNNY SCRIPT ("HUMBUG"), DARIN MORGAN ALMOST SINGLE-HANDEDLY REINVENTED THE SHOW.

8. THE COMEDIC ELEMENT – WHO WOULD EVER HAVE IMAGINED THAT AN EARNEST SERIES LIKE *THE X-FILES* COULD DO COMEDY WITH SUCH GUSTO.

9. INTEREST IN U.F.O.s AND THE PARANORMAL – WASN'T IT WHAT THE 1990s WAS ALL ABOUT?

10. STAYING POWER – HOW MANY TV SHOWS – NEVER MIND ONES WITH ROOTS IN SCIENCE FICTION – HAVE WHAT IT TAKES TO KEEP GOING AND PRODUCE CONSISTENTLY GOOD TELEVISION FOR NEAR ON A DECADE? NOT MANY, THAT'S FOR SURE!

MUSINGS OF A TELEVISION-PRODUCING MAN

by Dave Hughes

On 7 February 1997 Chris Carter gave a satellite interview, live from the Vancouver set of *The X-Files*, to an audience of nocturnal X-philes gathered at the National Film Theatre on London's South Bank. The 'Q&A' session followed a pre-satellite screening of Vince Gilligan's "Unruhe", and lasted for approximately one hour, during which time Carter candidly answered questions on a variety of topics. Here, as a record of the event, we present the highlights of the session, in which the questions asked by the audience have been edited for clarity.

What was the original impetus behind the creation of *The X-Files*?

From the beginning – I've made no bones about this – I set out to scare everyone with every episode, each week; every hour of the show is meant to scare the pants off you. But I think if you look at what the heart and soul of the show is, it's very hopeful and optimistic. It's about two people searching for truths and following their passions, and they really are romantic heroes in the literary sense. They are together on a quest, and I think that is really the secret to the success of the show, and less to do with what darkness there is in the show. I believe the same thing's true about my new show, *Millennium*, too: it has a very bright message at its centre which is hope for the future, and I believe the same can be said about *The X-Files*.

Did the success of the show come as a surprise to you?

No-one could have foreseen this success. There are so many truly miraculous things that have made the show what it is. First of all, the chemistry between David [Duchovny] and Gillian [Anderson] accounts for so much of the success of the show, but [also] the number of lucky things: [like] where we would set an episode in Florida, and then we would have six days of perfect blue Florida sunshine here [in Vancouver] in what was really the end of winter, where it's [normally] raining constantly. That luck, it's just one of the many amazing things that have happened on the show. I knock on wood still, and I'm going to here, and I try not to pinch myself.

Can you give us any insight into the original casting of Mulder and Scully?

I had written this script for imaginary characters, Mulder and Scully, and I had a casting director, Randy Stone, who was a big fan of David

Duchovny's. We saw a lot of men for the part, but [Stone] was very high on David, [and] showed me David's films. We brought David in; he read perfectly; it was a 'slam dunk'. With Gillian, it was a little different. We read a lot of women for the part, [but] she came in and I knew immediately she was Scully, even though she was rather dishevelled. She had just moved out of New York [and] she looked a little urban and funky, a little SoHo, and not at all like the Scully you see in *The X-Files*. But I recognised a seriousness and an intensity,

speaker that most of our TVs have, so the sound will be an amazing thing. Storytelling: you want to write for the big screen, and there are certain things that you do differently, and I think we'll be doing all of those. I really want to make it true to the television series, but there are certain small things that I can't do on the series - things I'd like to say, things I'd like to see - that I will be doing on the big screen. After all, there's no other reason to do a movie unless it has some things that the TV series couldn't offer.

Is it true the show is likely to come to an end after the movie?

Not in my mind. I think Fox has a big hit on their hands, and they're not going to let it die so easily. I recently was quoted as saying that I'm going to do the show for five years and that after the fifth year the movie will come out, and that will be the end of my involvement in *The X-Files*. I don't know if that's true or not, but that's as long as my contract is on the show.

What do you think about all *The X-Files* merchandising?

I've been in two minds about it. I was very resistant at first to do much merchandising, because I felt that it worked against the spirit of the show - if it felt like it was over-commercialised [or] over-sold, then it would feel somehow as if it were too 'pop', too mainstream; that it was trying to cash in on a good thing. So I've resisted putting too much stuff out there. Although there *is* a lot of stuff out there, it's kind of hard to find, which I think makes it that much more valuable [and] keeps the show that much more cool and cult, which is what I think of the show now: a very popular cult show.

> "I have had no experience with the paranormal, but i would love to... We want to believe that there is something beyond, something transcendent"

Could you see *The X-Files* continuing if either David or Gillian were to call it a day?

You know, I really don't want to think about it [and] I don't think I will have to think about it. I think that if they left I would anticipate that I might leave, but I don't know. Anything is possible, as you know from the show. It probably could go on without them, but it would have to be seriously re-conceived.

How did the *X-Files/Simpsons* crossover come about?

It was one of those little dreams come true. I'm a big fan of *The Simpsons*, and they just called us one day and asked if they could use Mulder and Scully on an episode, and there was not a moment's hesitation. We said yes; David and Gillian said yes; they sent a script up; we read it; we loved it; two guys from *The Simpsons* came up and worked with David & Gillian directing them for the voices... The amazing thing was how far ahead they were - they didn't finish that episode for about a year after David & Gillian had done the work on it. Mulder and Scully are actually the straight men, if you will, on *The Simpsons* - they don't provide much humour; they seem like sticks in the mud.

and I felt that she could play a young, recent med' school graduate who *did* want to work for the FBI, who *did* want to prove herself, who was ambitious, [and] whose parents may have had a problem with her going to the FBI when they had hoped for a career in medicine. It just seemed to fit.

Now, I brought her into the Fox executives and they didn't see it at all - I think because she wasn't the usual 'television tootsie'. So it took me some convincing and some foot-stomping, but after a while they relented and let me have Gillian. And I think that I feel vindicated and [that] they thank their lucky stars every day.

Where do you look for things that might make good *X-Files* stories?

Anywhere we can find them! It's the question that's often asked: where do the stories come from? They're very hard to find, which I think makes them special. We've done a lot of the big high points in the genre: vampires, werewolves, reincarnation; things like this. The farther the show goes - as we move towards the hundredth episode - these stories are harder and harder to come by. But usually they come out of science journals, magazines, [and] literature, because the stories are really built on the foundation of science. Then, from there, we can speculate, [and] ask the question 'What if?' What if this [scientific reality] was taken to its logical - or *illogical* - extreme? That's how the show works.

Can you give us any clues about the proposed X-Files movie?

I've begun writing it; I'm going to take off next Thursday [13 February] and devote myself to finishing the script, and the plan is to shoot it in June and have it ready to show in the theatres in the spring or fall of 1998.

In what ways will you be looking to expand from the television series?

I think there are things you can do with a feature budget, time and a big screen. I hope to spend more time on some visuals - some elements of storytelling that I couldn't do because of budgeting and scheduling constraints. I look forward to that big screen sound - that's going to be a real plus, and something that will really play to the strengths of the show. Right now all of us see an *X-Files* episode listening to it out of that tiny little

Does this mean that Homer is going to be in *The X-Files* ?

[Laughs] That would be a bit more difficult!

Is it true that Quentin Tarantino was going to direct an episode?

He was scheduled to. He had called me and asked if he could, [because] he's a fan of the show, [but] he is not a member of the Directors' Guild of America [DGA], and because Fox is a signatory to the DGA contracts, they couldn't hire him. The DGA would not allow him to work on our show, so it was a union problem that couldn't be worked through. He has chosen not to be in the union because it allows him to work with non-union crews and, I think, control the costs and budgets of his own movies.

How do you feel about shows that imitate *The X-Files*?

You have to be kind of flattered that people are cashing in, in a way, on your success. I see it more that I've opened the door on a genre that has been around for a long time, but was kind of forgotten. I didn't create it – I just re-investigated it, and it became an opportunity for people to come in and do what I do.

Is it true that William Gibson is writing a script for the show?

Yes, it's in the works. I've worked with him on the story for a while now, [but] then I got very busy and he got very busy... We have planned to get back into the story outline process again together soon, so that episode will be either in the fourth season or, more likely, the beginning of the fifth season.

Will Darren McGavin, star of *The Night Stalker*, ever appear on the show?

Kolchak: The Night Stalker was my original inspiration some 25 or more years ago now, [but] I've actually given up trying to put Darren McGavin on the show. He's either uninterested or unable to do it, which was kind of disappointing for us [because] we had high hopes of getting him on the show. Maybe it'll happen, I don't know; but we've given up for now.

Who is your average viewer?

There's a big following in the science community; there's a big teenage audience... There really is no average viewer, but the demographics tell me that more 18-49 year old men and women watch this show than most shows on American television, which is the big carrot out there because they have the most

money to spend. What I do is what goes between the commercials – that's the name of the game.

Do the difference between American and overseas audiences interest you?

It's difficult to answer the question because I haven't been over to see how people respond to it – although I hear things, I read things, there's a lot of talk on the internet, [and] there are a lot of letters sent to me. The show seems to be very popular with you people over there, and I'm just blessed with that and for that, as is the show.

I don't know if you react or respond to it in any way different than the American audiences, and if you do, I wish somebody could point that out to me, because maybe there's a distinction that I'm missing, and I'd be very curious to see the difference in the show's reception or *perception* on the different continents.

Which are your favourite episodes?

I have many, actually. From the first season, I loved "Ice", "Beyond the Sea", "[The] Erlenmeyer Flask..." Those are three going from the first year. Second year: the "Duane Barry"/"Ascension"/"One Breath" trilogy is very, very good. I loved "Colony" and "End Game" in that season, the two parter, [and] the three parter after that, the "Anasazi"/"Blessing Way"/"Paper Clip." But there are so many episodes also in addition to that: "Humbug", "Clyde Bruckman's Final Repose" – *all* the Darin Morgan episodes are favourites of mine.

We've had some very good episodes this year: I loved "Home", which was a very spooky episode. The writing team of [Glen] Morgan and [James] Wong came back and did a limited engagement of four episodes which turned out very nice for us this year, so it was great to have them back. They kind of replaced Darin Morgan, who's the brother of Glen Morgan; they came in and really filled up that slot. So, I think that those are some of my favourite episodes, but actually I have more favourite episodes than disappointing episodes, although I can more quickly name the disappointing episodes. But don't ask me to do that!

Glen Morgan says the background given for The Cigarette-Smoking Man in "Musings of a Cigarette-Smoking Man" is true, whereas you've said it isn't. Which is it?

Glen Morgan says it's true? It *is* called "Musings of Cigarette-Smoking Man," [and] it's based on his writings, which may or may not be fictional. I think the ambiguity is what drives the interest in that episode, which was very well written and directed by Morgan and Wong. I loved the ambiguity, where you don't know whether it's true or not, and I think that's the way I'll leave it.

Is it true that during the filming of "Memento Mori", David and Gillian improvised a kiss, which you decided to cut out?

You know, it's amazing – considering that I made a decision on that *less than a week ago* – that you actually know that! There was a kiss filmed; it was not scripted; it was not a romantic kiss; it was a warm, friendly kiss. I did not cut it out of the picture for any reason other than I felt that it didn't represent the moment that was being played – I felt that it was beyond or aside from that moment. So it really was an 'executive producer' decision to not show that kiss, [although] there *is* a very warm embrace [and] there *is* a kiss... but it is not a kiss on the lips.

Do you feel pressure from the fans to push the relationship further and further?

No, the fans really don't want me to do that. *You really don't want that to happen!* It really would spoil the dynamic of the show. I think the thing that gives it that classic sexual tension – in this case, a tension between the sexes – is that these two people share a goal and a passion. Sex confuses everything; sex gets in the way; and I believe in this case it would be something we would have to deal with and then move away from, and there would be nowhere else to go. Or we'd have to play it and get into a more tedious and complex kind of relationship that I'm not interested in exploring on this show.

Is there a reason why the episode titles are not shown on screen?

You know, that seemed to be a television convention, and when I came up with the show and the way I wanted to produce it, I didn't want to bow to any conventions – or as few as possible. And it's actually turned out to make the show a little more mysterious, because you have to work hard to find out what the names of those episodes are. If they're not listed in your local TV guide, oftentimes you'll have to go on-line, so it's just one [more] layer of mystery that I think adds to the show. In season two, I actually considered putting those titles on in some kind of mysterious way, where it wasn't quite obvious that they were there, [but] I tried a few tests and just decided to drop the idea all together.

Have there been any unexplained incidents on set?

The catering's often a little bizarre... [Laughs] Not really. We're up in Vancouver, Canada, where nothing too out of the ordinary happens. Actually, it's a wonderful place to be, and we have terrific crews, and I think they'd be too polite to tell us if anything out of the ordinary had ever happened.

What are you planning further down the line, after the *real* millennium?

That will be the end of both shows, as the world comes to an end! [Laughs] I really don't know right now. It's something that I think about. I'd like to get into the world of feature films. I'd like to do more TV series, but there are certain realities I'm dealing with right now, [such as] a lack of really good talented people to help me to do these shows. I'm finding that with two shows, I've scoured the town and the community to try and get people to come and work on these shows, and it's very hard to find people who share your vision and who want to work as hard as you need to work. The way I approach the show is a very 'hands on' and labour-intensive approach.

Has any episode ever had an 'official' response?

I've never actually had a government agency contact me with any concern about how I may have portrayed them, or when I've cast aspersions on any person's job or integrity. Maybe because they all feel so guilty, I'm not so sure! [Laughs] I had two Department of Defense special agents in my office yesterday who came by and wanted to shake my hand – they are big fans of the show – so the official response has usually been that: how can we get something with an autograph on it?

Lately there has been some tension between Mulder and Scully. Is the nature of the relationship going to change as the series goes on?

It ebbs and it flows, I think, to the rhythms of what we are feeling for the characters and about the characters and how the stories are progressing. We know what's coming, [and] we might want to play with some discord leading up to a series of episodes – a short mini-arc or something like that. I think we

feel those rhythms, and hopefully you feel them too. So, we're not going to go with anything more specific than a sort of writers' instinct.

How important is the music to you?

It's *extremely* important. Mark Snow is one of the stars of the show – he's a storyteller in his own right, [and] he gives the symphonic subtext and plays the moods and emotions so well. His scores are always best when they are actually least [obvious], and I think sometimes we've had too much music in the show lately, [which] is something I am very particular about, and every week I go over and listen to the music before it's put on the show, and work with Mark closely, so it's something that's very important to me and to the show.

One final question: does the series reflect your own views on the paranormal?

The answer is no. I really like that photo on Mulder's wall: I Want To Believe. I have had no experience with the paranormal, but I would love to. Since the death of my mother, I would love to see her return, to see her ghostly image at the foot of my bed; I would love to be in the desert or the hills or the mountains some night and see something I couldn't explain, [like] a UFO. I think it is tantamount to a religious experience, and it is really what we're all looking for: something that is beyond the mundane, temporal world we live in. We want to believe that there is something beyond, something transcendent. And I think that is what drives *The X-Files* and possibly *Millennium*, though not quite as much. It's actually better to be a sceptic and write these shows, because I think that it grounds the show. I think that my scepticism has been a good influence on the show; if I was an out-and-out believer, the show would be a little bit different and a little more... *unreal.*

With thanks to the National Film Theatre and Sky Television.

The X-Files **helped transform David Duchovny from an up-and-coming young actor into an international star**

DAVID IS
GOLIATH

BY ANNABELLE VILLANUEVA

G-man Fox Mulder was in the hospital with a grievous head wound. But the man who's played Mulder for several years, David Duchovny, doesn't seem bothered by the character's ill health. During breaks in filming, he sits near the rear of St. Mary Medical Center in Bakersfield, Calif., where the production is on location, still wearing his white hospital gown and head bandage costume while reading magazines or talking with new bride Téa Leoni via cell phone.

Shooting a scene where Mulder is visited by Walter Skinner and the Lone Gunmen, a hospital priest inadvertently interrupted the crew by delivering the morning prayer over an intercom. Duchovny suddenly leapt up, tearing the

gauze from his head and screaming, "I'm cured! I'm cured!" as the rest of the cast and crew dissolved into laughter.

The laid-back behavior and levity are characteristic of Duchovny's dryly self-effacing humor: It's well-known that the actor has no qualms about poking fun at his sex-symbol status by wearing teensy-weensy crimson Speedos on-screen. Of course, the casualness shouldn't be misunderstood—Duchovny takes Mulder, along with the rest of his acting, very seriously. Still, he remains low-key about his *X-Files* feature film performance, seemingly unruffled by the fact that the movie can push him over the brink of mere celebrity into Nicolas Cage-esque superstardom—a respected thespian who also can help carry

a big-budget summer blockbuster.

"I certainly approach my work on television the same way I approach [the film]," he says during a bit of down-time on the movie set. "I haven't made concessions or adjustments or intensifications for the big screen. I like to think that the character can exist anywhere without having to pump it up or bring it down or make whatever adjustments you might think you'd have to make just because, all of a sudden, it's a movie and not a television show."

Since *The X-Files* debuted in 1993, much of the mainstream press attention lavished on Duchovny has focused on his personality, his Ivy League education, his marriage, his looks. Frequently lost in that

INTERVIEW DAVID DUCHOVNY

media glare are his own thoughts about the role that thrust him into the spotlight. And to his real-life alter-ego, Fox Mulder's appeal doesn't just come from sly wit or handsome features.

"The most important thing for me about Mulder was the fact that he didn't care about what anybody else thought he was doing," Duchovny explains. "So he had a real 'screw you' strength. He basically was going to do what he was going to

do, which in most people's eyes was kind of a stupid endeavor for somebody with some of the talent he had, someone who was a respected young FBI agent to all of a sudden devote all his energy to chasing UFOs. Sometimes an audience may lose sight of that, because Mulder's always right, or at least 90 percent of the time we see that although he doesn't win, what he's saying is true. So it's easy to forget that he's kind of a loser, kind of a very odd guy who's made a really odd choice with his life.

"[But] I like to keep that idea alive. Whenever Mulder and Scully get respect or whenever people confer with them as if they're experts, I always think that it's the wrong way to go, because these people are not respected, they are not winners," he continues. "They're really on the fringe and really odd. And most respectable people think that they're just pissing away their time, which is true. The audience doesn't know that, because we're always right to them; we're their heroes. But the essence of the character always was that he didn't care that people thought he was a loser or odd or throwing away his talent."

During his *The X-Files* tenure, Duchovny has been given considerable input into the direction the role has taken in five years, a rare luxury for an actor. But his innate understanding of Mulder hasn't only earned him a Golden Globe Award and an Emmy Award nomination—it has impressed series creator Chris Carter enough that the two have collaborated on storylines.

SUPER DAVE: FBI Agent Fox Mulder journeys to the frozen north and battles aliens to rescue his partner, Dana Scully, from the alien cryo-tube [above and far right].

"The characters on a television show kind of evolve in a haphazard way, just as the scripts come in," Duchovny says. "All of a sudden one week you'll find out that you've got a mortal fear of fire, which we did the first year, which was never in the character as I conceived it or as Chris conceived it at any time. So depending on the week's work at hand, the character evolves. It's kind of false and true in that way—false in that the character just serves whatever is supposed to be served that week. [Yet] it's true in that, I guess, that's probably the way a [person] does evolve in life, because you don't plan the experiences you're going to have. So it is kind of cool in that way.

"But I think the character [of Mulder] was set from the beginning and the evolution has just been [through his] experiences," he adds. "As a character is brought out under more intense circumstances you get to see it more clearly. That's what's hap-

Which isn't to say the work isn't grueling. Despite avoiding fistfights and barely pulling out his gun in the film, Mulder suffers through a deadly obstacle course of explosions, killer bees, wayward helicopters, evil aliens and nefarious conspirators.

"There's no way that anybody could [actually] have done what [I'm supposed to] do on this movie," the actor says. And although many of the pyrotechnics were enhanced by special effects, several sequences were all too realistic. Duchovny remembers the chopper chase sequence as being particularly hair-raising, despite the reassurances of the stunt coordinators. "We were followed at an altitude that was a little too low for my liking—or at least my hair's liking," he says.

"A guy comes to you and says, 'Well, you know, the helicopters aren't going to land on you.' And you're like, 'Yeah, they shouldn't, I'm aware of that.' But they come awful close and they're really loud," he explains. "Again, once you've survived that and once you haven't been killed, you're grateful because you don't need to act. All you have to do is just exist in that moment, [when it's already] loud and scary and

"The most important thing for me about Mulder was that he didn't care what anybody thought. He had a real 'screw you' strength."

pened with Mulder. But I think he's always been who he is."

Even though Mulder's personality has remained somewhat constant since the series pilot, the role does veer into new territory with the feature film and its numerous high-intensity action scenes that give Duchovny and co-star Gillian Anderson a chance to flex their muscles. Fortunately, the former college hoops player loves getting physical.

"One of the things I like about the character is that he's very cerebral, but he can get out there and jump on a train and run around and get beat up. [In the feature film], there's a lot of physical stuff," he says, adding that he prefers a less-rehearsed approach to stunt work.

"I always want to shoot the first take because although [the crew] wants you to get used to the movement, I don't want to become accustomed to it. If, God forbid, you're ever around a bomb that explodes, you don't get to say, 'Look, can you just explode it in my face so I can get used to what [that's] like?' You want that kind of first-experience deal, which is always the best when you're acting."

windy and you're screaming. So it takes care of any other acting that you had to do. You just throw that out the window, 'cause basically, you're just trying to survive in this area. Which is fun, because the less acting you do the better.

"There's a lot of climbing, jumping, running, ducking, leaping [in the movie]. It's like playing a game," Duchovny continues. "As an actor, it's a good rest from the harder work of actually acting. It's fun to go out and jump off a building—that's actually the easy part. If you can't look scared jumping off a building, then you need help."

While the intense stunts may be a change-of pace for the actor, motion picture work isn't. Some might argue that Duchovny would have achieved stardom even without *The X-Files*—before signing on to the series pilot, he had made his mark with quirky parts in films like *The Rapture, Julia Has Two Lovers* and *Kalifornia*. But the acting bug didn't hit the New York native until he was in his 20s and started hanging around the prestigious drama school at Yale, where he was working on an English literature doctorate. He eventually dropped out of his Ph.D. studies and landed a few stage and TV commercial

"Our biggest challenge is to come up that are fun for us, and not think, 'Hmm

parts before nabbing his big break by playing another FBI agent—transvestite G-"person" Dennis/Denise Bryson on David Lynch's twisted cult hit *Twin Peaks*.

In fact, his career was so promising that the actor first hesitated when asked to audition for *The X-Files* pilot. The strength of Chris Carter's script eventually convinced him to take that chance, although it still took some time for him to realize how thoroughly that decision would change his life.

"I didn't really foresee it being any kind of series and stretching out the way it eventually did," Duchovny says. "I thought it was just going to be about UFOs and aliens, which I thought was an exhaustible subject matter. [Then around the first season] people would always preface something they'd say to me with, 'I don't watch TV, but I watch your show.' Now, some people are liars and guilty about watching tons of television. They tell David Hasselhoff, 'I don't watch TV, but I make time for *Baywatch*.' [But] the feeling I had was that we were a TV show that people who didn't watch television liked. We were giving [them] something different. We're not a soap opera or a cop drama or a medical drama, but we have aspects of all those shows."

Consequently, the series' skyrocketing success helped make Duchovny and Anderson the household names they've become. Since then, Duchovny's slowly come to terms with his fame, although it still is a subject that makes the reserved actor somewhat uncomfortable.

"As you would expect, I don't want to have anything to do with the show when I go home because I spend so much time doing it," he says. "So it's not like I log on. I'm just saying that word. I don't even know what it means. I don't have a computer. Do they still log on? Is that still current? I'm grateful to the original fans who got behind the show. [But] the way I see my job is to just do the best I can do and not even worry myself about whether or not it's what people want.

"I think one of the things we've avoided is actually trying to satisfy what people say they want," he continues. "Instead, we've been doing what we want to do and the by-product has been that they've been satisfied. You know, [in music] you always get an artist who either sells out or finds that people perceive him as selling out because he changes. And maybe he's changed because he was trying to anticipate the fan base, or maybe he changed because he wanted to. But it's perceived as selling out nonetheless. So I imagine there will be a time when we'll be perceived as selling out in some way. [Despite that], our biggest challenge is to come up with new challenges that we enjoy, that are fun for us, and not think, 'Hmm. What does the fan base want? Do they want to see Mulder and Scully kiss? Do they want to see more alien stuff or serial killer stuff?' What would interest us is more important, and I think that's why the show continues to be a success, because [we don't] cater to the phenomenon."

Now, *The X-Files* film promises to become a phenomenon itself, introducing an entirely new set of fans to intrepid agents Mulder and Scully and their ongoing quest for a greater truth.

"There's no secret password that you have to know to get this film," he explains. "Obviously there are some little inside jokes and things like that for fans. But I think there are a couple of scenes gracefully done where we've gotten the backbone out and given the back story: 'This is who I am, in case you didn't know, my name is Fox Mulder and I do this.' Whether they stand out as the bold-faced expositional things that they are or not has to do with the actor and writer. Some of [the series' mysteries] will be answered in the movie, but it's not the big answer. That wouldn't be like *The X-Files* to wrap it all up neatly."

The movie will be Duchovny's second starring role (he already toplined the 1997 drama/thriller *Playing God*) and an unprecedented opportunity to simultaneously play the same character on the big- and small-screen. He's excited about the prospect.

"I think [the series is] a natural for the movies. Because of the way the TV show is produced, there's always this idea that we're making little movies. So [we thought], 'Why don't we just go ahead and make a big movie?' Our two- or three-parters are sometimes released on video overseas as movies," he points out. "So there was always this idea that what we're doing already is big-screen worthy, whatever that means. We certainly approached it that way."

And Duchovny thinks this summer's *X-Files* movie might be only the beginning of the series' silver screen saga.

"My hope was that we would start it as a movie franchise and we could do a movie every four or five years, or whatever the demand might be," he says, optimistically. "I can see us doing three or four movies, easily. I think it's a serial first and foremost, and people identify with the characters, like James Bond or Captain Kirk or other serialized characters. Once you have a set of characters that people enjoy watching, then it's just a matter of putting them in new situations. So we'll see if people take to the characters."

So Mulder (and the actor who plays him) won't age badly? Duchovny, cracking a smile, offers his own opinion: "Oh, I'll age like Shatner." ●

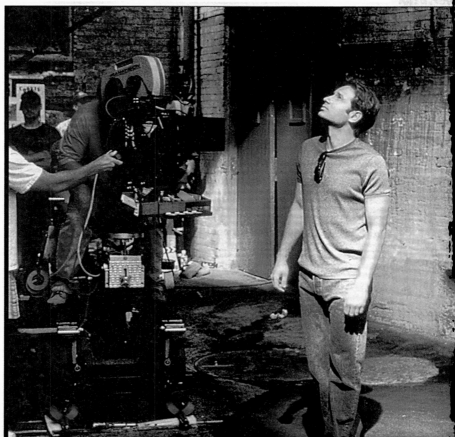

LIGHTS, CAMERA, ACTION: Despite the feature film's dark and sinister atmosphere, Duchovny helped keep the atmosphere on the movie set light with his witty wise-cracks

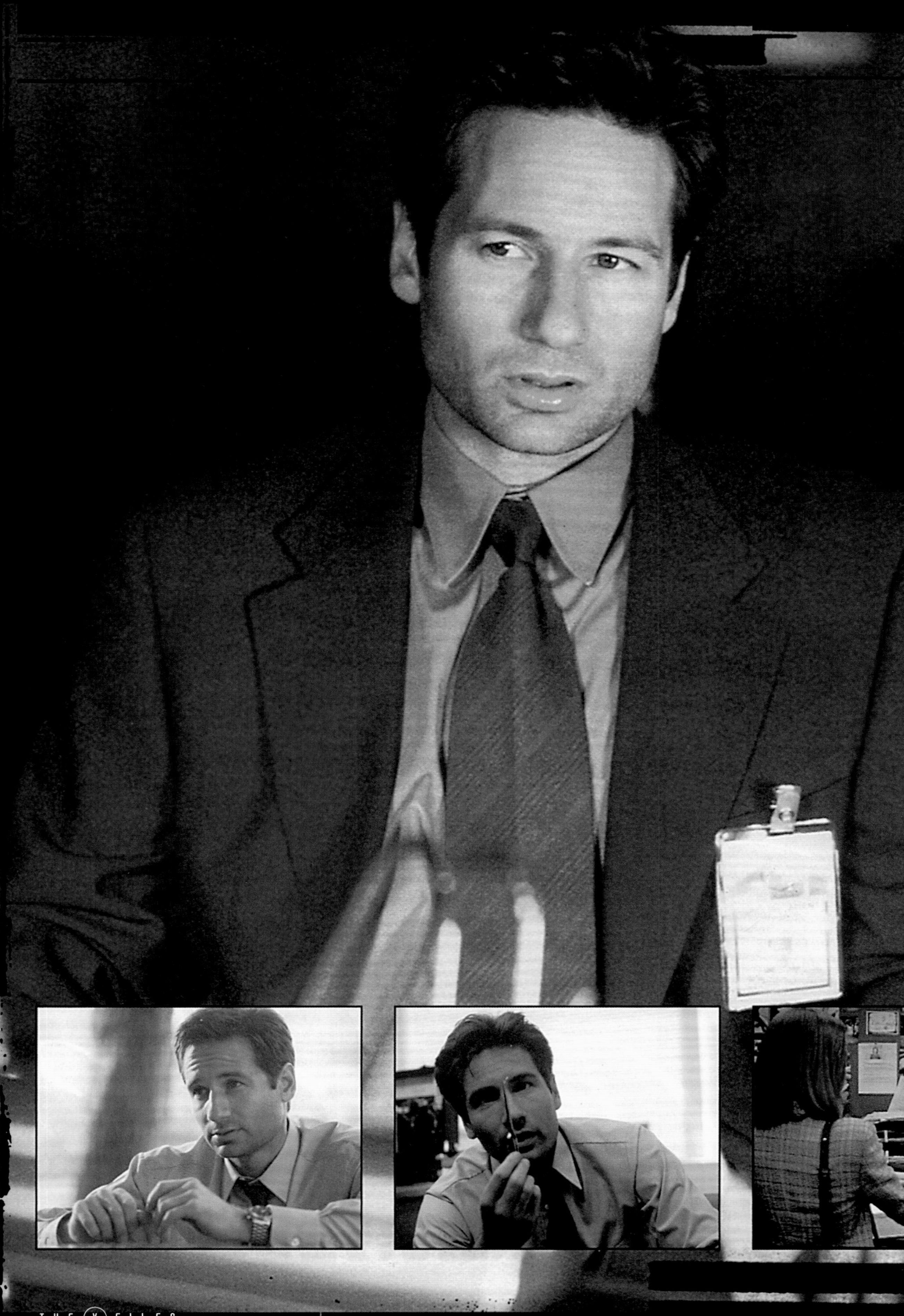

FBI CASE STUDY:
SPECIAL AGENT FOX MULDER

```
AGENT FILE:          BORN:
FOX MULDER           OCTOBER 13, 1961
EDUCATED:
PHD, OXFORD UNIVERSITY
FBI ACADEMY NICKNAME:
"SPOOKY"
X-FILES PARTNERS:
SPECIAL AGENT DANA SCULLY, SPECIAL
AGENT ALEX KRYCEK (DECEASED: 2001)
ASSIGNED TO X-FILES: 1993.
DISMISSED FROM FBI, 2001.
```

AGENT ANALYSIS: K. STODDARD HAYES SHARES HER VIEWS ON "SPOOKY" MULDER AND HIS WORK AT THE FBI.

Fox Mulder has spent most of his F.B.I. career dodging bullets. Not just the lead kind, but bullets of discipline fired by his superiors: investigative hearings, disciplinary transfers, even recommendations that he be dismissed. Yet in the beginning, Mulder seemed to his superiors to be a very promising young agent. Known as the best analyst in the Violent Crimes section, he made his reputation by catching a notorious serial killer. He was rewarded by being given greater freedom to pursue investigations that interested him. Then Mulder discovered the X-files, and his career took a sharp left turn into the wilderness of official disapproval.

What the Bureau hierarchy thinks of the X-files can be seen the moment his new partner, Scully, goes in search of his office in the pilot episode. No large upstairs suite with panoramic views, the X-files office is relegated to a back basement hallway filled with storage shelves. In answer to Scully's knock, Mulder calls out, "Sorry, nobody down here but the F.B.I.'s most unwanted." Scully of course walks in anyway. When she explains that she has been assigned to work with him, he retorts, "So who did you tick off to get stuck with this detail?" and, "I was under the impression you'd been sent to spy on me." (Pilot)

Working on the X-files has left Mulder's reputation irredeemably tarnished in the eyes of his colleagues and especially his superiors. He's considered an eccentric, and worse, a maverick, out of the Bureau mainstream. Yet despite his cynical reception of his new partner, out of the mainstream is exactly where Mulder wants to be. Since he was 12 years old, he's been obsessed with the mystery of his sister Samantha's disappearance, and the hope of someday encountering the extra-terrestrials he believes abducted her. We see in "Paper Hearts" just how vulnerable Mulder is, when any case seems likely to reveal information about Samantha's fate. He needs so desperately to find out what happened to her, that he'll believe almost any likely theory that might support his faith in her abduction.

The X-files is Mulder's best means to pursue this mystery. Mulder gets all the bizarre cases no one else wants to touch: the psychic serial killers, the mutant monsters, the grotesque ritual murders. And because the Bureau would prefer to ignore these freakish cases, Mulder is allowed to work largely undisturbed by bureaucratic oversight.

The exception is any case involving extra terrestrials. By the time Scully is assigned to the X-files, Mulder already knows that his quest has brought him to the edge of very deep waters. He tells

her that he is being kept away from classified files, by someone at the highest levels of power. We learn very quickly that the conspiracy that's getting in Mulder's way extends both inside and outside the F.B.I. And this is the real key to Mulder's fall from official approval. Virtually every time that

Mulder finds himself in danger of reprimand, transfer, or even dismissal, the motive behind the discipline is not Bureau protocol – keeping a maverick in line. The motive is to stop Mulder from exposing the truth about the alien colonization, and the men who are in league with humanity's would-be conquerors. Yet this conspiracy is far from unified, and that's Mulder's salvation. While the Cigarette-Smoking Man and his allies leverage their power in the Bureau to push Mulder away from the truth, others within the same conspiracy, such as Deep Throat and his successor, X, see in Mulder a means to bring the truth to light.

Mulder's reputation as a kook has always cut two ways. It does give him more freedom to pursue unconventional lines of investigation, such as spray painting X's on a country road, or

asking questions about werewolves. His colleagues and superiors have learned to tolerate these eccentricities in "Spooky" Mulder. Yet being an eccentric also works against him when his superiors, or the shadow conspiracy that controls them, want to keep him in check. They can always find a reason to justify disciplinary actions against an agent who breaks the rules as often as Mulder does. This is Section Chief McGrath's intent when he brings Mulder up on charges of insubordination and misconduct. Both Mulder and Scully think McGrath will succeed.

"I'm surprised I lasted this long," says Mulder, as he prepares to receive judgment.

(Continues Overleaf)

TRUST
SOMEONE

Mulder's relationship with Skinner, his immediate superior, can be as ambivalent as any in the X-files. At least with the Cigarette-Smoking Man, Mulder always knows he is dealing with an enemy. With Skinner, Mulder has often been unsure. Here are a few of the cases where Skinner has proved to be Mulder's staunch ally, protector and friend:

"Ascension" – After the X-files are shut down, Skinner orders them opened again, in response to Scully's abduction.

"One Breath" – When Scully reappears in a hospital, near death, Skinner can't openly give Mulder the Cigarette-Smoking Man's address, but he makes sure that Mulder gets the information, smuggled in a pack of Morleys.

"Memento Mori" – As Scully's cancer progresses, Skinner refuses to let Mulder make a deal with the Cigarette-Smoking Man to cure her. Instead, he secretly makes a deal that puts him in Cancer Man's debt.

"Redux" – When Mulder and Scully allow the F.B.I. to think Mulder has shot himself, Skinner guesses the truth, and withholds evidence from the Bureau, to protect Mulder until Mulder comes into the open again.

"DeadAlive" – Skinner insists on exhuming Mulder to see if he, like Billy Miles, is still alive. Later he pulls the plug on the comatose Mulder, to prevent him from becoming an alien replicant.

"Existence" – When Krycek is about to shoot Mulder, Skinner shoots Krycek.

But not everyone in the conspiracy thinks Mulder is a total liability, as McGrath discovers when Deep Throat reverses the Hearing's decision against Mulder.

"His insubordination is in the end far less dangerous than having him expose to the wrong people what he knows," says Deep Throat, to justify protecting his secret ally. ("Fallen Angel")

Bureau policy is also a cover-up for the real motive in assigning Mulder a partner who will discredit his work. The Bureau may want a scientist to keep the X-files grounded in solid investigative technique, but the conspiracy wants a credible, impartial outsider to debunk Mulder's crazy theories, so no one will believe him. It's Mulder's good fortune – or perhaps his destiny – that the agent assigned as his watchdog is Dana Scully. No doubt she was chosen not only because of her impeccable scientific credentials, but because of her unimpeachable integrity. No outside authority could ever suspect the young Agent Scully of being part of some shadowy conspiracy. Hence she seems the ideal, impartial agent to keep Mulder's work from becoming a serious threat to the conspiracy. At least, that was surely the plan, as Section Chief Blevins implies when he orders her to bring her scientific objectivity to bear on the X-files.

Unfortunately for the conspiracy, they chose their impartial tool too well. Mulder's suspicions of Scully evaporate

almost immediately, as he recognizes that she shares his devotion to the truth, though she has very different ways of finding it. Before the end of their first year of partnership, Scully has become Mulder's trusted partner and closest friend. After the Bureau orders the X-files shut down and the agents reassigned, Mulder's new watchdog, Krycek, reports to his superiors that Scully remains a serious problem. Even though she has been separated from Mulder, she still contributes to the threat he represents. The Cigarette-Smoking Man's solution to this problem – make Scully disappear – shows us how important Scully is to Mulder's work, in ways neither Scully nor his enemies nor Mulder himself could ever have predicted.

If Samantha makes Mulder vulnerable, Scully makes him invincible. She's the one person he can count on to back him up, to keep his feet on the ground, and to tell him honestly when he's wrong, or when he's right. The intent of the Syndicate is, of course, to weaken and distract Mulder by threatening his partner. But in fact, every time Scully is endangered, Mulder becomes a relentless, unstoppable adversary. When she's abducted by Duane Barry, when she's dying of cancer, when she's abducted and infected with the alien virus, Mulder will go to any lengths to save her.

The "Gethsemane"/"Redux" trilogy is the most dramatic example of this. Mulder is on the brink of suicide, believing his U.F.O. obsessions are a huge lie created by a government conspiracy, and that this conspiracy caused Scully's cancer, just to make him believe the lie. Then he learns that he is under government surveillance, and Scully collapses, near death. Mulder ultimately gets a cure for Scully's cancer, smashes through the conspiracy aimed at

destroying Skinner, and brings down both Blevins and the Cigarette-Smoking Man. So much for weakness and distraction!

Even after Mulder learns the truth about Samantha's death, he continues his quest to expose the truth about the alien conspiracy, until he himself suffers the fate of so many whose lives he investigated. He is abducted, infected with an alien virus, and left for dead. Ironically, though all the abduction investigations of the past seven years haven't been enough to end Mulder's F.B.I. career, his own abduction accomplishes this. Once he's dead, the Bureau can close his agent file. When he returns to life, preserved by the alien virus, all they have to do is refuse his application for reinstatement to the X-files. When he joins an X-files case anyway, and it goes wrong, it's easy for Bureau authorities to lay the blame on Mulder and dismiss him.

Yet Mulder is still so much a threat to the conspiracy that they set him up for assassination. Soon after the birth of Scully's son, Mulder goes into hiding, because certain elements within the F.B.I. will kill him, if they can find him. Mulder's long time adversary, Deputy Director Kersh, is a prime suspect in this plot. After Kersh is exonerated of all wrong-doing by the investigation, he reveals to Doggett that it was he who warned Mulder to escape. Even in absence, Mulder still has the power to make his enemies divide against themselves. And not even the end of his F.B.I. career can bring the end of his work on the mysteries of the X-files. ●

AGENT ANDERSON

In an exclusive interview for

The X-Files Magazine,

Gillian Anderson

reflects on her nine years playing

Agent Dana Scully, as she faces the

future without her alter-ego. Interview

by **John Reading**

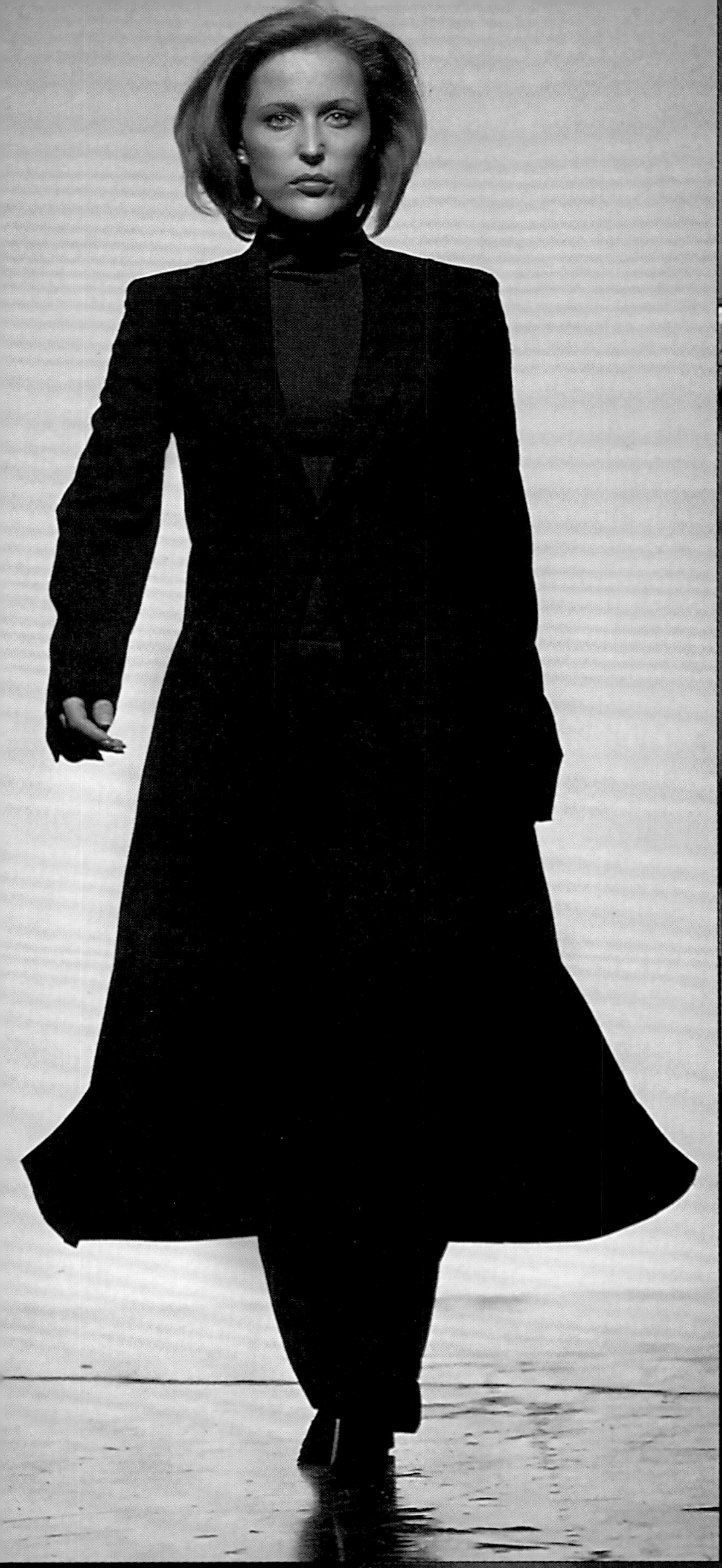

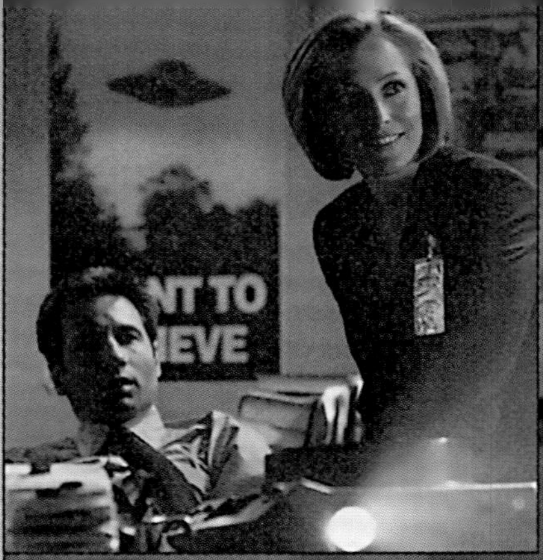

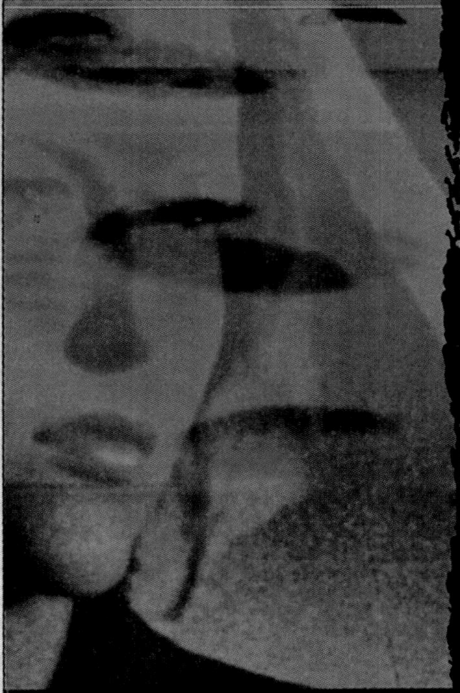

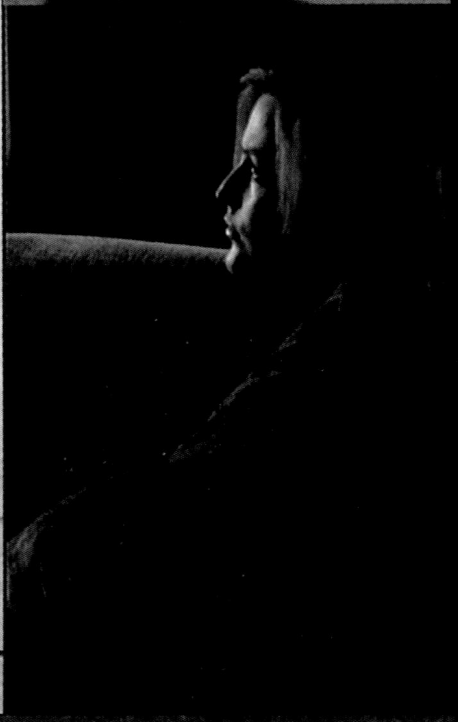

TROUBLE-SHOOTING IN "PAPER HEARTS" AND "ORISON"

It's all just starting to dawn on Gillian Anderson. The *X-Files* television series is over. She spent nearly one-third of her life portraying F.B.I. Special Agent Dana Scully on the show, first opposite David Duchovny as Fox Mulder and, later, opposite Robert Patrick and Annabeth Gish as John Doggett and Monica Reyes.

Along the way, Anderson made time for a wide range of other experiences, both personal and professional. She married, divorced and became a mother during the show's run, and helped raise nearly half a million dollars for Neurofibromatosis, Inc., a charity dedicated to those, like Anderson's brother, who suffer from this genetic disorder that causes tumors to form on a person's nerves. The actress also managed to squeeze in performances in such films as *Chicago Cab*, *The Mighty*, *Playing By Heart* and *The House of Mirth*, and lent her voice to the likes of the animated feature film *Princess Mononoke* and TV shows such as *Fraiser*, *Harsh Realm* and *The Simpsons*. Closer to home, Anderson wrote and directed the "all things" episode of *The X-Files*.

Now, however, it's time to get on with the rest of her life and career. We caught up with Anderson just as filming on the series was approaching its end, engaging her in a wide-ranging conversation about matters past, present and future as they relate to both *The X-Files* and to Gillian Anderson.

THE X-FILES MAGAZINE:
So what are your thoughts on this major chapter of your life closing?
ANDERSON: This is so surreal. I swear to God it's only started to hit me over the past couple of days. It feels like the nine years was so short. You know what I mean? While we were in the middle of it I felt that it would never end and now all of a sudden it just feels unfathomable.

So does that mean you don't want it to end?
No, no, no. I think ultimately that it's good. I think it's good for everybody and I think that everybody has put in such a huge effort over the years in really trying to keep the quality of the show up, to continue with its integrity as much as we could. There's a time for everything to end and I think this is the right time, I think everybody in their own way is excited about moving on to other things. But both things can co-exist; one can be sad and in the process of mourning and at the same time be excited and hopeful for the future and change.

After nine years, is there a favorite episode that stands out in your mind?

I felt akin to ("all things"). It certainly wasn't one of my favorite episodes, but the process of it was exhilarating and rewarding. There are a few that I liked, that were fun. "Bad Blood" was a bit of a comedic episode that I felt was fun and smart and well written. Our schedule is so crazy that it's hard for me to keep them straight. I'm terrible at that, so I couldn't even begin to tell you favorites, but you know there are some.

The X-Files went from cult favorite to pop culture phenomenon. Let's talk about the so-called craziness of the fans.
I haven't been feeling the craziness of it lately. We're pretty well protected from that. It all just feels like there's another entity out there that's kind of breathing

"I live a very **quiet**, private life and every once in a while it feels abruptly **jarred** by somebody who's extra-enthusiastic."

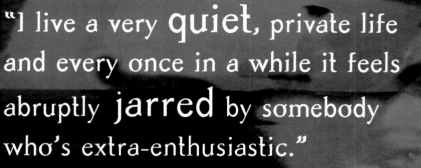

ABOVE: SCULLY IN "THE TRUTH"; TOP
RIGHT: SAYING GOODBYE TO MITCH
PILEGGI ON THE SET OF THE SERIES
FINALE; MIDDLE: "BIOGENESIS";
BOTTOM: DIRECTING "ALL THINGS"

with the same heartbeat as we are and they support us.

I don't experience a lot of craziness. We don't get a lot of visitors on the set. Once in a while we do and people burst into tears and stuff, but the crazy period of time was earlier on and I didn't even realize that that was crazy until it stopped being crazy. Then I thought, "Oh God, that *was* crazy!"

But you must go to restaurants and get recognized?
Yeah, but it's not on the same level as other people have. It's not what Gwyneth Paltrow has, where you can't sit in a restaurant without the entire restaurant stopping and trying to listen to your conversations. So I'm blessed in that way that I don't have the pressure of that in my life. I live a very quiet, private life and every once in a while it

feels abruptly jarred by somebody who extra-enthusiastic.

OK, let's get into the show a bit more. The past couple of years have focused not on Mulder's story, but Scully's. She was the anchor. What's your take on the character's evolution and where she's at as we build to the end?
Well, it's happened by necessity because of the fact that David was

going to be leaving. I think that for the first year he was gone the writers did a very good job of keeping him in the public consciousness even though he wasn't around. It was remarkable. It's interesting how if someone is talked about, it feels as if they're present even though they're not. So they were very successful in doing that. The show certainly did start out as Mulder's quest. The show was primarily about his character and his genius and his revelations, and Scully's job was to kind of help solidify that in the questions she would answer. They created a whole partnership, but it was 70/30, then it got to 60/40 and then to 50/50. And I'm not talking financially.

This season, Scully spent a lot of time with baby William and away from Doggett and Reyes. What did you make of that turn of events?
That's interesting. I don't know about this whole baby thing. It certainly adds a level of complication to the filming! I think it added an interesting storyline, but it's also been complicated. How do you involve Scully in the cases they're investigating to a degree without the audience thinking, "Well, where's the baby and why isn't she home with him?" And if she *is* with the baby the fans are going, "We want her out in the field. We don't want her home with the baby." It was a very fine balance they had to play.

Speaking of kids, how excited is your daughter Piper about the likelihood of having you home more often?
Well, she's not necessarily going to have me back home. She's going to be doing a lot more traveling is what she's going to be doing.
   I don't know what she's feeling right now. I mean, we've had a couple of conversations about it and she's just at that age right now where she's starting to understand what it is that Mommy's been doing for her lifetime. And I think she has, for the first time, a bit of a romantic view of what that is, and I'm trying to break that down as quickly as possible!

How do you feel about David coming back for the finale?
I think it's great. I didn't realize how important it would be for that to happen. When I heard I was very excited and he called me and we had a conversation about the fact that he was coming back and possibly going to

be directing something. I guess I didn't realize how much I was missing him and how integral he was [to the show], and I didn't realize that we needed his presence to make a necessary closure.

You and David started on this journey together. How differently do you think you might feel if he didn't come back to close things out?
I don't think I would have known that until the very end when I would have thought, "Well, wait a minute. This isn't right. This isn't right." I'm very glad that the show is completely ending now because I have a feeling that, even though I would have mourned to a certain degree in saying goodbye, it wouldn't have been as clean. I feel like we have an opportunity now to really tie it up in a whole and constructive way.

What will you miss most about The X-Files?
There are many, many things that I'm going to miss. I'm really going to miss

David and Kim (Manners) and Chris (Carter). I think my body is going to keep expecting to do something familiar that it's not going to have an opportunity to do. I'll have the hiatus and then come July it will kind of feel like, "Well, something's supposed to happen now, right? I'm supposed to go on a sound stage." So it will be interesting to watch how it transpires in my body and in my psyche.

Would you even for a second consider jumping into another TV series?
No, I'm just done. Please, it's been nine years. There are so many other things to do, so many other things not even in the business that I want to do… and in the business, but in other ways. Eventually, after I do some features, maybe if HBO asks me to direct something, I might do that. But there are so many things I want to do first.

How about the next X-Files feature?
Well, there's one that they're hoping to do in the next couple of years. That I would definitely do.

TEN OF THE BEST

With over 200 episodes to choose from it's been difficult – but Martin 'Editor' Eden has picked what he thinks are the 10 best Scully episodes! (Okay, so he cheated and did best 'storylines' in some cases, but what the heck…)

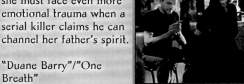

"Beyond the Sea"
Scully's father dies, and she must face even more emotional trauma when a serial killer claims he can channel her father's spirit.

"Duane Barry"/"One Breath"
Scully is 'abducted' and returned shortly afterwards in a bad state. Will she pull through?

"Irresistible"/"Orison"
Scully becomes the next target for death fetishist Donnie Pfaster in "Irresistible," and they have their final, fatal confrontation in "Orison."

"Leonard Betts"/"Memento Mori"
Scully discovers that she has cancer and must deal with the terrifying consequences.

"Never Again"
Feeling low, Scully gets herself a new tattoo, and seeks solace with Ed Jerse – who has a rather bizarre tattoo of his own.

"Christmas Carol"/"Emily"
Tragedy strikes Scully as she discovers she has a daughter, and loses her soon after. She says her final goodbye to Emily in "All Souls."

"Patient X"/"The Red and the Black"
Scully sees a U.F.O.! But will she remember it…?

"Milagro"
Scully has a very dangerous liaison with Mulder's new next-door neighbor.

"all things"
Scully meets an ex-lover and faces a turning point in her beliefs.

"William"
A disfigured Jeffrey Spender makes Scully realize that she must give up baby William for his own safety.

"ON THE SET OF "THE TRUTH"

Any concerns about ending the show now and then having to turn up on the set of an *X-Files* feature a year or so down the road?
No. I've got a lot of stuff that I'm going to be doing between now and then that will be feeding me creatively in completely different ways. So when an *X-Files* film eventually presents itself, it will feel more like a reunion, I think, than something to dread or be afraid of.

Chris was asked about the meaning of the tagline "Trust no one," and he said, to paraphrase, "I live in Hollywood, I work in Hollywood." Do your

experiences in Hollywood make you think the same way?
I don't trust anybody. I don't trust anybody in Hollywood or Ohio. No, that's not true.

But does working in this business, if nothing else, make you more cynical?
Probably, I think. It's interesting, because what I've heard about that aspect of the business is much more devastating than my experience. Because I don't tolerate that, and I don't behave in that way with people, I have a tendency to bring people into my experience who do not behave that way, because there's no

room otherwise. And so I don't have that experience very much. I generally work with and get into business with people who are very on the line and honest and straightforward.

You're currently gearing up to do a play and a movie. What can you tell us about those two projects?
I optioned something that I'm going to adapt and direct eventually. Hopefully I can start writing over the summer. It's a book called *Speed of Light*, by Elizabeth Rossner (see boxout). It's a beautiful little book. But I'm not sure when I'm going to be able to get to that. I'm looking for

Written by Elizabeth Rossner, this debut novel sees the adult children of a holocaust survivor learn about grief, forgiveness and the power of bearing witness from a Latina housekeeper who has also been victimized by government-sponsored genocide. Together, they overcome the tragedies of the past to reconnect with one another and the world around them.

Late last year, Gillian Anderson put up her own money to option the novel which she will adapt to make her feature directorial debut now that *The X-Files* is over.

"Directing was a transformative experience for me, one that I really enjoyed," Anderson told *Variety* last year. "Then when I picked up this book and started reading the poetry of her words, I found myself trying to visualize where the camera should be, the colors of the characters, the texture of the shots. It felt so intimate and natural, like I wrote it myself. I took the steps to option it, something I'd never done before. It's a beautiful piece that needs to see the light of day and hopefully I can do it justice."

different film projects for the summer and then I'm going to do a play in London in October and then maybe a feature after that. Or I might take a little time off. The play is a new Michael Weller (show) and it's called *What the Night Is For*.

How full an experience has this show been for you? You started as a young unknown and you're leaving as a mature woman and famous and respected actress.
The fact of the matter is that I grew up during the course of this show. I started when I was 24 and ended at almost 34. That's almost a third of my life. I was young and naïve and impressionable and didn't have a clue about the business or anything at that time. Then, to grow up and to make mistakes along the way and to experience my life while trying to be somebody else (Scully) and try to be something other than myself for 18 hours a day was an interesting task. I also was doing that very publicly. So, as I've said, it's been… surreal. ●

FBI CASE STUDY:
SPECIAL AGENT DANA SCULLY

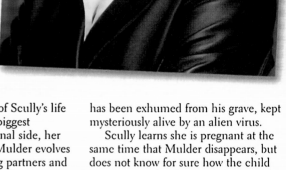

```
AGENT FILE:        BORN:
DANA SCULLY        FEBRUARY 23, 1964
COLLEGE MAJOR:     ADVANCED DEGREE:
PHYSICS.           DOCTOR OF MEDICINE.
RECRUITED TO FBI: 1990.
ASSIGNED TO X-FILES: 1993.
X-FILES PARTNERS: FOX MULDER 1992-2000
(EXCEPT FOR A PERIOD IN 1994 WHEN THE
X-FILES WERE CLOSED); JOHN DOGGETT, 2000-2001
CURRENTLY ASSIGNED TO TEACH AT
THE FBI ACADEMY IN QUANTICO
```

AGENT ANALYSIS: K. STODDARD HAYES PROVIDES HER TAKE ON SCULLY'S LAST TWO YEARS ON THE X-FILES

When Special Agent Dana Scully was first assigned to the X-files, she had only two years' experience in the FBI. As Fox Mulder's partner for the next eight years, she has had a wider range of experiences than most people would see in a lifetime. She has been abducted and made the victim of bizarre experiments; she learns that she can't have children; and develops cancer. She loses her father to natural causes, and sees her sister murdered. She and Mulder discover a huge conspiracy of alien colonization and human/alien cross-breeding. And she investigates enough paranormal cases to fill an entire file room. Is this exceptional? Since the same years of Mulder's life have been equally tumultuous, we have to conclude that this is normal life for an FBI agent on the X-files.

It's the last two years of Scully's life that have produced the biggest upheavals. On the personal side, her close relationship with Mulder evolves from the trust of working partners and friends, to the intimacy of lovers. Then Mulder disappears, presumably abducted. Months later, he is found, dead, and she has to bury him, and mourn him. Then she learns that he has been exhumed from his grave, kept mysteriously alive by an alien virus.

Scully learns she is pregnant at the same time that Mulder disappears, but does not know for sure how the child was conceived. After a pregnancy and delivery beset by conspiracies and indestructible alien replicants, she attempts to settle down to the ordinary life of a mother with a new baby and the baby's father, Mulder. But before she and Mulder can explore this new stage of their relationship, he is forced to go into hiding to escape those trying to kill him. And just when she thinks her son is a normal baby after all, she discovers that he may have paranormal powers, and that his conception may be linked to a secret government program to genetically engineer super soldiers.

On the professional side, after working with the same partner for eight years, Scully has to adjust to a new partner. And just when she begins to cement a good working relationship with Doggett, she has to start her maternity leave. After the birth, instead of returning to the field work that has occupied most of her career, she is assigned to teach at the FBI Academy.

On a day-to-day basis, working with a new partner may be more challenging

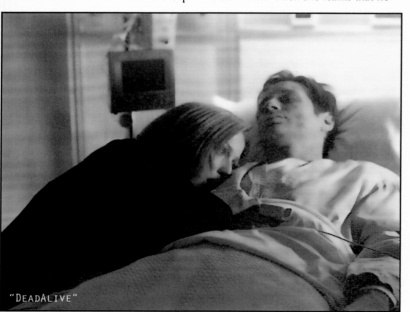

"DEADALIVE"

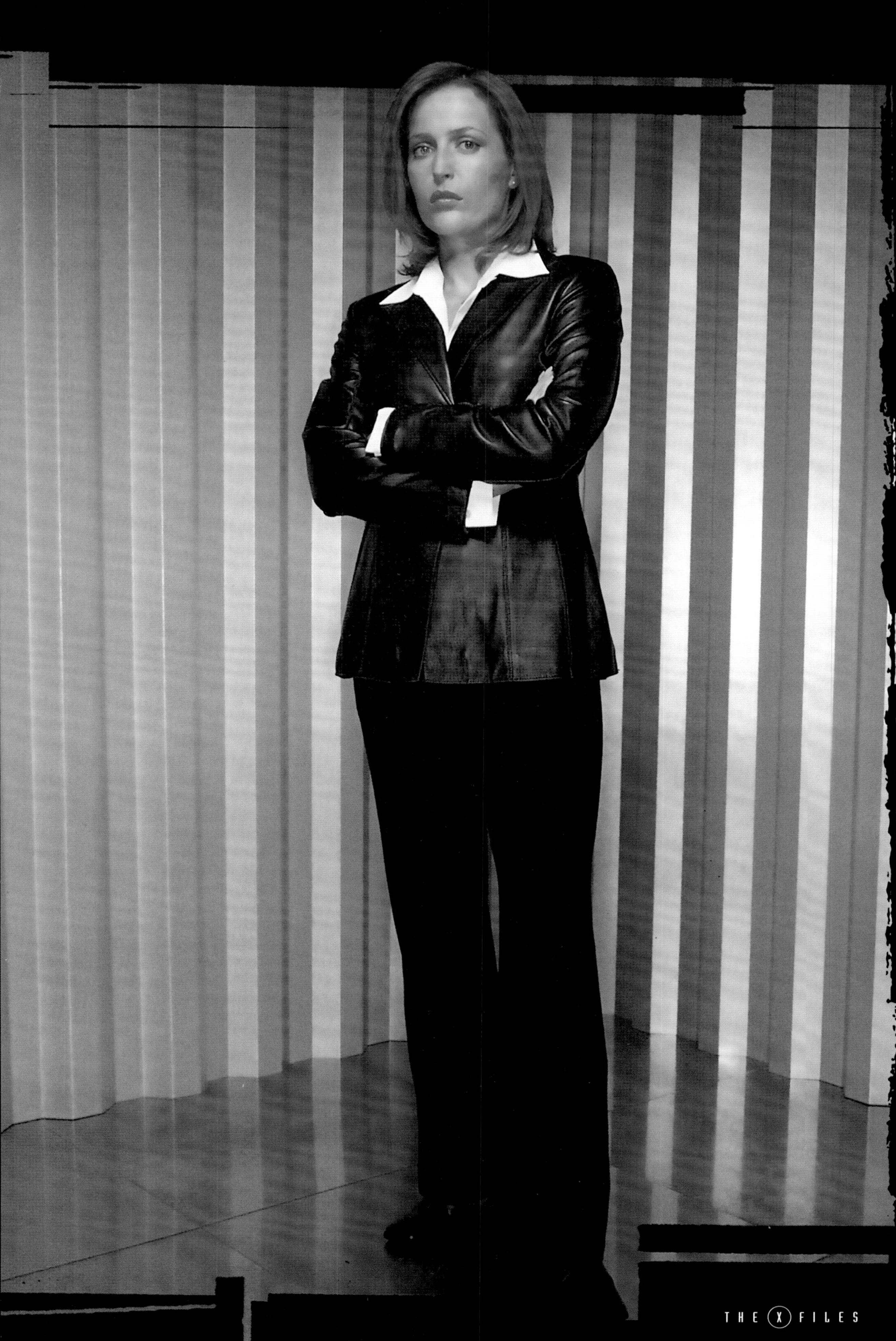

DANA SCULLY

DANA SCULLY

than it appears in comparison with the other changes in Scully's life. In Mulder, Scully had a partner whom she knew cared about her as deeply as she cared for him. They knew each other's ways of working, each other's fears and obsessions and infuriating foibles. She trusted him, and she could use her solid scientific approach to ground his more fantastic theories. Doggett brings her more than the very human stress of getting used to a new face and personality in place of the one she misses: different habits, different sense of humor, different professional values. Even under ordinary circumstances this might be difficult. Working on the X-files, though, is never ordinary, especially now. Scully doesn't know if she can trust Doggett to back her up in the dangerous Bureau politics that surround the X-files. And she is afraid that he will treat her as an alien-obsessed crackpot, instead of a solid scientist and investigator.

This fear seems foremost to Scully during their first murder investigation ("Patience"). Abbott, the local detective, treats Scully with barely concealed hostility, and tries to enlist Doggett to join him in dismissing her

observations as fantastic. While Doggett doesn't scoff at her, he doesn't seem to be leaping to her defence, either. Finally, when Abbott accuses Scully of jumping at "whatever explanation is the wildest, the most far fetched," Doggett firmly takes him aside. The camera lets us see the stern expression on Doggett's face, so we can guess that he's telling Abbott to back off, respect his partner, and do what she says. But Scully can't see her partner's face, or hear what he says, and she's afraid he's joining with Abbott to undermine her work.

"What did you say to him?" she demands. He answers that he told Abbott to dig up the body she ordered, because she is a "leading authority on paranormal phenomena, and who are we to argue with an expert?"

"I am not an expert. I am a scientist who happens to have seen a lot," Scully insists.

After this, things start to get better between Scully and Doggett. After a fruitless nine-hour stakeout makes Scully wonder if she isn't trying too hard to force the facts into shape, Doggett wonders if she is trying too hard to be Mulder. Then he adds, "I don't think you're wrong, Agent Scully. I'm no Fox Mulder, but I can tell when a man's hiding something."

Still, it takes a long time for her to trust Doggett completely. At the end of her next case, in which Doggett has to rescue her from a murderous cult ("Roadrunners"), she has to apologize to him for leaving him out of the investigation. And it's many weeks before he learns that she is pregnant. Though she tells him she kept the secret only because she didn't want to be forced out of the FBI, by excluding him, she has classed him with those not to be trusted, rather than those, like Skinner and Mulder, whom she trusts.

And all the while she is adjusting to Doggett, she has to carry the load of her fears for Mulder. It's impossible to overstate the impact on Scully of Mulder's disappearance and death. Though she seems to keep soldiering

"INVOCATION"

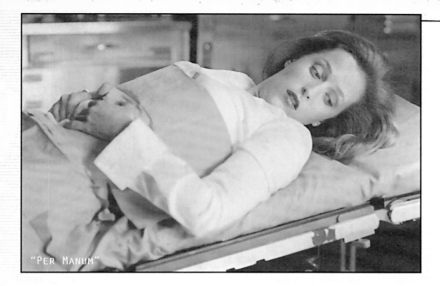

"PER MANUM"

on, the delicate way Skinner and Doggett treat her, each time they break news concerning Mulder, shows how much they fear each new development is going to hurt her. As they get closer to finding Mulder, Scully's fears of loss grow overwhelming. The autopsy of a man who was abducted with Mulder is almost more than she can bear. "I don't know how she's doing it," says Doggett, "with everything she's feeling, what she's afraid of." ("This is Not Happening")

She tries to prepare herself a little, by recounting to Skinner a conversation she and Mulder had about starlight. But it's not enough. When Mulder is found dead, and Jeremiah Smith, the only man who might help him, disappears, Scully's cry of anguish

sums up everything she feels: "This is not happening!"

Scully has three months to mourn for Mulder. Those months pass in a flash of television time, so before we really have a chance to see the effect of Mulder's death on Scully, she gets him back. The tearful joy on her face, when he wakes up and greets her with a joke, and the way she quietly rests her head on him, show that with him back, her world has miraculously righted itself.

Scully now has three people she can count on to protect her and her unborn child at any cost: Mulder, Skinner, and Doggett (who has brought in a fourth, Monica Reyes). But all of them together are not what saves her and the baby. The replicants, led by the indestructible Billy Miles, find the remote birthplace. However, as soon as they have one look at the newborn, they all leave mysteriously, and the agents conclude that the baby is an ordinary human baby, after all.

That feeling of relief lasts only until the next wave of revelations, which

"LORD OF THE FLIES"

send Mulder into hiding and raise grave questions about William. It's hard to say which frightens Scully more: the possibility that William might be other than a normal child, or the possibility that she might lose Mulder to his enemies. When Doggett first tries to tell her that her baby may have some connection to the super soldier program, she says flat out, "I don't want to hear this. My baby is fine." When he persists, she asks him to leave and not come back. It's as if she has so recently gotten over her fears that the baby is an alien hybrid, that she can't deal with the possibility that something else might be wrong. ("Nothing Important Happened Today")

Yet at the same time, she is so afraid for Mulder's life that she tells Skinner she won't tell Mulder about her fears for the baby, because it's too dangerous for him to come back to the FBI. Weeks later, when Doggett tells her someone is trying to contact Mulder with information about the super soldier program, she even lies to her former partner, telling him that she doesn't know where Mulder is or how to contact him.

Doggett confronts her on this at once: "How long are you going to do this? Refuse to trust me, or anybody? How else are you going to get him home?" Scully doesn't have an answer for him. ("Trust No 1") Her meeting with the Shadow Man, and his revelations about how closely he has been watching her and Mulder, terrify her even more. Between her longing to see Mulder, and her desperate need, for William's sake and for Mulder's, to get information about the super soldiers, she sends for him. Then the Shadow Man springs his trap, and the closest Scully gets to Mulder is to watch his train go by. As much as she longs to see him, she is far more relieved, in the end, that he has apparently escaped his enemies. She tells him in her final email of her hope for another time, when it will be safe for him to return.

With more than half of The X-Files' final season still to run, it's impossible to guess what new threats and revelations Scully will have to face. We can only be sure that she'll do whatever it takes to protect her son and her soul mate. ●

THE ROSTER

ASSIGNMENT: Provide a list of FBI employees who have made an impact on the last nine years of *The X-Files*.
RESEARCHER:
Martin Eden, with help from Robin Benty and Kate Anderson.

Division Chief Scott Blevins
(Played by Charles Cioffi)
First appearance: Pilot
Notes: Brought Mulder and Scully together on the X-files, but was ultimately revealed as the man who tried to betray them.
Current status: Deceased – shot by mysterious gunman in his office.

Agent Frank Burst
(Played by Vic Polizos)
First appearance: "Pusher"
Current status: Deceased – suffered heart attack (induced by Robert 'Pusher' Modell).

Agent Collins
(Played by Steve Bacic)
First appearance: "Pusher"
Notes: Set himself on fire (under the influence of Robert 'Pusher' Modell). He was saved by Scully.

Agent Tom Colton
(Played by Donal Logue)
First appearance: "Squeeze"

Notes: Brought Eugene Victor Tooms to the attention of Mulder and Scully.

Agent Gene Crane
(Played by Kirk B R Woller)
First appearance: "Within"
Notes: A member of Doggett's task squad during the hunt for Mulder. It soon became apparent that Crane was really an alien Super Soldier.
Current status: Deceased – possibly...

Agent Arthur Dales
(Played by Fredric Lane (young Dales) and Darren McGavin (old Dales))
First appearance: "Travelers"
Notes: Arthur Dales was the first agent to work on the X-files (with a little help from his assistant Dorothy).

Agent John Doggett
(Played by Robert Patrick)
First appearance: "Within"
Notes: Former marine and NYPD detective.
Current status: Doggett is now assigned to the X-files.

Assistant Director Brad Follmer
(Played by Cary Elwes)
First appearance: "Nothing Important Happened Today, Part 1"
Current status: Overseeing the X-files.

Agent Diana Fowley
(Played by Mimi Rogers)
First appearance: "The End"
Notes: Worked twice on the X-files

– first with Agent Mulder, and then some years later with Agent Spender.
Current status: Deceased. Murdered for her betrayal against the conspiracy.

Agent Leyla Harrison
(Played by Jolie Jenkins)
First appearance: "Alone"
Notes: Working in the accounts department of the FBI. Helped out Doggett on an X-file when Scully took maternity leave.
Current status: Still an FBI agent.

Agent Lucy Kazdin
(Played by C.C.H. Pounder)
First appearance: "Duane Barry"
Notes: Was involved in a hostage situation involving Duane Barry.

Agent Michael Kinsley
Played by Scott Burkholder
First appearance: "Detour"
Current status: Unknown. Presumably still an FBI agent, still partnering Agent Stonecypher, and probably still attending FBI creative team seminars.

Agent Alex Krycek
(Played by Nicholas Lea)
First appearance: "Sleepless"
Notes: Krycek partnered Mulder on the X-files during Scully's disappearance. He didn't hang around long in the FBI...
Current status: Deceased – shot by Skinner.

Agent Jerry Lamana
(Played by Wayne Duvall)
First appearance: "Ghost in the Machine"
Notes: Approached Mulder and Scully whilst on probation from a murder case involving a company called Eurisko.
Current status: Deceased – Agent Lamana died in an elevator crash in the Eurisko building.

Agent James Leeds
(Played by Kevin McClatchy)
First appearance: "Via Negativa"
Current status: Deceased – found

dead in his car with an axe wound while investigating a mysterious cult.

Section Chief Joseph McGrath
First appearance: "Fallen Angel"
Notes: Headed an enquiry over the conduct of Agent Mulder. Attempted to fire Mulder but was overruled.

Agent Fox Mulder
(Played by David Duchovny)
First appearance: Pilot
Notes: Nicknamed 'Spooky,' Mulder was the driving force behind the X-files for many years.
Current status: Having left the FBI, Mulder is on the run from aliens.

Agent Greg Nemhauser
(Played by Greg Thirloway)
First appearance: "Grotesque"
Notes: Assisted Agents Patterson and Mulder in a serial killer case, possibly involving demonic possession.
Current status: Deceased – became one of the victims of the serial killer, and was discovered encased in a clay gargoyle.

Agent Bill Patterson
(Played by Kurtwood Smith)
First appearance: "Grotesque"
Notes: Assisted Agent Mulder in a serial killer case. Patterson in fact turned out to be the murderer.

Agent Danny Pendrell
(Played by Brendan Beiser)
First appearance: "Nisei"
Notes: FBI lab tech who assisted Mulder and Scully on various cases. Had a crush on Agent Scully.
Current status: Deceased – he took a bullet which was meant for Scully.

Agent Reggie Purdue
(Played by Dick Anthony Williams)
First appearance: "Young at Heart"
Current status: An old agent friend of Agent Mulder's, Purdue brought Mulder to the attention of

an apparently resurrected criminal known as John Barnett.
Current status: Deceased – strangled to death.

Agent Monica Reyes
(Played by Annabeth Gish)
First appearance: "This is Not Happening"
Notes: Specialist in cases involving satanic and ritualistic abuse.
Current status: Reyes is now assigned to the X-files.

Agent Peyon Ritter
First appearance: "Tithonus"
Notes: New York City field agent, partnered Agent Scully in an investigation involving bizarre circumstances surrounding an Alfred Fellig. Ritter shot Fellig – and Scully too, by accident. Scully escaped death.

Agent Lewis Schoniger
(Played by Stanley Anderson)
First appearance: "Closure"
Notes: Agent Schoniger assisted Scully's queries about her partner Mulder's behavior.

Agent Dana Scully
(Played by Gillian Anderson)
First appearance: Pilot
Notes: A former doctor, worked with Agent Fox Mulder on the X-files for several years.
Current status: Teaching at the Quantico FBI Academy.

Agent Chesty Short
(Played by Andy Umberger)
First appearance: "Requiem"
Notes: Was appointed the unenviable task of investigating Mulder and Scully's expenses over their seven years on the X-files.
Current status: Unknown, probably auditing somewhere.

Assistant Director Walter Skinner
(Played by Mitch Pileggi)
First appearance: "Tooms"
Notes: Oversaw Mulder and Scully's work on the X-files for many years.
Current status: Still working for the FBI.

Agent Jeffrey Spender
(Played by Chris Owens)
First appearance: "Patient X"
Notes: Worked alongside Agent Fowley on the X-files for a short period of time.
Current status: Deceased – found shot dead in the X-files office.

Agent Angus Stedman
(Played by Lawrence LeJohn)
First appearance: "Via Negativa"
Current status: Deceased – found dead in his car with an axe wound. Agent Stedman had been investigating a mysterious cult.

Agent Carla Stonecypher
(Played by J.C. Wendel)
First appearance: "Detour"
Current status: Unknown. Presumably still an FBI agent, still partnering Agent Kinsley and probably still attending FBI creative team seminars.

Agent Barrett Weiss
(Played by Andrew Johnston)
First appearance: "Colony"
Notes: Assists Mulder and Scully in an investigation into the deaths of various doctors.
Current status: Deceased – died in a confrontation with the Alien Bounty Hunter.

Agent Jack Willis
(Played by Christopher Allport)
First appearance: "Lazarus"
Notes: Shot by Warren James Dupre while trying to prevent an armed robbery with Agent Scully.
Current status: Deceased – having just survived his gunshot wounds, 'Willis' kidnapped Agent Scully and soon after died of diabetes-related complications. ●

Z' OF FBI

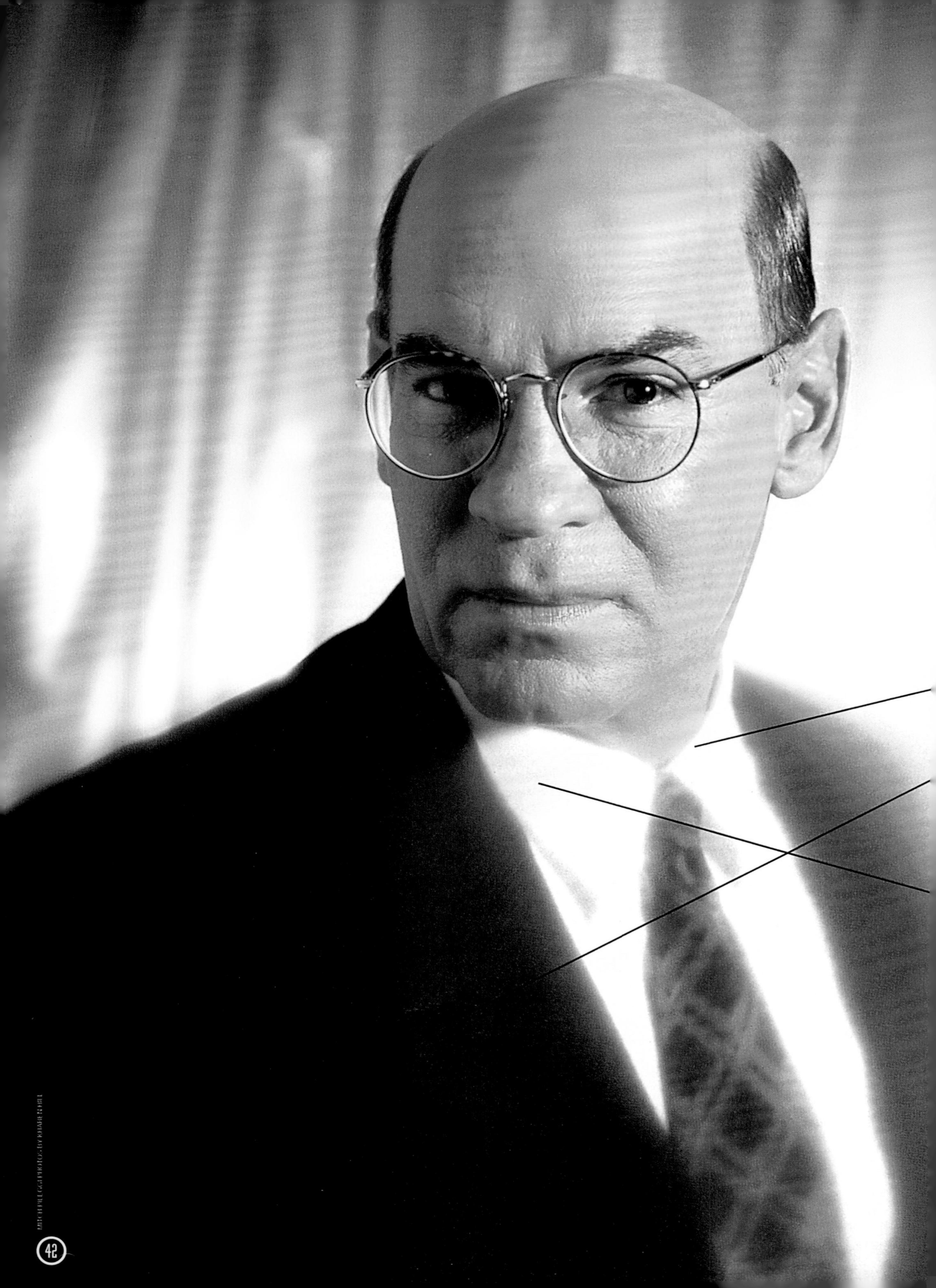

MITCH PILEGGI PHOTOS BY KHAREN HILL

mitch pileggi reflects on walter skinner's role in the X-files mythology

WHO'S THE BOSS?

Mitch Pileggi chuckles when asked if there's any chance for a Walter S. Skinner *X-Files* spin-off. "Oh I don't think so," he says, laughing.

The amused response reflects the 46-year-old actor's humility. Even after watching his role as the FBI assistant director grow in both complexity and frequency of appearance over the course of the last five seasons, Pileggi remains surprised at the loyal legion of fans he and his stern FBI alter-ego have attracted.

"I don't even know the [extent of the] character's popularity," he says. "I haven't had the time to really sit in on any of it, because I'm not on the Internet—I'm totally computer ignorant. [But the response] is interesting and very flattering. I'm happy they like what I'm doing with the character. I don't think it'll affect how much he's on the show, though."

Though the Mitch Pileggi Estrogen Brigade and sundry other Internet-based Skinner boosters are proof of the actor's current fan-favorite status, the Pileggi/*X-Files* combo wasn't an instant success. In fact, Pileggi unsuccessfully auditioned for other

BY Annabelle villanueva

guest parts on the show before winning the role of Skinner. Four years after the first appearance of the gruff-but-lovable assistant director (in Season One's "Tooms"), he's enough of a series fixture to merit an appearance in *The X-Files* feature film. It's a welcome big-screen return for Pileggi, who was best-known in his pre-*X-Files* days for a turn as a psychotic murderer in Wes Craven's 1989 thriller *Shocker*. His latest movie role is far less horrifying—while Skinner and his position within the Bureau remain enigmatic, the intense ex-Marine's some-times-ambiguous relationship with his agents promises to gain some clarity in *The X-Files* movie.

"My character is there to support them and try to get the rest of the people to understand that what they're doing is not a bunch of hog-wash, but is valid," Pileggi explains. "For a long time, the fans have not been sure of whose side [Skinner is] on, and if he's using [Mulder and Scully] to promote his own agenda. But I think if you go back and watch some of the episodes and the movie, you will find that he's an ally, a friend. He's put his job and his life on the line to help them accomplish what they're doing and to save them from whatever disasters they come up against."

Pileggi's innate understanding of the character helped him get a handle on Skinner's film role even though he didn't know how the character would evolve in the show's fifth season (which was shot in the months after the movie had wrapped).

"After playing him for so long, I know how he would react in this situation," Pileggi says. "I think there are ele-ments of Skinner's personality, his character, in what I'm doing in the movie, that have been developing over the past couple of seasons. And they'll just continue to build, to grow. I think the nature of the character and who Chris and I perceive him as being and the interaction that Skinner has with Mulder and Scully will dictate how he develops and how he comes to be where he's at this point in time."

PRINCIPAL SKINNER: "ZERO SUM" [LEFT], "PAPER CLIP" [RIGHT] AND "AVATAR" [BELOW RIGHT]

Besides, it's not as if Pileggi is unaccustomed to being in the dark about *X-Files* storylines. "It's tough in some respects [not knowing how plots will unfold], but knowing that 95 percent of the time the writing is going to be really good gives you a lot of confidence going into the unknown," he adds.

While Skinner ended up keeping a lower profile this past season, Pileggi doesn't grumble. In fact, he's quick to point out that Mulder and Scully's work remains the soul of the show, and the nature of their investigations necessarily sends them out in the field and well away from the assistant director's office. The season still managed to fulfill at least one of Pileggi's professional dreams, anyway—the chance to

chew scenery with his wife, Arlene, who is Gillian Anderson's stand-in on *The X-Files* set. Even before she and her future husband began dating, Arlene wanted to play Skinner's secretary. She finally got her chance in the Vince Gilligan-scripted standout "Bad Blood."

"It was really cool," Pileggi says enthusiastically. "Initially, she was just going to be an extra, just sitting there and eyeballing [Mulder and Scully], and then they gave her some dialogue, which was really neat. So I got to do a scene with my wife."

Although Pileggi relishes his role, he admits that playing a recurring character can have some drawbacks. "Sometimes it is [difficult] to get back into the groove of a character," he says. "The first couple of scenes and first couple of days you're kind of grabbing for what you've been doing in the past. I just have to refresh my memory about who this guy is and what he does and who he's dealing with."

He didn't have any problems finding his acting rhythms for the feature film, however, where the occupational short-hand he already had developed with David Duchovny, Gillian Anderson and director Rob Bowman proved invaluable.

"As actors, we all know what [the other actors] are going to do," he explains. " I don't know if it's a comfort thing or what, but we can just go onto the set and do our job and still have fun."

The laid-back actor's go-with-the-flow-and-have-fun attitude is pretty far removed from the assistant director's intimidating, by-the-books nature. Yet the role is very personal for the actor, who frequently mentions his late father's influence in shaping the character.

"I got lucky, I guess, that they wrote a role for me that I just kind of fell into," he says. "A lot of the character is based on my father, who was an administrative-type on a Department of Defense contract with the Air Force [in the Middlè East]. And I remember him as a child, watching how he dealt with his personnel. Although his position was in a different sphere, [he acted] very similarly to the way Skinner does."

As instrumental as those memories of his father are to his perfor-

X-Files will give me a better chance of getting roles in movies and just doing meaty character roles in the future."

Until then, he's helped fill his spare time by making personal appearances at the X-Files Expos and by hosting a couple of popular *Magic's Biggest Secrets Finally Revealed* specials for Fox (the first of which was the highest-rated special in the network's history). "Magic is pretty cool," Pileggi says. "It's fun finding out how they do stuff. And they pay well, too, which is nice—I'm gonna have a baby to feed!"

Pileggi says he and his wife tape and watch every X-Files episode, partly to see their work, but also partly because they're huge X-Philes themselves. .

"I think [the feature film] made [the audience] use their own imagination and made them think, which is one of the things I think is so great

"if you watch some of the episodes and the movie, you'll find that skinner's an ally, a friend. He's put his job and his life on the line to help them." – Mitch pileggi

mance, they didn't give Pileggi everything he needed to play an FBI G-man, especially considering that the actor never studied with advisors about the role. "I found out at one point [in the fourth season] that I was shooting the gun wrong after holding it wrong," he remembers. "Rob [Bowman] pointed out to me exactly how I should be

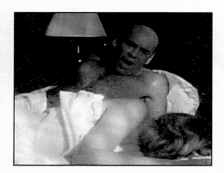

holding it. So you'll get help wherever you can get it. Even from a director." He laughs heartily. "Just kidding, Rob."

Now with *The X-Files* film's release and the show's production moving from British Columbia to Los Angeles, Pileggi's life

looks to grow both professionally and personally. He and Arlene became parents in spring 1998, and they look to permanently move into a California house they bought in 1997. Because his recurring role sometimes gives him several weeks off in-between Skinner appearances, he hopes to use the spare time and proximity to Hollywood to expand his movie career. Pileggi recently announced that he and his agents have decided that *The X-Files* would remain his only television foray, with the rest of his time devoted to finding film roles—hopefully ones more diverse than the heavies he'd been typecast as in the past.

"I'd like to start doing some small character roles in movies and build my career from there," he says. "I don't think it's likely that I'll be cast in a lead in a major film, but perhaps people's exposure to me in *The*

about the show—it brings the viewer into play. They're invited to participate in what we're showing them, and I think that the movie did the same thing."

And as for his role as Skinner, Pileggi seems rather content with the way the FBI supervisor has developed. "I think they've really gone into a lot of areas of the character that I've wanted them to go into," he says. "His relationship with Mulder and Scully really has evolved to what it is now. Except for more, I don't know what else I could want or ask for." ●

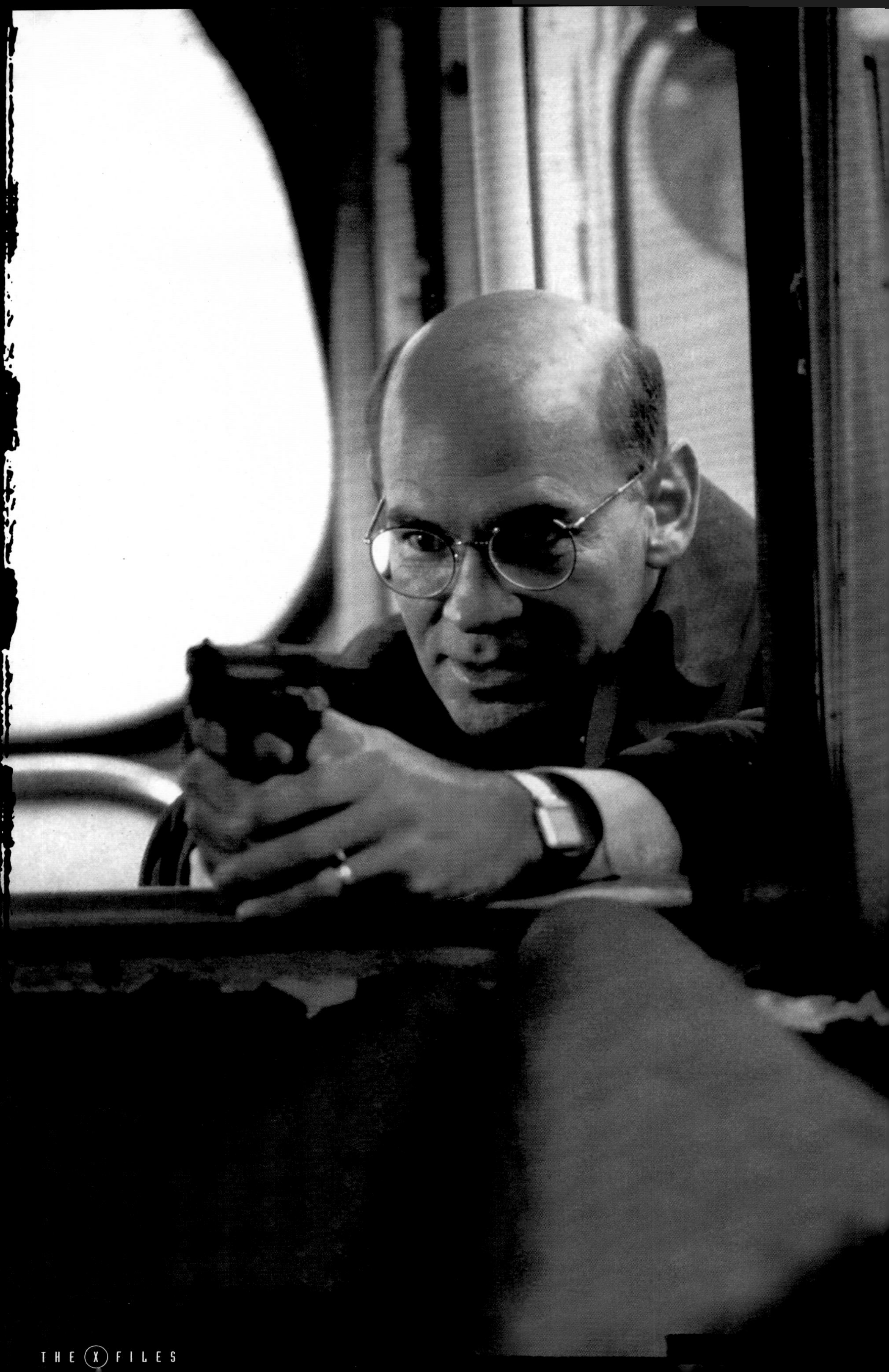

F.B.I. ASSISTANT DIRECTOR WALTER SKINNER

K. Stoddard Hayes

reflects on A.D. Skinner's years

on the X-files

What makes a good boss? If you're hiring a corporate manager, you might want a person who makes his employees productive and always serves the interests of the company. If you're writing a TV drama, your ideal boss isn't that perfect manager, but a man who is ever torn between his obedience to the higher-ups, and his strong sense of responsibility for his subordinates. Enter Walter Skinner, F.B.I. Assistant Director, often the immediate supervisor to the agents of the X-files.

Skinner is the perfect boss for the X-Files. Respected and competent in the Bureau, he has an authority the agents have to respect; he's clearly someone who's going to create dramatic problems if they cross him, as they so often do. At the same time, he is so private about himself that Mulder and Scully don't even know he is married until they meet his wife during a case. Though Skinner is not a liar like the Cigarette-Smoking Man, he rarely reveals everything he knows or everything he intends. And what better way to keep the heroes and the audience guessing, than to have them work for a man whose intentions toward them are never clear?

In many of his minor episodes, Skinner has only the simple role of

'the boss.' He's the person who gives the X-files agents their orders to investigate or (more dramatically) to leave a case alone. He is the provider of vital plot information about a suspect or a situation, such as the news that a suspect has diplomatic immunity. He may arrive with backup for the agents in a dangerous situation, or even rescue them in a crunch, as he does at the end of "Field Day." And he receives the reports of the agents (with varying degrees of scepticism), and hence becomes an ear for their conclusions, metaphysical, philosophical or forensic.

As the boss, Skinner's appearances are most reliable, and most memorable, whenever one of his agents is hurt. When Mulder is frantically searching among the charred bodies in "The Red and the Black," it's Skinner who tells him that Scully is not among them. In "4-D," Skinner calls Reyes with the news that Doggett has been shot. And a list of the scenes in which Skinner visits one of his agents in hospital might take up half a page.

These hospital scenes show very clearly what kind of boss Skinner is. The kind who cares for his agents as individuals, more than he cares for the company's interests – at least as those interests are often defined by Skinner's

superiors. Like any boss who has invested more in people than in product, he knows his people's weaknesses and fears, as we see when he orders Mulder away from the investigation of Scully's abduction ("Ascension"), and tries to protect Scully from bad news about Mulder's abduction ("This Is Not Happening"). He knows their strengths, as we see when he refuses to accept Mulder's resignation from the X-files, because he knows that the Bureau needs Mulder's tenacity and courage in the pursuit of the truth ("One Breath"). It's a hospital scene that shows the depth of Skinner's care for his agents. When Mulder reports that Scully's cancer has gone into remission, Skinner gasps, "That's incredible news!" And he smiles – one of the rare occasions that we ever see Skinner smile ("Redux II").

When the X-files pass into the charge of new agents, we learn that Skinner's care isn't limited to his long-time associates, Mulder and Scully. His loyalty extends to their successors, Doggett and Reyes, as we see in "John Doe," when Kersh orders Skinner and Reyes to leave the search for the missing Doggett to the Mexican

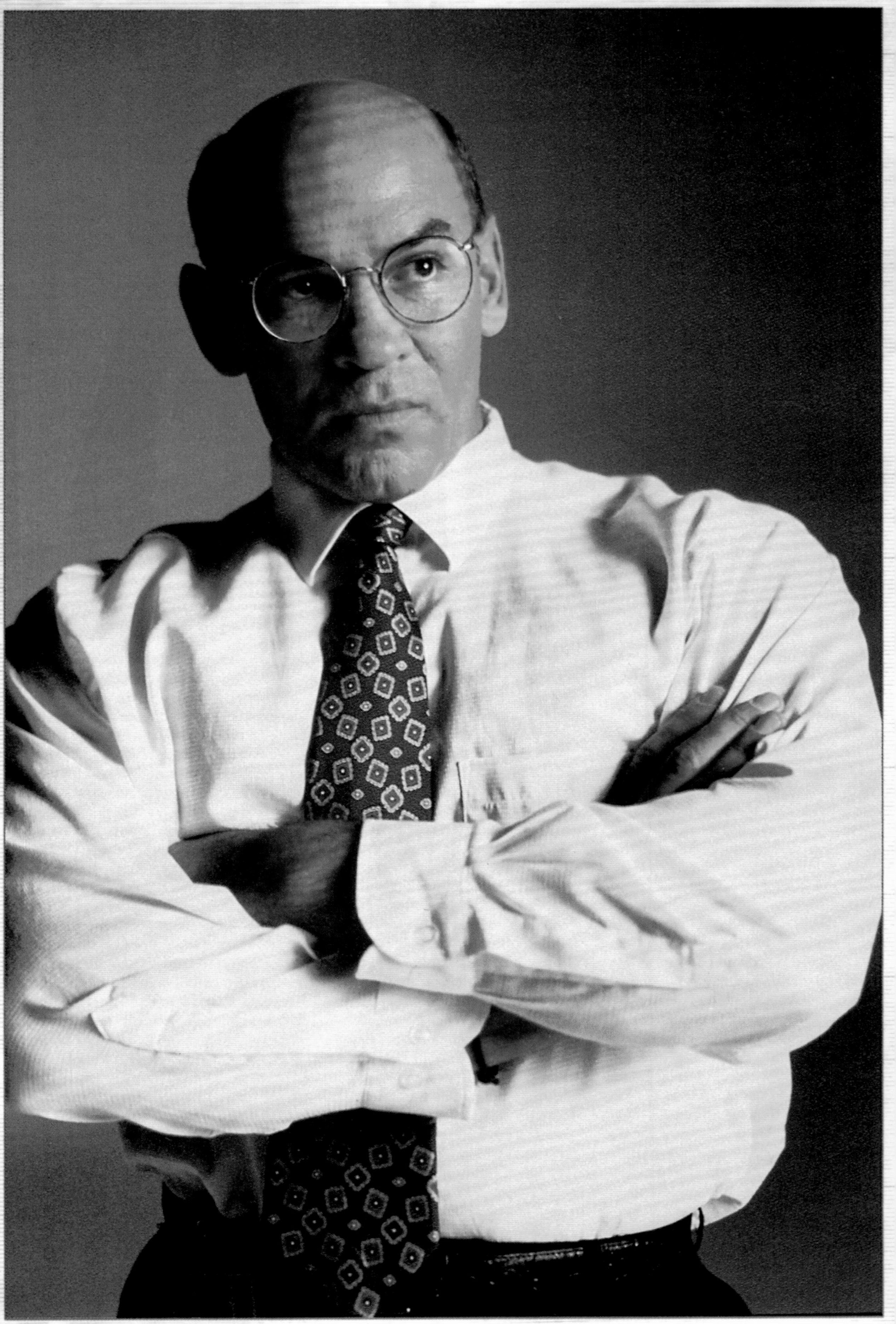

authorities. How closely Skinner adheres to Kersh's order can be seen when he himself leads the cavalry, in the form of the Federales, to the rescue of Doggett and Reyes.

Skinner's life gets most interesting for us, and most difficult for him, whenever he is caught between the conflicting interests of the agents who work for him, and the superiors to whom he is accountable. In the corporate world, this balancing act may be only a matter of diplomacy and politics, and the penalty is losing your job. In the F.B.I., where the bureaucracy itself is a tool of the alien conspiracy, keeping your balance is all too often a matter of life or death.

Skinner first shows his skill at this balancing act in "One Breath," when Mulder demands contact information for the Cigarette-Smoking Man. Skinner refuses. But a few hours later, he has the address smuggled to Mulder in a pack of cigarettes. In "The Blessing Way" and "Paper Clip" he steps clearly over the line to take sides with Mulder and Scully. He tells them he can use the digital tape to protect their lives and gain their reinstatement. And in his secret confrontation with the Cigarette-Smoking Man he shows his heart for the first time, in the way he speaks to the man who has tried to murder Mulder and Scully, and caused the deaths of Mulder's father and Scully's sister. "This is where you pucker up and kiss my ass. You listen to me, you son of a bitch!"

It would take too long to list all the times Skinner has come out on the side of the X-files agents, even against orders. When Scully identifies a faceless body as Mulder's, Skinner suspects that Mulder may still be alive. But he keeps his suspicions to himself, to protect both Mulder and Scully, until Mulder emerges from hiding ("Redux"). When they have been removed from the X-files and from his supervision, they break into the X-files office, and he tries to warn them they

GREAT SKINNER MOMENTS

"Anasazi", "Paper Clip" and "The Blessing Way"
Skinner becomes a major player for the first time, when he gets involved in the fate of the digital tape. He has a gunpoint standoff with Mulder and Scully, and later puts a metaphorical gun to the Cigarette-Smoking Man's head.

"Piper Maru" and "Apocrypha"
As the agents have their first encounter with the Black Oil, Skinner is shot by a Syndicate trigger man.

"Tunguska" and "Terma"
Skinner makes his apartment a "safe house" for Krycek, by handcuffing Krycek to his balcony in winter weather.

"Memento Mori"
After refusing to let Mulder bargain with the Cigarette-Smoking Man, Skinner makes his own deal with the devil, to save Scully's life.

"Zero Sum"
Skinner becomes a pawn in a plot of the Cigarette-Smoking Man, poses as Mulder, and almost gets framed for another murder.

"Redux" and "Redux II"
The shadow Bureau hierarchy sets up Skinner for a fall when Blevins tells Mulder to save his own career by naming Skinner as a mole.

"S.R. 819"
Skinner is infected with a deadly alien nanovirus controlled by Alex Krycek.

"Biogenesis" and "The Sixth Extinction"
Skinner is forced to become Krycek's informant, and to watch Mulder go

apparently insane from the influence of an ancient alien ship.

"Brand X"
When a tobacco company whistleblower dies mysteriously before he can testify, Skinner gets a rare opportunity to exchange his desk for investigations in the field.

"Hollywood A.D."
Skinner goes Hollywood when he brings a screenwriter friend into the X-files to do research for a movie.

"Requiem", "Within" and "Without"
Skinner witnesses Mulder's abduction, and finds himself completely ostracized from the F.B.I. hierarchy as he and Scully try to investigate Mulder's disappearance.

"This is Not Happening"
Skinner tries to shelter Scully from an investigation of returned abductees; an investigation that forebodes the direst news of Mulder's fate.

"DeadAlive"
When Billy Miles is found alive, Skinner orders Mulder's exhumation, then has to choose between Mulder and Scully's baby.

"Existence"
As the agents try to protect Scully and her unborn child, Skinner has a near fatal close encounter with Billy Miles; and finally gets payback by shooting Alex Krycek.

"Provenance" and "Providence"
Skinner is caught between the F.B.I. bureaucracy and his X-files agents when an investigation of a U.F.O. cult endangers Scully's baby.

are about to be apprehended ("Two Fathers"). He secretly brings Kritschgau to Mulder's hospital room in the hope that Kritschgau may be able to help Mulder's condition ("The Sixth Extinction"). And when Mulder is abducted, Skinner is so outspoken in his conviction that the investigation ordered by Kersh is a cover-up, that Scully has to restrain him so that he won't be suspended ("Within" and "Without").

There have been times when Skinner has appeared to be working for Krycek, or for the Cigarette-Smoking Man, since both have gained leverage over him in different ways. Yet if there was any serious doubt about whose side Skinner is really on, consider that he has twice been targeted for assassination or professional disgrace ("Piper Maru", "Apocrypha" and "Avatar"), and both times, the motive has been to deprive the X-files of his protection.

Yet because of Skinner's trademark reserve, even after eight years, we can still be kept guessing about his intentions, if not his true loyalties. After his staunch support of Scully,

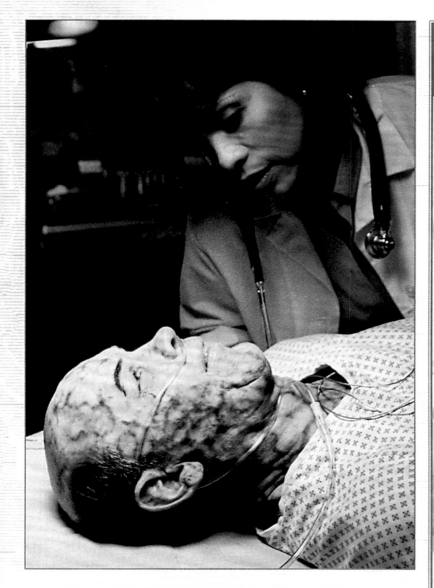

Mulder and Doggett through the events of Mulder's disappearance and the birth of Scully's child, we expect him to be completely on the agents' side. But in the U.F.O. cult investigation of "Provenance" and "Providence," Skinner appears to have switched sides again. He seems to be cooperating with Kersh, Follmer, and the bureaucrats who interrogate Scully, and try to keep Doggett and Reyes away from what should be an X-file investigation. It's Doggett, with his own strong sense of loyalty and square dealing, who challenges Skinner on this. His challenge shows how much the X-files agents have come to count on Skinner.

"I don't understand, none of us do, why you're keeping their secrets?" he says. To Doggett and his comrades, the X-files and the bureaucracy are an "us" against "them" opposition, and Skinner belongs among "us" not "them."

Skinner has the same reasons he always has, though he doesn't reveal them until later. The F.B.I. has an unconfirmed report that Mulder may be dead. Skinner was with Scully through all the anguish of Mulder's abduction, death and revival. Having seen her suffering then, he's trying to protect her now from an investigation that he fears may be unbearably painful to her. And no doubt his silence is also partly due to orders from his superiors, who are trying to keep the U.F.O. cult investigation as secret as possible.

As always, though, Skinner can find small ways to subvert his orders, and look after his people. When an undercover agent dies in his hospital bed, Skinner's superiors order him to find Reyes and Scully, who were with the man moments before, and bring them to account for themselves. Instead, Skinner warns his agents that they should get away before they can be questioned. It's just one more way he shows that his true loyalties lie with his agents, and with the truth.●

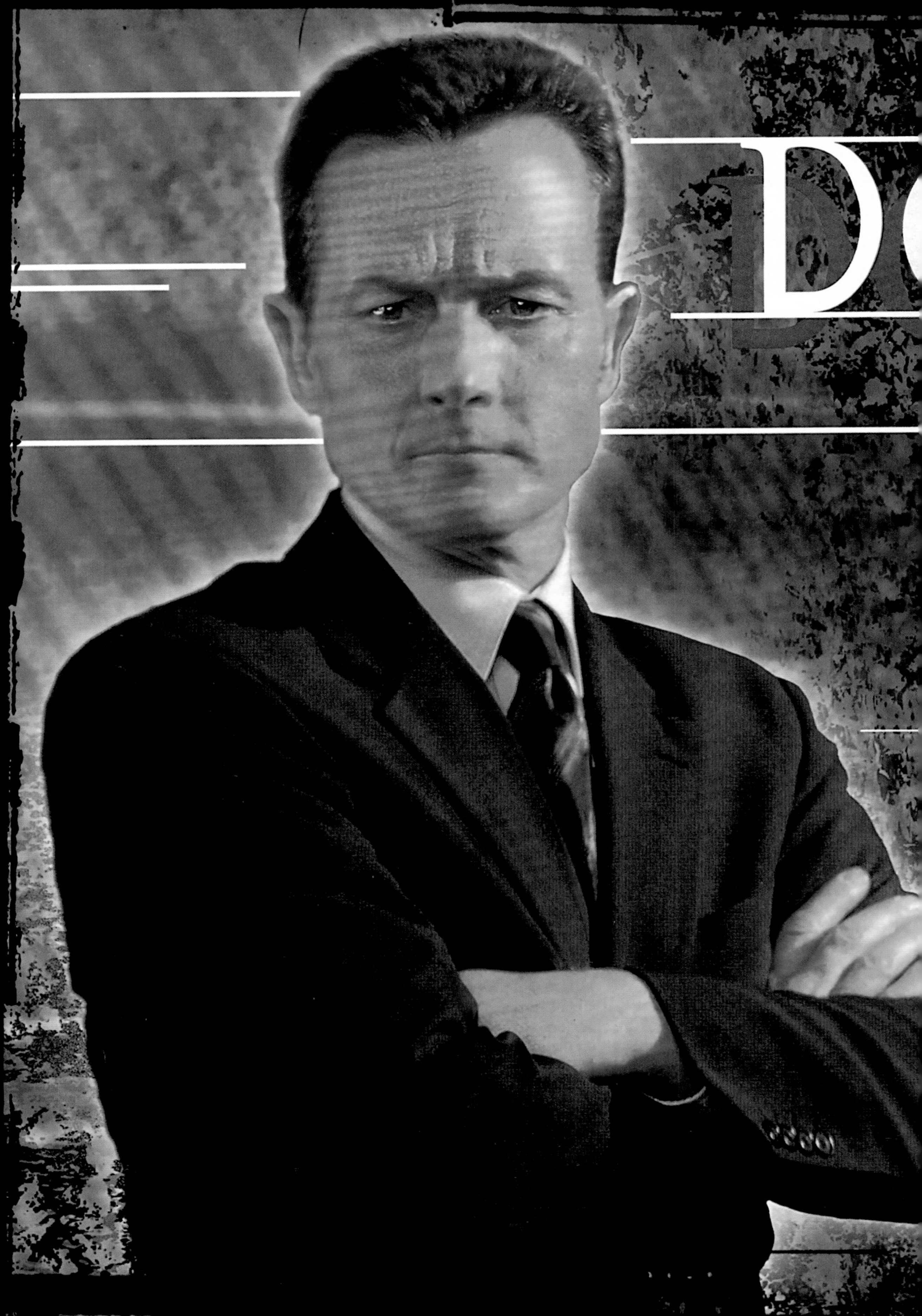

OGGETT
PURSUITS

HE AMAZED US ALL IN SEASON EIGHT, AND NOW HE'
SET FOR BIGGER AND BETTER THINGS IN SEASON NINE.

ROBERT PATRICK CHATS

ABOUT SPECIAL AGENT JOHN DOGGETT.

Interview by Ian Spelling

"I love our show," Robert Patrick enthuses of *The X-Files*. "A lot of people love *The X-Files*. Hopefully, it's a good diversion. One of the big things about *The X-Files* is that it's often about questioning authority and not just accepting everything your government tells you is true. I think a lot of it applies right now, in this new world we're in since September 11. That's a big thing. Plus, I'd like to think that our characters are heroic and patriotic and on the side of good. They're not nearly as heroic as the real police and firemen, but our intentions are good. We, as actors, are trying to make our characters people of virtue."

Patrick, of course, joined *The X-Files* in Season Eight as Special Agent John Doggett, the man brought in to head up the investigation into the disappearance of Fox Mulder. Doggett initially displayed plenty of doubt. But based on what he himself saw and experienced – everything from shapeshifters to possible alien babies, from death to rebirth (via regurgitation!) – he is becoming increasingly faced with the possibility that perhaps Mulder wasn't crazy and that perhaps Dana Scully had every reason in the world to believe in Mulder and his cause. Heck, by the end of Season Eight, after dealing with the imminent arrival of Scully's baby, interacting a few times on missions with Mulder, and facing the possibility that he himself possesses some sort of psychic ability that may tie into the death of his son, Doggett was very close to becoming, well, less of a doubter...

"I thought there were a number of important episodes and moments," Patrick says of Season Eight. "I think there were a lot of stand-alone episodes we did that were good experiences and good episodes. The one that sticks out is `Via Negativa'," he says of the episode which earned *The X-Files* its second viewer discretion warning for graphic content (the first being for Season Four's "Home"). "That was the one where Doggett's mind was possessed by the leader of a religious group that was invading people's psyches and getting them to commit

MULDER AND DOGGETT IN "VIENEN"

ON THE HUNT IN "MEDUSA"

these atrocities on his behalf. He started to get into my head. That was a great experience as an actor. It was challenging and a lot of fun. So far as specific character moments, I think he gained Scully's trust and respect. He came through in the sense that he found Mulder. He gained respect for and insight into Mulder and what he's done. He was a man of his word and accomplished his goal, and all the while he did that protecting Scully, watching after her and her best interests. Even though he loves Scully, he realized that he was there to protect her, and he didn't intrude on her relationship with Mulder. He stood back and respected that. I thought that was a great thing.

"I was also pleased with the scenes between Doggett and Mulder," Patrick continues. "I thought they were great, and Chris Carter and Frank Spotnitz did a great job of respecting both characters, allowing them to get together and find respect for each other. I really loved the way they wrote those scenes.

David Duchovny, the actor who of course portrayed Special Agent Fox Mulder from the very first episode, left the show at the end of Season Eight. Patrick comments on the actor and their brief working relationship. "I think David and I both responded as actors with mutual respect toward each other, and that carried over to the characters. It all went hand-in-hand. You also have to realize that a lot of what Chris and Frank wrote reflected what was going on

"I was pleased **with the scenes between Doggett** and **Mulder**. Chris Carter and Frank Spotnitz did a great job of respecting both characters, allowing them to get **together and find** respect for each other."

in real life, in terms of me being a new actor on the show. Mulder and Doggett did a few missions together, but we were bitching in the corners of the office. It's his office and I have respect for that, but I'm now there and I have a job to do. So what do I do? I can't not have a backbone. I think Chris and Frank did a great job writing that transition and I commend David for the way he handled it. I thought it was first-rate all the way down the line."

So, did Duchovny ever approach Patrick and say, either directly or in essence, 'I'm not coming back. It's all yours. Good luck'? "David and I had a couple of conversations about it and they went like this," Patrick recalls. "David said, 'Man, I'm having fun. This is fun. I'm really enjoying working with you.' I said, 'Yeah, I think it's great. I want you to come back whenever you want and I hope you know that.' He said, 'I do and I will, maybe. I've got to see how things progress and how they write.'

"That's how it went for a while," says Patrick. "Then, as things progressed, I got the sense that he wanted to stick with his game plan of saying goodbye and moving on. But I never got a definitive [answer] until the end. He said, 'Hey man, you've got a great job. You're doing a great job. Just have fun with it.'

"He probably decided that, after eight years, enough was enough," Patrick continues. "I'm not going to speak for him, but I want to convey that it was a great experience working with him. I think he really enjoyed it. But I think as he got back into it, he thought, 'You know, I said I'm going to walk away and I'm going to stick to that.' He never flatout said that to me, but that was the sense I got."

Once it became clear that Duchovny was not coming back, the fate of the series was thrown into question, and not just because of Duchovny's departure. Carter, just before the eighth season kicked off, signed a one-year contract. And as the season ended, Carter had yet to sign on for year nine. Fans wondered if Carter would relinquish his day-to-day writing and producing duties. He did return, but only at the very last minute,

after Spotnitz and company had started work on upcoming episodes.

Then there was the matter of Gillian Anderson. She was under contract for a ninth season, but made it clear in interviews that she'd prefer to move on with her career and spend more time with her daughter. Patrick, meanwhile, stood on the sidelines and awaited word of the show's fate, though he figured it would all work out.

"I'm going to be presumptuous and say I don't think there's ever been a show like *The X-Files*," he says. "It's an expensive show. It's a fantastic-looking show. They tell stories no other show tells. They try to do things on *The X-Files* in 8 days of shooting an episode that are incredibly difficult. The hours

are grueling. We hear from other people on other one-hour dramas about their 12-hour days, and we'll be in our 18th hour. The schedule is grueling. There's not a lot of free time. There were some times last year when I was really treading water, going, 'My God, I hope I make it.' It can be a little overwhelming, not just for me, but also for the whole crew because the show is so ambitious and there's so much money behind it. We sometimes do 80 hours a week. Chris takes two weeks off a year, but otherwise he's got to eat, drink and sleep *The X-Files*. The whole thing is on his shoulders. I'm sure he probably gives it some thought. 'Do I want to continue?' I know how hard Gillian works. And she's been there from the beginning. I know

CHRIS CARTER AND ROBERT PATRICK ON THE SET OF "PATIENCE"

"I'd like to think that our [X-Files] characters are heroic and patriotic and on the **side of good. They're** not nearly as heroic as the real police and firemen, but **our intentions** are good."

"Even though [Doggett] loves Scully, he realized that he was there to protect her, and he didn't intrude on her relationship with Mulder."

how hard David worked. I know how hard I work. That's why I'm excited that the show is now more of an ensemble show. If it's an ensemble, there are more people and that eases everyone's workload. It's certainly easier than having just two people who are in every scene together. We can spread the workload around. So if Chris and Gillian are tired, it has nothing to do with the show, the subject matter or the enthusiasm we all have for the creative part of the show. I think it's just the arduous schedule that gets to you.

"As I said last year, when I started on the show, I focused on the work, did the best I could and figured 'Whatever happens, happens.' And I kind of feel I stuck to that game plan and it worked, thank God. The fans stayed tuned and they seemed to accept Doggett as a new character. I don't think his being there threatened anybody. I think people, even the Mulder fans, felt that Doggett was there to support all the good work that Mulder had done. And that worked dually, as characters and actors. I think the fans also realized that I was there to support David and all the good work that he'd done."

Season Nine got underway in the US in November with the "Nothing Important Happened Today" two-parter and the show has indeed morphed into an ensemble series. Doggett is partnered with Special Agent Monica Reyes, a

relationship that's complicated on several fronts. On the professional end of the equation, they work well together. She believes in Doggett and does her best to support him, both on the usual investigations into the unusual and also in Doggett's pursuit of Deputy Director Kersh. Kersh is emerging as a major nemesis, a shadowy figure not unlike Assistant Director Skinner in the early days of *The X-Files*.

On the personal front, Reyes seems well aware of Doggett's suppressed psychic abilities and might just be in love with the guy. That last point's a sticky wicket, for Doggett seems to be interested in Scully, Scully still feels affection for Mulder (even though he's on the run from the aliens and had to leave baby William behind) and Reyes is fending off the unwanted affections of her snide and oily former beau, Assistant Director Brad Follmer, who looks to be as out to get Doggett as Doggett is out to get Kersh.

"I like what's going on," Patrick enthuses. "I want to continue on with this theme of Doggett having virtue, being morally sound and patriotic. He believes in his country and yet he's willing to question authority and question everything, really. There's a fine line in that. I keep talking about the fine line that John Doggett walks, and I want that to be defined more. I also think Doggett's going to have to deal better

with the situation involving his son and the premonitions. I didn't realise, going into the show last year, that Doggett had some sort of questionable paranormal experience relating to his son. That happened about midway through the season and it was a good thing. Maintaining your knee-jerk scepticism when you've taken a shotgun blast, been spit out by a shaman and come back to life… how can you got through that and maintain your scepticism? That's been one of the challenges of my job. Doggett has to stay somewhat sceptical, but hopefully that will help him be able to be a little more open to some of the things he comes into contact with as a result of being on the 'X'-files.

"I also think he's going to have to resolve some things with Scully and Reyes. There's a lot going on there. I've gone to Scully for some help and she doesn't want to help me. Doggett finds himself alienated. Nobody wants to help him out. The only person on his side is Reyes. So, in effect, Doggett and Reyes are the new Mulder and Scully. I want to see what happens with his relationships with them."

Might that entail Doggett engaging in a romance with either of the ladies? "I would really like it," Patrick replies playfully as the conversation comes to an end for now. "Doggett would really like it, I should say. You know what I mean? It would be great for the character." ●

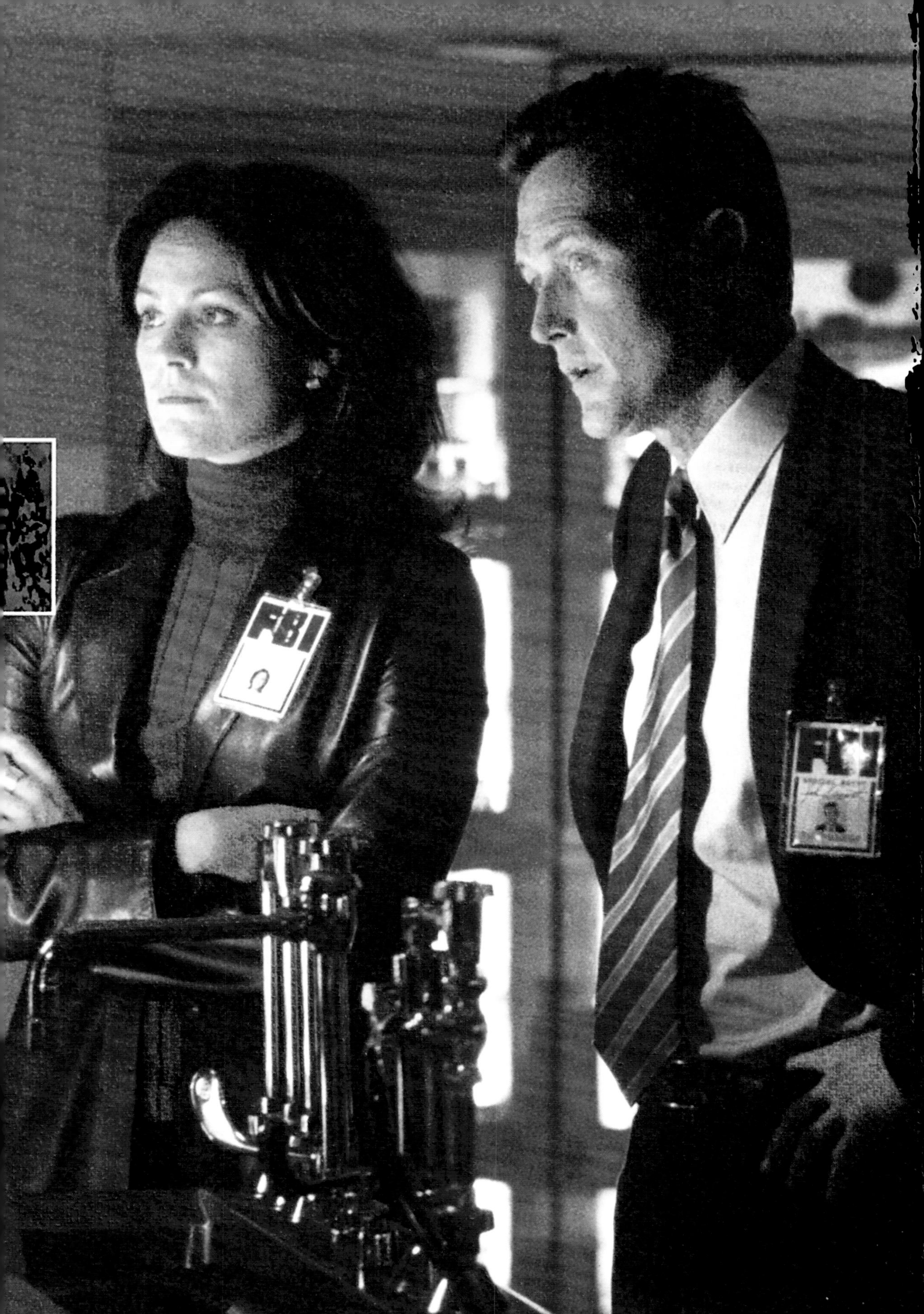
FBI
FBI

DOGGETT AND NEW PARTNER REYES IN "NOTHING IMPORTANT HAPPENED TODAY"

FBI CASE STUDY:
SPECIAL AGENT JOHN DOGGETT

AGENT FILE:
JOHN DOGGETT
ASSIGNED TO X-FILES, 2000
CAREER HISTORY:
FORMER MARINE AND NYPD DETECTIVE
PERSONAL: HIS SON LUKE WAS ABDUCTED
AND MURDERED IN 1997 AT AGE 7. THE
CASE IS STILL OPEN.

John Doggett hates playing games. He is as open and direct as law enforcement work allows, and insists that those he works with be equally direct with him. When he is first assigned to the X-files, the whole issue of paranormal phenomena seems at first like just another game, played by people like Mulder and Reyes, who would rather seek a supernatural explanation than a simple criminal one.

As a sceptic, Doggett fills the role that Scully had when she began work on the X-files. And in that role, he pushes both Scully and Skinner into the true-believer role that was once Mulder's, as they try to convince him that there might be paranormal explanations for Mulder's disappearance.

As Doggett steps into Scully's shoes, he follows the same road of belief that she did. Like Scully, he instinctively seeks the rational, real-world (and, in Scully's case, scientific) explanations first, and only looks at the paranormal with great reluctance, when no other possibilities are left. When Reyes uses paranormal evidence to link a series of murders with the three-year old murder of Doggett's son, Doggett's first reaction is, "Not this again!"

Yet he has seen enough, and is honest enough, that he has to begin to question his own scepticism. He asks Scully why she began to believe in the paranormal.

"I realised it was me – that I was afraid to believe," Scully answers.

Her words force him to examine his own fears. He tells Reyes, "I gotta believe that I did everything I could to find my son. I gotta believe that I did everything I could to save him, to get him back safe, to not let him down... These other possibilities that you talk about – if they're real, then that's something else I coulda done to save my son." ("Empedocles")

Once Doggett starts coming face to face with the paranormal, it's Scully's turn to help him, as Mulder helped her, to come to terms with one of the realities of the X-files – that most of the time, the truth will remain buried. In "Medusa", Doggett is determined that the chief of the Boston MTA should be held accountable for opening a subway tunnel that contained a deadly biological pathogen. When Scully points out that they have no evidence, Doggett can't believe it. He saw the organisms on his own skin and saw the results in the burned flesh of the victims, and he knows the MTA chief was more concerned with his rush-hour schedule than with protecting lives. But there's that word, "evidence". As Mulder and Scully have done countless times before, he has to learn to let it go.

Doggett's relationship with Scully in some ways parallels Scully's with Mulder: the sceptic facing their own beliefs, and the new partner winning the believer's trust and respect. At the core, though, his feelings for Scully are

"WITHOUT"

pure John Doggett. As a law enforcement officer, he believes he owes his partner complete loyalty from the start. He'll cover her back no matter what he thinks of her beliefs. But it very soon goes beyond that. Through the whole year, whenever Scully is in danger, when her pregnancy is threatened, or even when she's upset and grieving for Mulder, Doggett's overriding concern is always her well being. Yet he also cares enough to let her do what she must. When Mulder is exhumed alive and brought to the hospital, Doggett tries to spare her the pain of seeing him in this condition.

"I need to see," she says.

"I know," he says gently. "But I wish you wouldn't." ("DeadAlive")

What does Doggett see in Scully that makes him care so deeply, in such a short time? Probably the same quality that Skinner and Mulder saw: an honesty that goes right through her. And for Doggett, that may be the most important quality anyone could have. Like him, Scully doesn't play games.

It's also a measure of how much he cares for her, that he understands that he will never be first in her life. When Doggett sees Mulder in the hospital, awake for the first time since his death, and Scully lying on his shoulder, Doggett just looks at Scully for a long moment, then he walks away alone. They don't need him, and he knows it.

Doggett especially hates being used as a pawn in someone else's game. When Absalom, who is holding him hostage, is shot by a government sharpshooter, without any attempt at negotiation, Doggett knows something is wrong. He goes to his informant Knowle Rohrer for information, then realises afterwards that the information Rohrer gave him was intended as bait for Mulder. Doggett has been used to set Mulder up. He risks his own life to go into the ambush and warn a very sceptical Mulder, just in time to let both of them escape. ("Three Words")

Deputy Director Kersh is the champion game player in Doggett's professional life. He has chosen Doggett as an important strategic piece that will let him shut the X-files down for good. He counts on Doggett to prove that Mulder's disappearance has nothing to do with extra-terrestrials. And he

"WITHOUT"

assumes, because Doggett is a straight-arrow agent and a credit to the FBI (a complete contrast to the maverick Mulder), that Doggett will accept a promotion, and get out of the dead-end X-files assignment as quickly as possible.

The moment when Doggett joins the meeting with Skinner and Kersh in Kersh's office is a remarkable benchmark in Doggett's arc. He began the season as the outsider and adversary, apparently opposed to the true believers, Skinner and Scully. When Doggett sits down next to Skinner, it's apparent from the glances he gives Skinner, even before a word is spoken, that he considers himself on Skinner's side, not Kersh's. And he very quickly breaks Kersh's bubble of complacency, by

refusing to jump at the promotion Kersh offers. He has too much integrity to walk away from what he considers unfinished business. More than that, he is too shrewd to miss Kersh's intentions, and too stubborn to let anyone use him for their own games.

"It's not my career he's thinking of," he tells Scully later. "In six weeks, you go on maternity leave. If he transfers me out, he gets to lock that door for good... We still got an open file on this case, and I got big questions." ("DeadAlive")

Doggett may never be a true believer in the X-files. Yet he has learned that Earth-bound forensic science can't explain everything and that the need for the X-files will always be there. ●

- K. Stoddard Hayes

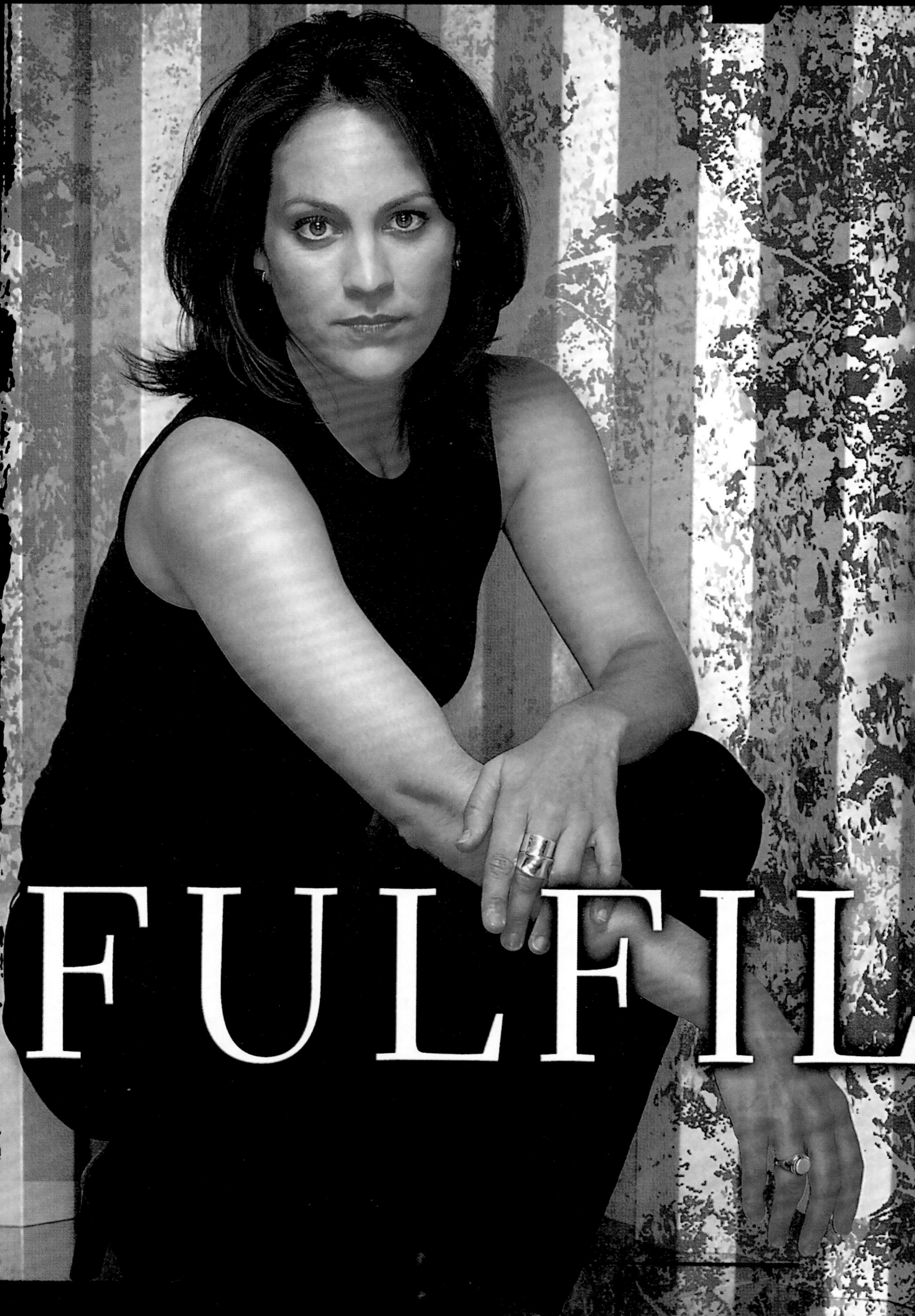

FULFIL

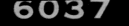

AFTER AN IMPRESSIVE DEBUT AS SPECIAL AGENT MONICA REYES IN SEASON EIGHT, ANNABETH GISH HAS CONTINUED TO BRING A FRESH FEEL TO *THE X-FILES*. THE ACTRESS CHATS TO IAN SPELLING ABOUT HER – AND HER CHARACTER'S – PROGRESS.

From that deliriously odd and decidedly personal X-file called expectation versus reality, Annabeth Gish observes the following so far as her character, Special Agent Monica Reyes, is concerned: "I thought that she might be more esoteric, more ethereal, based on the way that Chris Carter and Frank Spotnitz presented her to me at the beginning, when we first talked about how Reyes would develop," the friendly and soft-spoken actress says. "But I think, actually, that might have been my own misconception, because she's also an FBI agent and she has to have a lot of practical, tactical and logistical skills that she can perform. I don't know that any agent could perform all those skills and be too esoteric and ethereal. So the performance aspect

that's been the most challenging is being a detective, as opposed to being a spiritual, open-minded woman. The way she is now, she's a bit of both. She's an FBI agent who has a bit of the ethereal in her. Chris and Frank are cultivating that more and more, but she has to deliver when it comes down to wielding a gun and doing her job. That's been interesting for me."

Asked about her initial reaction to her character, Gish is full of enthusiasm. "I liked Reyes' disposition right away," she says. "She had a willingness to believe without knowing much. She was open-minded and had this attraction to the other realm without pure, direct experience of it. I don't think Monica had seen alien spacecraft before, but it was in her

GISH
LMENT

Interview by Ian Spelling

ANNABETH GISH

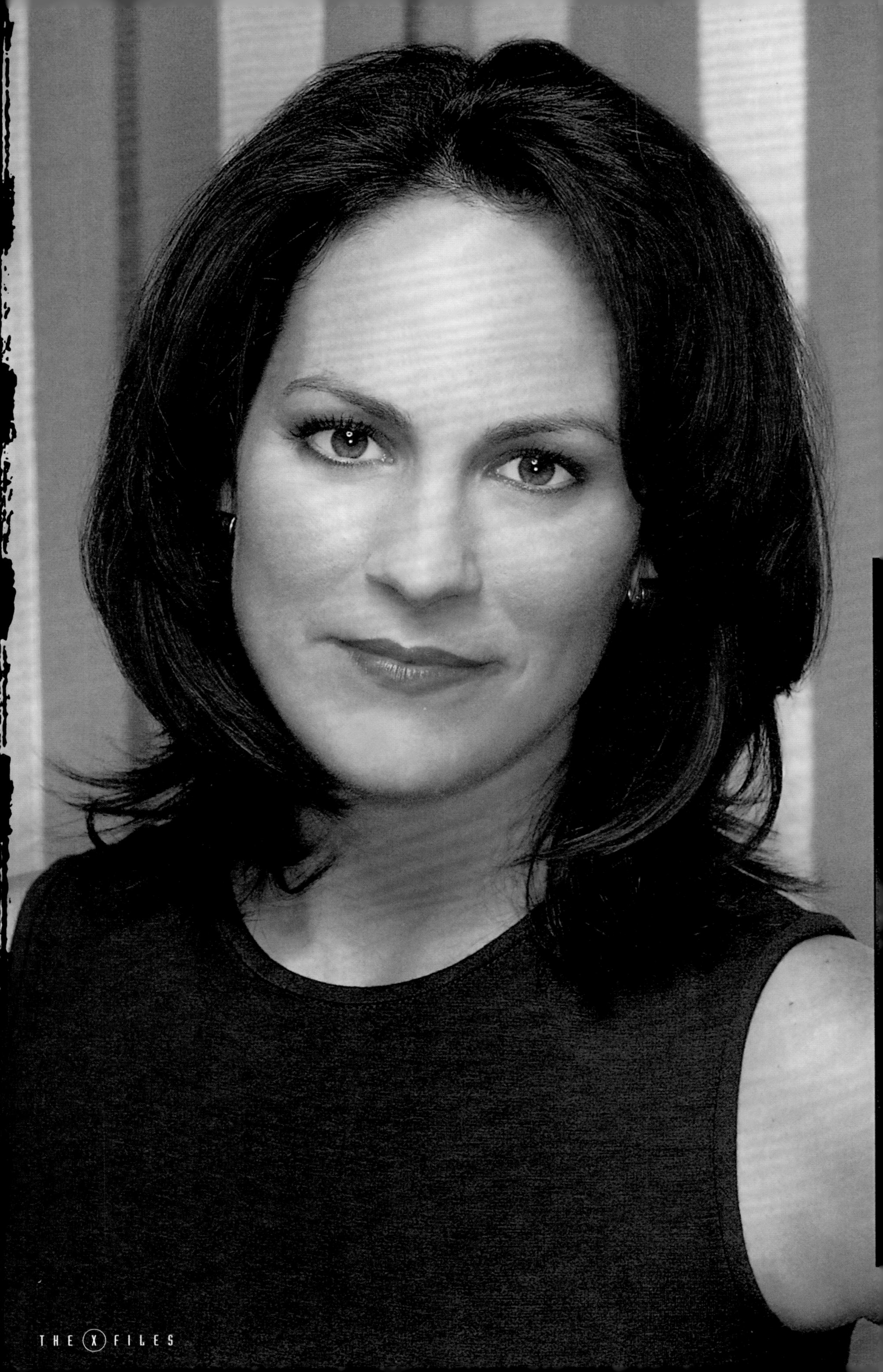

"I liked Reyes' disposition

right away. She had a willingness to believe without **knowing much."**

nature to have a sensitive, mystical thirst for whatever is out there. We've touched on that and I hope it's an aspect that they'll really pursue. There's also a lot about her past that I don't know yet. I've sort of collaborated on our ideas about how she came to be here. They're giving me some roots to feed on, but as with any series the characters evolve as the stories evolve. So I think that Chris and Frank are discovering who Monica is, just as I am. It's happening simultaneously and I like what I'm seeing. What else would I like to

"HELLBOUND"

know about her? I'd like to know about her experiences with her family, her mother and father. I think there's some mystical aspect to her background, and I'd like to explore that or at least touch on that. I think that knowing what happened in the past will give you a better understanding of why she is who she is now. I also want to know why she's into the occult."

Gish arrived on *The X-Files* scene late in the eighth season, appearing first in "This Is Not Happening" and then returning a few episodes later for "Empedocles," "Essence" and "Existence." The character was quickly partnered with Special Agent John Doggett (Robert Patrick) and thrown into the mix as Doggett and Scully (Gillian Anderson) dealt with the return of Mulder (David Duchovny) and the impending birth of Scully's baby. The realm of series television was pretty new to Gish, who'd acted in the short-lived show *Courthouse* and a bunch of made-for-TV movies, including *Scarlett, Don't Look Back, God's New Plan* and, most recently, *The Way She Moves.* However, Gish is best known for her work in such features as *Desert Bloom, Mystic Pizza, Wyatt Earp, Nixon, Beautiful Girls, Steel,* the box office hit *Double Jeopardy* and the soon-to-be-released independent features *Buying the Cow* and *Race to Space,* the latter of which co-stars James Woods, Jake Lloyd of *Star Wars: Episode I – The Phantom Menace* fame, and *X-Files* veteran John O'Hurley.

Gish quickly discovered that *The X-Files* production team spends more

days shooting an episode than just about any show on TV and that those days can easily run 12 or 14 hours or even longer. And, just as the rigors of weekly television were new to Gish, so too was much of *The X-Files* universe. "I was a casual *X-Files* watcher, but you have to understand that I've never been a religious watcher of any television program," she says. "I'd definitely watched the first few seasons while I was in college. That was a big Friday night thing, watch *The X-Files* before you go out. As for the entire mythology… man, I tried to download some of it on the computer before I started with the show and it was so extensive and so deep and profound that I was kind of intimidated and daunted. The good thing was that Monica Reyes doesn't have to know everything. She, like I was, was walking into the mythology kind of blind."

By the time Season Nine rolled around, Reyes was on hand as a full-time presence, while Mulder vanished into the night, Scully spent much of her time at her new job at Quantico, and Doggett tried to fill Mulder's shoes, win Scully's affections and trust, and solve cases – of both the standalone and mythology variety – with Reyes. Meanwhile, with each passing day and each passing case, Reyes seemed to grow fonder and fonder of Doggett. Where any of this is leading, Gish has no idea. "The frustrating thing about series work is that you don't know the entire story and you have to wait to know it," explains the actress, who was born in Albuquerque, New Mexico, and now lives in Los Angeles. "And even

"**I watched** the first few seasons while

I was in college. That was a big Friday night thing, watch

The X-Files before you **go out."**

"NOTHING IMPORTANT
HAPPENED TODAY"

partner a housewarming gift of Polish sausage with mustard. The banter is sweet and when one character affectionately wipes some mustard off the face of the other, there's no denying the sexual tension. Gish's face registers comfort, warmth and familiarity, while Patrick's betrays that plus a touch of confusion: "Hmm, I think this woman

al. It's not like any of us are standing around, stomping our feet and saying, 'Get the limo to take me home!' We're all about the work and we're all dedicated to the work. I think Chris sort of demands that. He chooses actors who can execute that way, under these conditions."

Gish has been called upon to do some strange things in a handful of her previous projects. She, along with Cameron Diaz, Courtney B. Vance and Ron Eldard, wined, dined, mur-

"I want to know
what's going on between Doggett and Reyes. There's
this **unrequited love.**"

is into me." Later, that scene gains relevance and impact when Doggett ends up paralyzed. "It was awkward for Robert and me to film that [mustard-wiping sequence] because we haven't gone there romantically as our characters," Gish notes. "But that scene was so good. And the word is calibrate. That's the perfect word. It's frustrating, as I said, not to know where things are going, but it's also great as an actress to always have an obstacle. My relationship with Doggett always has an obstacle in the way. Either he doesn't want to love me or he's in love with Scully. I don't know if he even recognizes that Monica loves him. It'll be very interesting to see how they play it out, but Chris and Frank haven't told me anything."

W hile many of her scenes pair her with Patrick, Gish has found herself part of an ensemble cast. That's been another new experience and one quite to her liking. "The amazing thing about Chris and Frank is that they have the ability to find actors who are interesting and as talented as hell," Gish enthuses. "They really do attract great actors, from the main parts to the recurring parts to even the smallest roles. David, Gillian, Robert, myself and Cary are completely different beings. I think we each have very different characteristics and qualities, and that's good for the show. The one thing we all are, though, is dedicated and profession-

dered and buried Jason Alexander, Ron Perlman and others in the black comedy *The Last Supper*. And, hell, she acted with Shaquille O'Neal in the comic book-based big-screen epic, *Steel*. *The X-Files*, however, regularly requires that Gish participate in a variety of crazy things, the kinds of things that prompt her to call her friends and family after a day's work and, sometimes, right after she wraps a scene. "Doing some of the stuff in 'Lord of the Flies' was pretty darn weird," she says, laughing. "Getting in that plastic sheath [which served as spider webbing] was pretty weird. I've had to look at hamburger meat that was used as the brain in a skull. Delivering the baby [in 'Existence'] was pretty wild. One of the most exhilarating experiences was doing the episode with the ship ['Nothing Important Happened Today, Part II']. That explosion scene was one of the most extensive stunts I'd ever been a part of and it was totally exciting."

G ish was obviously disappointed by the news of the series' cancellation. She wanted the show to continue and she wanted fans to give her and the show – which she acknowledges was starting to morph into something new – a fair shake. "I think people like what I'm doing," she says, bringing the conversation to an end. "I'm sure there are those who are very loyal to Mulder and Scully and don't want to have anything to do with Reyes and Doggett. As a whole, though, I think people are seeing good work and a good show." ●

though you don't know it you have to play it out every week, a little bit at a time. So there are pieces of the puzzle that don't quite fit or don't match up yet or that are missing. That's one of the things that's frustrating as an actress. I want to know what's going on between Doggett and Reyes. There's this unrequited love. They've set up that Scully loves Mulder, Doggett loves Scully, Reyes loves Doggett and Follmer, Cary Elwes' character, loves Reyes. So they've set that up and it's all unrequited. I think there's a lot of sexual tension going on. And I think they should explore that, dammit!"

The ongoing, teasing, will-they/won't-they nature of the romantic situation between Reyes-Doggett forces Gish and Patrick to carefully calibrate their performances, both when the characters are together and when they're apart. A longing glance here or there might suggest something to the audience that Carter and Spotnitz never intended to convey. No episode highlighted the point better than "4-D," the parallel universe show. Early on, Doggett brings his

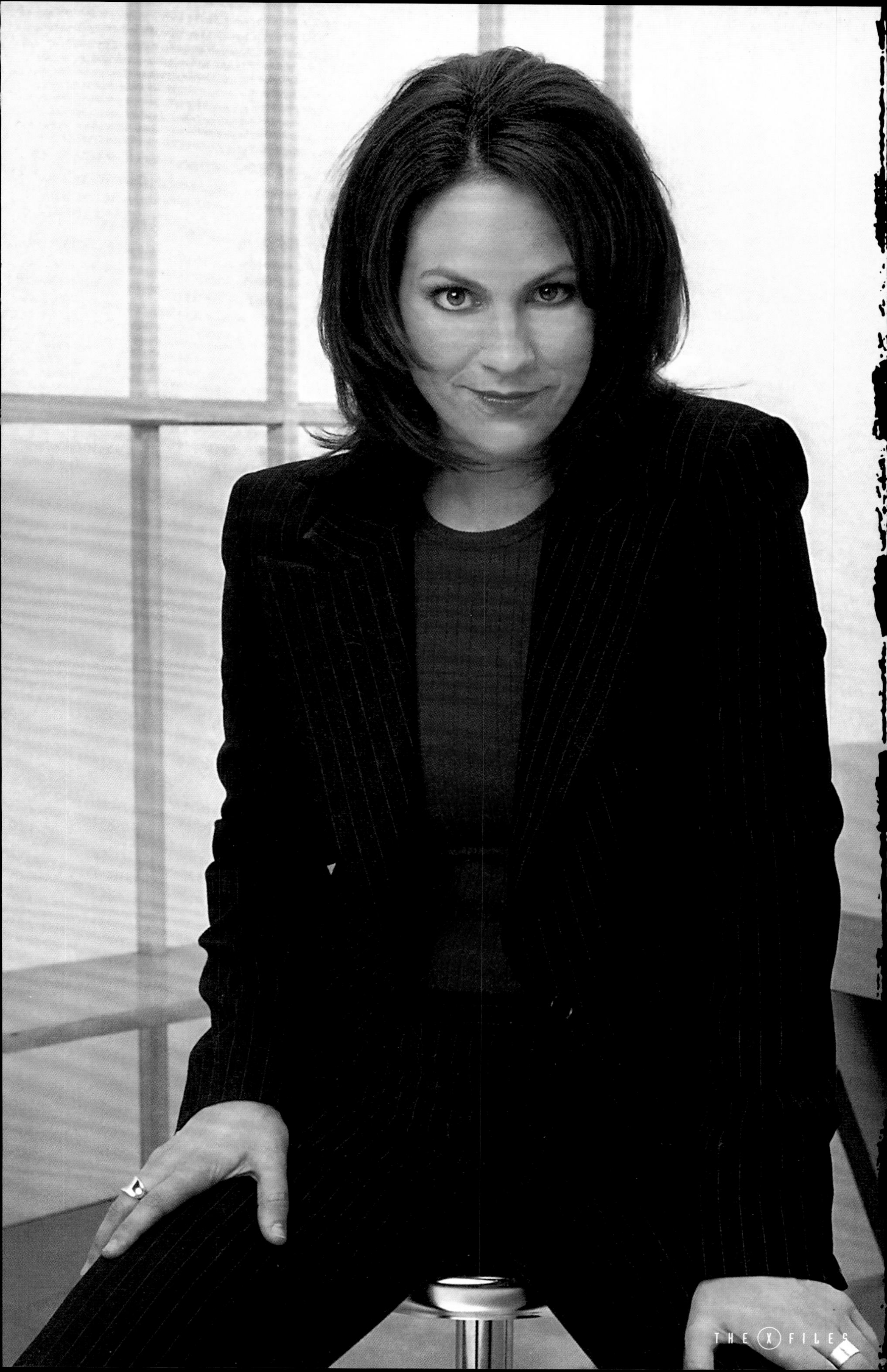

ANNABETH GISH

Where's Mulder's bedroom? What about his TV? Why is there an "X" on his computer? While we weren't able to solve all the mysteries of the agent's bachelor pad, we did unearth some interesting finds.

EXHIBIT A

Exhibit A: The item on the scale is a smudge stick, traditionally used by Native Americans to cleanse a dwelling of bad spirits. Above, Mulder and Scully demonstrate the finer points of lounging around the house in "Redux" and "The End."

McIntyre
Thornton
y Kharen Hill

EXHIBIT B

Exhibit B: It appears to be a cluttered desk just like any other, except for all those classified FBI documents, one vaguely obscene artist's model and a computer screen sporting a red "X." The scarlet letter, which is removed when the apartment set is in use, indicates that the monitor is equipped with video playback capabilities and differentiates the machine from others belonging to the set decorating department.

EXHIBIT C

Exhibit C: Yes, those are real fish swimming in Mulder's tank, and when the agent is away, the X-Files' crew is kind enough to feed them. The plastic aquarium decoration at the far right is a replica of the legendary statues of Easter Island.

Exhibit D: Mulder's idea of a coffee-table book, Playpen Magazine, is actually a mock-up created by the art department, not a real publication. The take-out menu beside the ashtray is, however, from a real Los Angeles eatery. Above, Scully attempts to summon X in "Herrenvolk."

EXHIBIT D

EXHIBIT E

EXHIBIT F

Exhibit E: After a long day chasing aliens and cracking conspiracies, nothing hits the spot like a handful of chocolate-covered cookies and a protein drink!

Exhibit F: When he's not working on the Sabbath, junk-food junkie Mulder likes to nosh on some Matzo crackers. Of course, he's too busy to wash dishes.

When not shooting in Scully's apartment, the crew removes her PowerMac G4 computer.

Due to snacking crew members, this candy jar contains pineapple-flavoured candy (not the most popular flavour) and a note begging the crew not to eat all of the contents.

The photo wedged inside this frame is of set decorator Tim Stepeck's grandmother, circa 1942.

vitamin E

Intrepid FBI agent by day. Feng Shui acolyte by night. Courtesy of *The X-Files* set decorating department, *The X-Files Official Magazine* takes a tour through our favourite heroine's apartment to discover the softer side of Scully.

The set decorators' personal junk mail finds a new home on Scully's entry desk.

DANA'S DIGS

PHOTOS BY VERN EVANS

So far, Scully has only made tea in this kitchen, but she's fully stocked for an Italian feast if the mood strikes. (Yes, there is silverware in the drawer!)

silverware drawer

Weird medical news clips and postcards adorn Scully's fridge.

The back of the refrigerator was removed for a scene in Season Seven's "Orison" to allow the camera to shoot through the fridge as Scully opened the door. Unfortunately, the scene ended up on the cutting room floor.

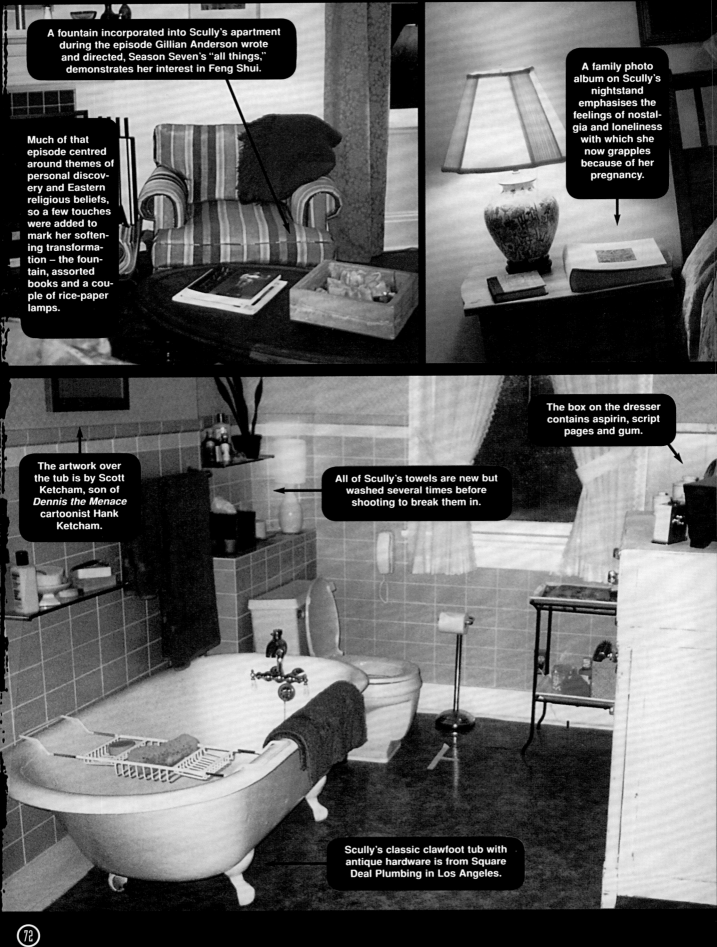

A fountain incorporated into Scully's apartment during the episode Gillian Anderson wrote and directed, Season Seven's "all things," demonstrates her interest in Feng Shui.

A family photo album on Scully's nightstand emphasises the feelings of nostalgia and loneliness with which she now grapples because of her pregnancy.

Much of that episode centred around themes of personal discovery and Eastern religious beliefs, so a few touches were added to mark her softening transformation – the fountain, assorted books and a couple of rice-paper lamps.

The box on the dresser contains aspirin, script pages and gum.

The artwork over the tub is by Scott Ketcham, son of *Dennis the Menace* cartoonist Hank Ketcham.

All of Scully's towels are new but washed several times before shooting to break them in.

Scully's classic clawfoot tub with antique hardware is from Square Deal Plumbing in Los Angeles.

rice-paper lamp

Unless something is scripted, Scully's dresser drawers remain empty — except for the occasional wad of marker tape, stray script pages and spare light bulbs.

The yellow tape by the toilet is Anderson's mark for Scully's bout with morning sickness in a scene from the Season Eight premiere, "Within." (The camera crew uses this tape to "mark" actors' positions for camera movement and focus purposes.)

James Pickens Jr. made quite an impression on *The X-Files* back when he appeared for the first time as F.B.I. Deputy Director Alvin Kersh in "Beginning," the sixth season opener. He immediately stirred up antipathy in Agents Fox Mulder and Dana Scully and, as a recurring character, returned again and again to cause them grief. Even as Robert Patrick and Annabeth Gish arrived on the scene to play, respectively, Agents John Doggett and Monica Reyes, Pickens was there as Kersh, a thorn in everyone's side, a mystery figure who seemed to possess some mighty dirty hands. But are his hands really dirty? Is he a good guy or a bad guy or something in between? Even as *The X-Files* races to the end of its run, those questions remain as yet unanswered. *The X-Files Magazine* recently caught up with Pickens – whose credits range from the films *Menace II Society*, *Nixon* and *The Ghosts of Mississippi* to *Bulworth*, *How Stella Got Her Groove Back* and *Traffic*, to regular roles, recurring parts and guest spots on such television shows as *L.A. Law*, *Roseanne*, *The Practice*, *JAG*, *Seinfeld*, *NYPD Blue*, *The Pretender* and *Philly* – to discuss his thoughts on the end of *The X-Files*, his plans for the future and a few things in between.

THE X-FILES MAGAZINE: In general, do you like science fiction?
JAMES PICKENS, JR: You know what? I'd always been a science fiction fan, which is why I kept asking myself why I never watched *The X-Files* before I came onto the show. My son would watch it from time to time and he tried to fill me in on what had gone on when I got involved. But I was a big fan of *The Outer Limits* back in the 60s. I was a big fan of *The Twilight Zone*. I loved science fiction and horror, so it's been a hoot to finally get a chance to be involved on this level to it. The closest I'd really come before *The X-Files* was *Rocket Man*, and that was really more of a slapstick comedy than anything else. So I'm glad I got to do *The X-Files*. It's been a ball.

What would you say have been some of Kersh's best bits?
There was a really nice scene in "Nothing Important **Happened Today**, Part II" where I dressed down Cary Elwes' character. Follmer came to me trying to backdoor Doggett about some information pertaining to the whole Super Soldier controversy. I pretty much told him, "I know what you're trying to do and I'm not going to be a party to

that. I'm still your superior and I won't be involved in any clandestine stuff." At least he doesn't want to get involved in any of Follmer's clandestine stuff. I liked that. Last season I had a great scene in which I pretty much told Doggett I had been supplied with information regarding Mulder – information that he couldn't get any other way. I liked that because I came at Doggett in a different way. I didn't come at him as dogmatic and pragmatic as usual. I came at him with some genuine concerns.

You've worked with some interesting people on the show over the past few years. What can you say about such folks as Gillian Anderson, David Duchovny, Robert Patrick and on and on?
Robert is a hoot. He keeps everybody up on the set. He's a very funny guy. He's really quite funny. Robert's also a wonderful, wonderful actor. I've enjoyed his work even before we started working together on *The X-Files*. So I was a fan.

THE

DIRECTO

Ian Spelling chats to James Pickens Jr., the man who has played intimidating Deputy Director Kersh for the past few years on The X-Files.

DEPUTY
OR'S CUT

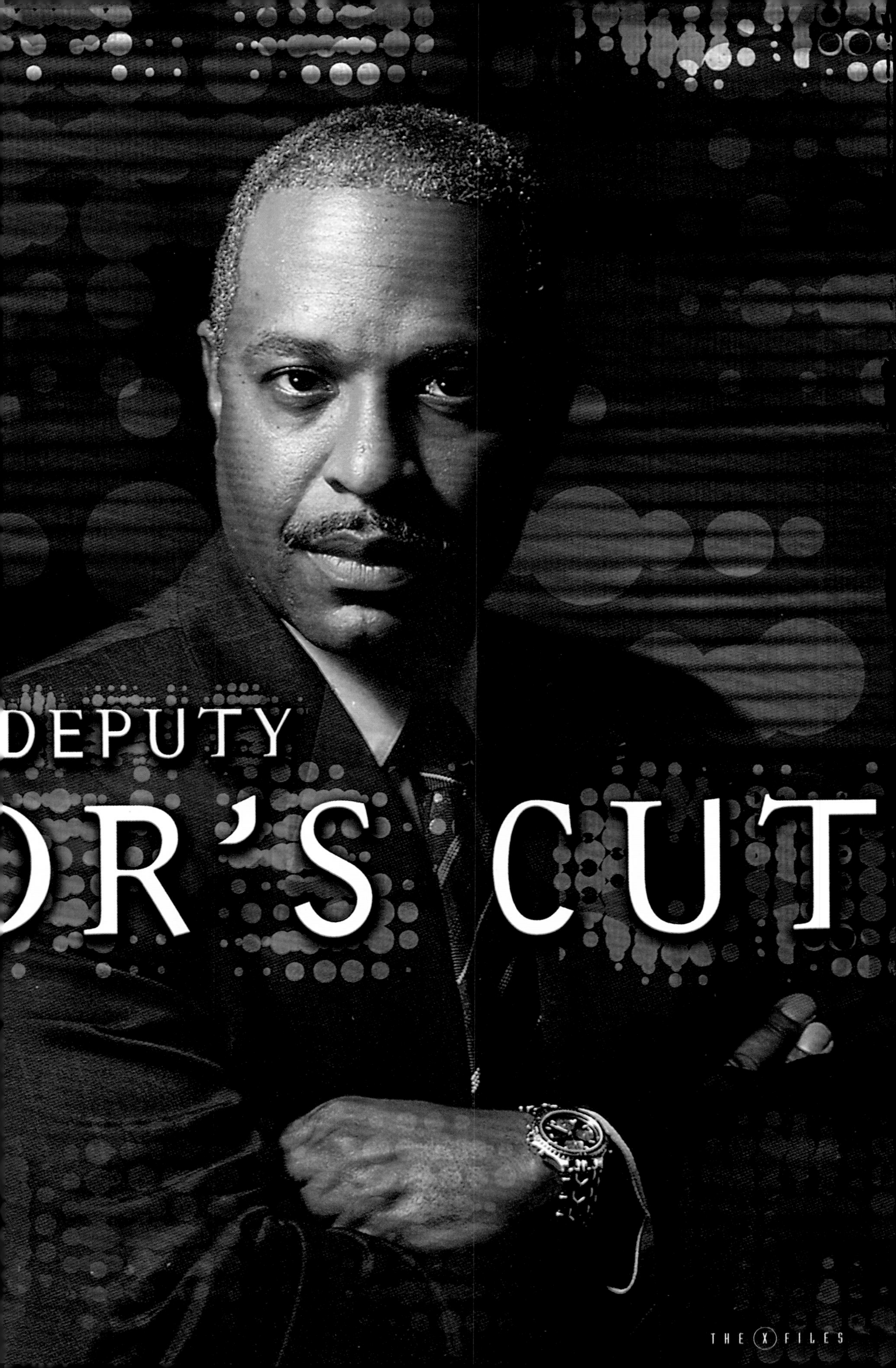

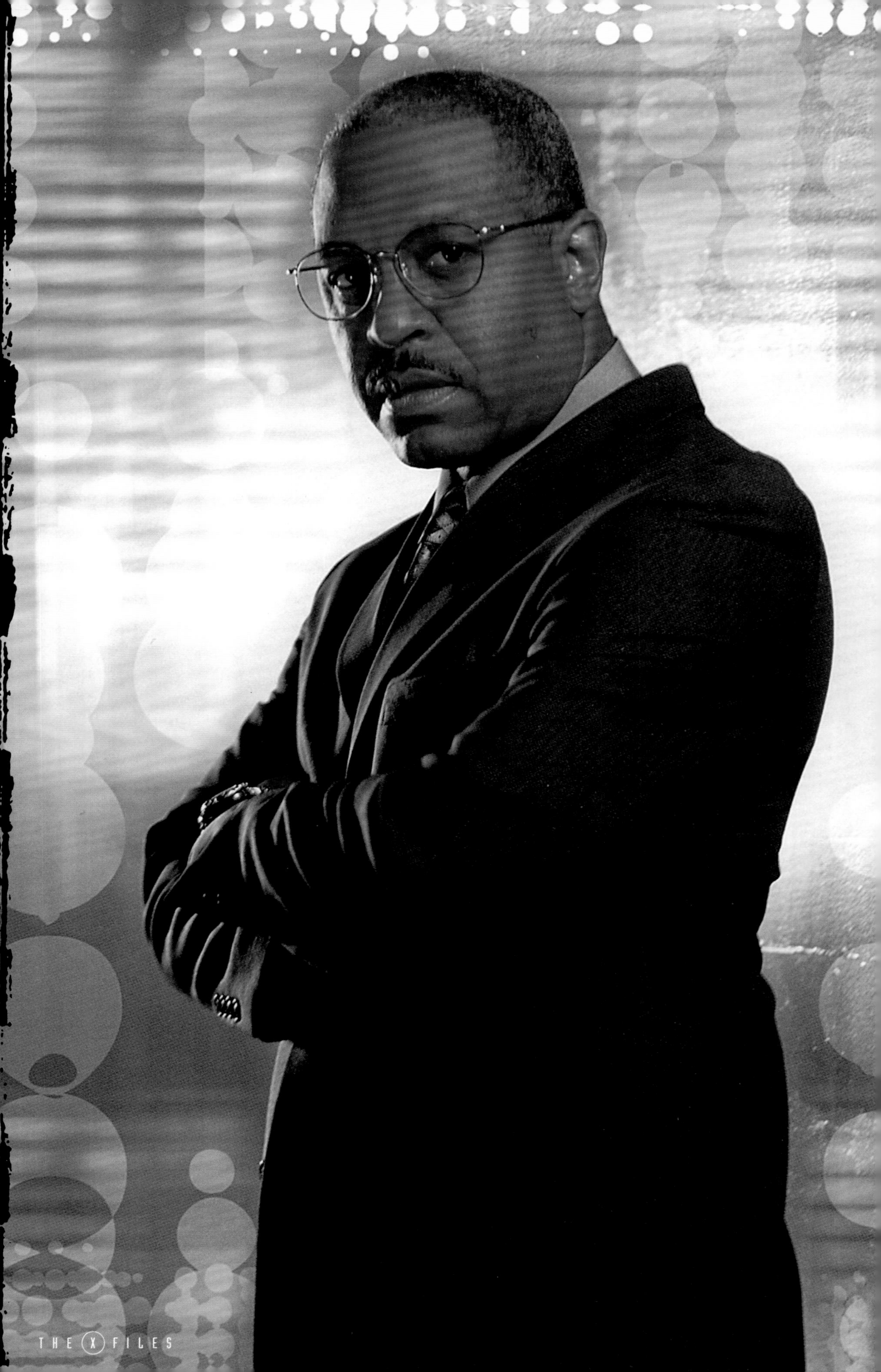

"Robert [Patrick] is a hoot. He's a very funny guy. He's also a wonderful, wonderful actor."

Annabeth is wonderful. She's a very beautiful lady, very focused. Besides bringing an element of beauty to the show, I think she brings a different kind of pathos to what's going on than the Scully character. There's a determination in Reyes that's very interesting to watch. It's hard to take your eyes off her.

I've always enjoyed all the work Cary's done. He's been in a lot of interesting movies. He brings a whole different flavor to *The X-Files*. Follmer is kind of somewhere between Doggett and Kersh. He's definitely in it for his own interests, so he brings that almost slithering, Dick Dastardly-like element to the show. Follmer's kind of slick, and I like that. It mixes things up. Everyone's peeking at his cards, but he keeps on playing, and Cary does a great job of making him interesting.

People really love to hate Kersh. Were you at all surprised by the intense reaction to him?
I was surprised. I started out as a recurring guest star on the show. I've been in this business for close to 25 years. I started as a New York stage actor and I've been out here in L.A. for the past

11 years. I'm very proud of the work that I've done, but I have been most recognized and approached more often as a result of *The X-Files* than anything else I've done. Men, women, it doesn't matter. They are intrigued by the character. I can't tell you why, other than the fact that they don't know what's behind the face. They don't know what Kersh's intentions are, and hopefully I can keep them guessing. I've had people say everything from Kersh is an alien to he works for the Cigarette-Smoking Man. And I like that. It keeps folks guessing and I guess that keeps folks wanting to see which way he's going to go.

What was your reaction when you heard about the show calling it a day?
Chris [Carter] called me to tell me. Not too many shows have been on the air for nine years. It's always sad when something like that comes to an end. But it's like everything else in life. Things have to come to an end.

Can we assume, if Kersh doesn't die before the last episode airs, that you'd be open to reprising your role in the next X-Files feature film?
Most definitely. No one has to twist my arm, not at all.

You've completed a couple of upcoming films. What can you tell us about Homeroom?
I'm very excited about that one. It's an independent. It was written by a young guy who is making his directing debut after doing a few short films. There are a few elements of the whole Columbine situation, although it is not about Columbine. It takes elements from all of these tragedies, in terms of school shootings and kids who feel like outcasts or on the fringe and can't find any way to vent except to [get involved] in these terrible tragedies. I play the

principal of a particular school where such a tragedy has occurred. I feel guilty because it was my vote that rejected a ballot to get metal detectors at my school. As a result a shooting occurs and some students are killed, so I try to justify to myself whether or not this would have happened had I done something different. You see my interaction with the parents of the victims and my interaction with the friends of the students who perpetrated the crimes and with the students themselves. It's a pretty involved character and I think it's going to be a really interesting little film.

And you've also got a role in Red Dragon.
They're shooting it now. I play a veterinarian and I have a scene with a live Bengal tiger, which was really a hoot. That was really interesting. Anthony Hopkins is reprising his role as Lecter and Edward Norton is playing the manhunter. My scenes were with Emily Watson and Ralph Fiennes. Emily plays the blind girl and Ralph is the Tooth Fairy. Harvey Keitel is in it, too. Brett Ratner has great energy. He asked for me. I'd auditioned for another role, and they wanted to go another way on that. But he was such a fan that he said, "Look, man, please, please. I've got this role, can you do it?" I said, "Great." I was a fan of his work, and if anybody can pull this off, I think he can. I think he's looking forward to the challenge, because most people think of him as the director of the *Rush Hour* movies. He's got the right temperament and he definitely knows what he wants. When he doesn't know something he's not averse to deferring to someone who can help him. That's all you can ask for in a director. He also kinds of leaves the actors alone and lets us do what we do. I think *Red Dragon* is going to be a hell of a movie. I'm excited to see what happens.

James Pickens Jr., thank you very much. ●

RETURN

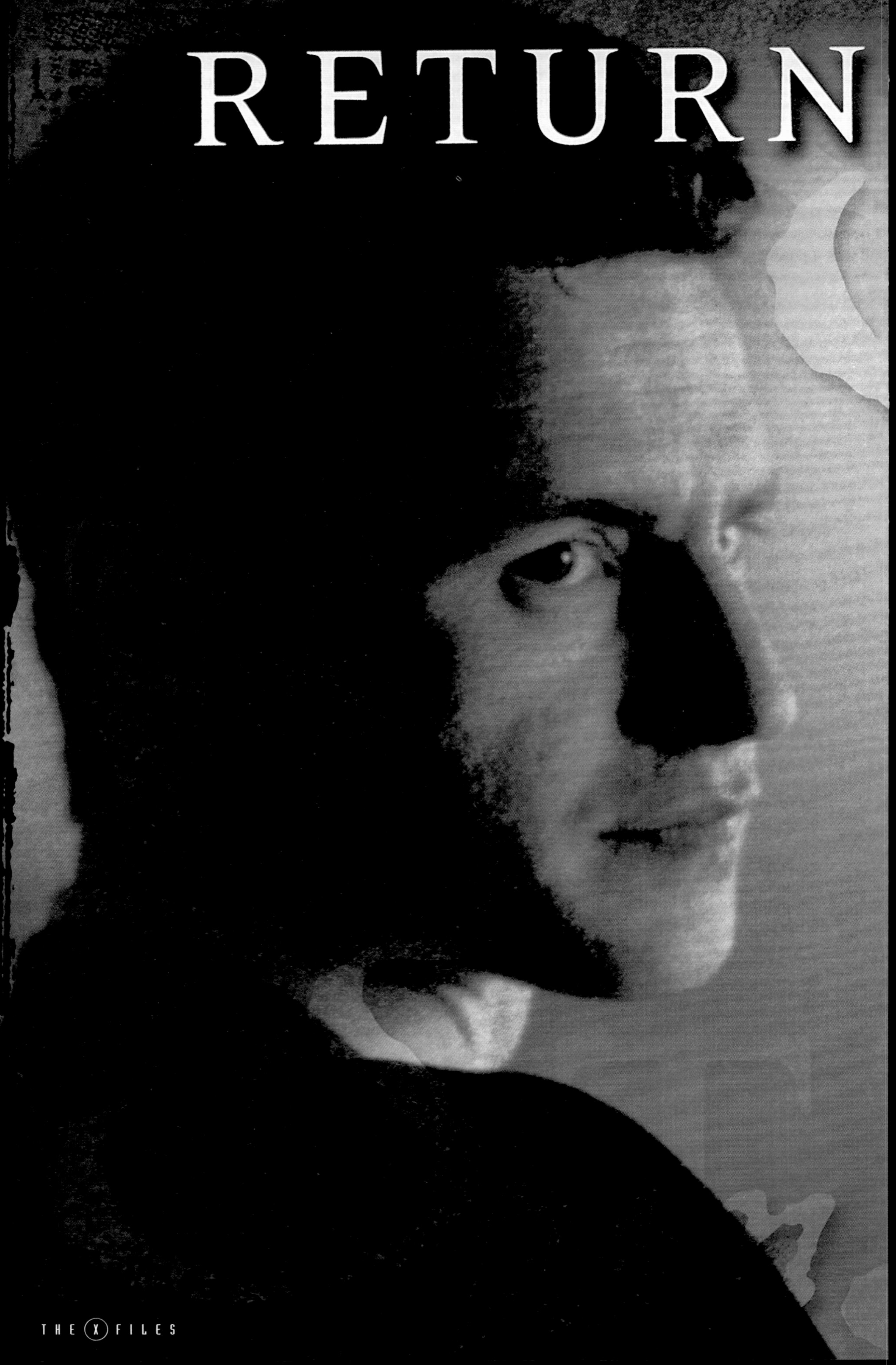

TO Spender

Ian Spelling chats to Chris Owens who appeared several times on *The X-Files*, and made a welcome return as Jeffrey Spender at the end of Season Nine

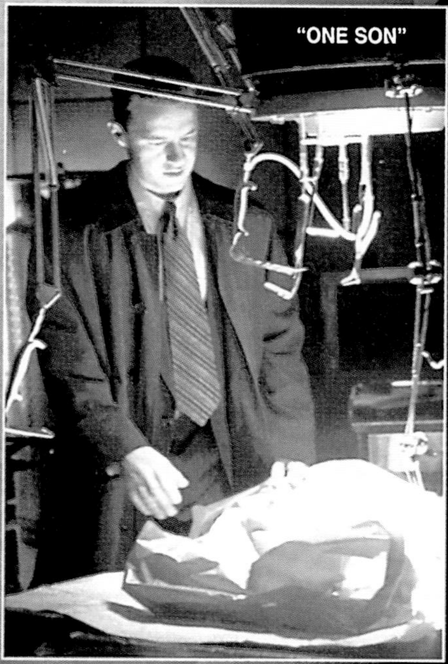

"ONE SON"

The X-Files TV show is gone, but it's far from forgotten. Fans will surely remember the central figures who contributed to transforming the show from cult series to pop culture icon: Chris Carter, David Duchovny and Gillian Anderson, as well as Mitch Pileggi, Robert Patrick, Annabeth Gish, and William B. Davis. They'll remember the likes of Tom Braidwood, Bruce Harwood and Dean Haglund, not to mention Nicholas Lea, James Pickens, Steven Williams, Laurie Holden and John Neville, all of whom made their mark as recurring supporting characters. And they'll also vividly remember Chris Owens, who stepped into several roles over the years and can even lay claim to an extended *X-Files* connection – his sister guest-starred on the show as well.

"I guess I've got a little place in the history of *The X-Files*," Owens says. "I think I was brought in more often as different characters than anyone else. I can't tell you how thrilling that is. I played the younger version of the Cigarette-Smoking Man (in "Musings of a Cigarette-Smoking Man" and "Demons"). I played the Great Mutato (in "The Post-Modern Prometheus"). I played Jeffrey Spender a bunch of times (in such episodes as "Patient X," "The End," "The Beginning," and the "Two Fathers"/"One Son" two-parter, which served to reveal that Mulder and Spender are, as the children of Cigarette-Smoking Man, half-brothers; the character's mother is Cassandra Spender, portrayed on the show by Veron

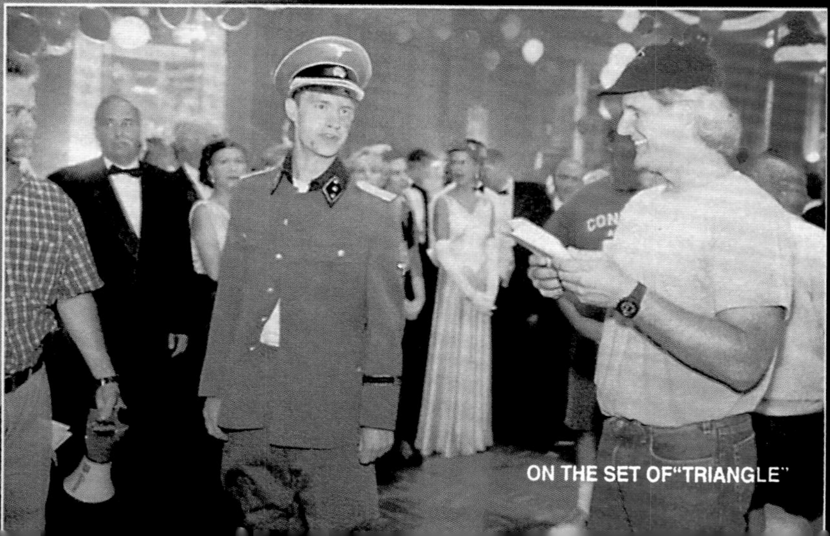

ON THE SET OF "TRIANGLE"

Cartwright). And I played the Nazi officer in 'Triangle' during the sixth season.

"I felt like I went full circle on the show," Owens reveals," because just as the show was ending I went down and played Spender again in 'William,' the episode that David Duchovny directed. That was Spender coming back. I've recuperated from the gunshot wound.

of Season Nine Spender has survived.

"It's funny," continues Owens, "because after I took the bullet in my last two-parter I told my wife, 'Don't be concerned. There's plenty of work to be done on *The X-Files* yet. This happens to all the characters.' But then I didn't hear back from them for a couple of seasons and I had to assume at that

point that Spender was in fact dead and buried. I actually had a contract to do several more episodes (during Season Six), so I was disappointed when no one called me. Then I received a call from David Duchovny saying that he was going to be directing an episode of the show and he wanted to bring Spender back. That call came completely out of the blue. It was a wonderful surprise. When they told me about Spender also coming back for the finale I was pleased, but not quite as surprised.

"I received a call from David Duchovny saying that he wanted to bring Spender back. That call came completely out of the blue. It was a wonderful surprise."

I'm assuming I was up in a cabin in Quebec. The Cigarette-Smoking Man and I take turns using the cabin. The whole place smelled of Morleys. Anyway, Spender was also injected with an alien virus that burned me from the inside out. So I was once again under lovely prosthetics, worked on by the best in the world. I had a great time. One night, at four in the morning, I was dancing in the makeup trailer with the makeup people. It was a pretty funny sight. And then I got to come down again to work on the first part of 'The Truth.' I'm very happy to say that at the end

"Getting the call to do 'William' was the bigger shock," says Owens. "It was great to hang out with David again. He and I had gotten pretty friendly a few years back, and we'd tried to stay in touch, but it was hard because he was in LA and I was still up here (in Canada). So, he had me over the house for some dinner again and I hung out with him and Tea Leoni, which was really wonderful. At the end of my last day on 'William,' after I'd been in make-up for 17 hours, David was kind enough to arrange for a 90-minute massage. So clearly, he's an actor's director.

"I also got to work a lot with Gillian in 'William,' which was wonderful. Actually, I had a few scenes with Robert Patrick and Annabeth Gish, too. I enjoyed doing that very, very much. They're a couple of terrific actors as well. It was very interesting to come back again after three years. I wasn't sure if I'd be able to step right back into character. But the crew made me feel so comfortable; it was a lot of the people

SPENDER AND MULDER IN "THE END"

who were there in year six. Gillian and David were there to talk to, too. After a day or two I was right back in *The X-Files* mode. I was surprised how quickly it came right back.

"To tell you the truth, I'd stayed on top of the show for a while after I did my last episode, but then I sort of dropped off and went on to other things," he continues. "I hadn't seen the show in almost two seasons when David called about 'William.' So, as I said, getting back into the whole loop of the show was fun. I did a little bit of catch-up. It was fun to revisit.

"I got a lot of information about what was going on from doing the first part of the finale, actually," says Owens. "I'm a character witness for Mulder, who's been put on trial. I'm also there to help confirm his conspiracy theories. I'm not sure how successful I am in helping him, but I do give it my best shot. It was interesting to go from trying to debunk everything Mulder and Scully did to being there at the end to defend Mulder. Now that I've done these last couple of episodes people are asking me again if I think I've played the character for the last time. I can honestly say, even with the show ending, I don't know. I love working with Chris and the gang. It was great to go back and get reacquainted with everyone. I hope it's not the end. I hope I can squeeze into the next *X-Files* movie or maybe some other project that Chris or David does."

Though he may be best known for his assorted stints on *The X-Files* (and also for his guest spot on *Millennium* as Deputy Bill Sherman in the episode "Monster"), Owens is a working actor with a range of other credits. He offers to fill us in on his exploits since the "Two Fathers"/"One Son" two-parter aired more than three years ago. "Let's see," begins Owens, who currently resides with his wife in Toronto, the city in which he was born. "I did an independent film up here in Canada called *The Uncles*. I was fortunate enough to get a Genie nomination for best performance. The Genies are the Canadian equivalent of the Oscar. That was really nice. The film was a comedy-drama. Kelly Harms played my brother and Tara Rosling played my sister, and we had a terrific little script. I played a guy who tries to hold together his Irish-Italian family. His sister's stealing babies because she hasn't got one of her own. His brother won't go to school. And he's having an affair with his boss's daughter. So it's a family comedy drama. I did a couple of other independent features and TV movies (including *Python, A Glimpse of Hell, My Louisiana Sky* and

"I had a few scenes with **Robert Patrick** and Annabeth **Gish**, too. I enjoyed doing that very, **very much**. They're a couple of terrific actors."

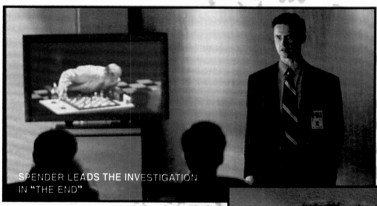

SPENDER LEADS THE INVESTIGATION IN "THE END"

The Happy Couple). And I also did episodes of *LEXX* ("Texx Lexx") and *Mutant X* ("Interface"), continuing with the sci-fi theme. They were fun to do. I also did a few days on a film called *The Farm*. That was with Al Pacino, which was exciting. That's a C.I.A. thriller and I play a C.I.A. recruiter. I can't seem to get away from sci-fi and spies, but it's a great way to make a living. What else? I've got a couple of other things in the works, but I don't know yet for sure if they'll be happening. I've read for roles and had a couple of meetings. There's a Canadian series up here that I could end up on as a regular. That would be very nice. But it's funny; even though there was a three-year hiatus for me, I'm recognized by fans for my work on *The X-Files*. And I'm fine with that. It's very gratifying. I want to do other things as an actor, but it's an honor to be recognized for something as unique and popular as *The X-Files*. I'm incredibly grateful for the whole experience.

"What's funny is that my sister appeared on the show, too." Owens adds as the conversation comes to an end. "Her name is Shelley Owens. She appeared in 'Conduit,' episode three of the first season, I think it was. She was living in Vancouver, so she was in there long before I was, paving the way for me, I guess. She was thrilled when I got on *The X-Files*. But she does always like to point out that she got there first!" ●

After being scared witless in season eight's "Alone," who'd have thought Agent Leyla Harrison would return for more in season nine? Jolie Jenkins talks to Joe Nazzaro about playing an X-files groupie.

According to Jolie Jenkins, Leyla Harrison is an X-files geek and proud of it. "She's kind of a nerd," she notes in describing the over-eager FBI agent, "in that she knows every single detail of every single case, and I love that about her."

Harrison made her series debut in the eighth season episode "Alone," in which she appeared as Agent Doggett's newly transferred partner, armed with an encyclopaedic knowledge of the X-files. The character proved popular enough to bring back; Jenkins recently wrapped up "Scary Monsters," her second episode of the series, and she insists that Agent Harrison is still very much a wide-eyed innocent. "She's happily back in accounting now, but still follows up on every case because she's such a huge fan, and ends up uncovering something in the expense reports that she finds interesting. She tries to talk Scully into believing that it's an X-file she's uncovered, so she's definitely still the eager, wide-eyed girl, who's going to get to the bottom of this even if it kills her.

"Leyla keeps going to Scully, but that doesn't work out, so she goes to Robert and Annabeth's characters and tries to get them riled up behind her. I think they've even taken Leyla to the next extreme with this episode. I so appreciated the comedy in the first episode, where she's alluding to all of Mulder and Scully's previous cases, and they continue that with this episode, which was a lot of fun."

As to whether or not Agent Harrison will survive her second encounter with The X-Files, "I don't think she'll be back, but she does survive," says Jenkins. "You'll see, but she has some problems in the second episode as well. But she does survive, and I think they've got a lot of loose ends to tie up now, because they've opened up a lot of jars."

Jenkins had already auditioned for The X-Files several times before "Alone," but this time, the actress thought she had a small advantage. "About a week before the role needed to be cast, the casting director Rick Millikan had seen an episode of The West Wing that I'd done," she explains. "That character was a young professional, and I don't think Rick had seen me that way before, so when he saw that episode, maybe he thought I'd be perfect for this."

In terms of how to play the character, "I knew she came from accounting, and she was the quintessential fan of the X-files, so I knew the bare bones facts about her. Frank did say to me later, when we were on set, 'You were really eager, but you didn't have a ditzy blonde thing going on. You were eager and naïve, but you could tell that this girl was smart and she wasn't an idiot.' I think there probably were some fans who thought, 'Kill her, let the lizard eat her!' but I'm so glad that it didn't, because I had such a good time coming back the second time."

The actress praises her co-star, Robert Patrick, with whom she had most of her scenes in "Alone." "When I got the job and read the script and saw that there were so many scenes with him, I thought, 'Oh God, he plays all these scary bad guys! What if he's mean, or we don't get along and I have to work with him in all these scenes?' but it ended up being so wonderful. We had a lot of fun on set, and when I came back for the second episode, almost all of my scenes are with Robert and Annabeth, and the three of us had such a great time, laughing ourselves sick. It makes for such a great experience, especially when you're working overnight and 14-hour days."

Jenkins spent less time with David Duchovny, but enjoyed the opportunity of working with him, notably the closing hospital scene. "He and Gillian were both very nice, but I didn't really get to know them like I felt I got to know Robert or Annabeth, because I had so many scenes with them. It was super fun, especially the hospital scene, to be with the two of them. It was fun to just sit there on the bed and think, 'Oh my God, here I am with David Duchovny and Gillian Anderson!' It was kind of surreal."

Life has been busy for Jolie Jenkins in recent months, between getting married, moving house, and making the rounds for pilot season, but she hopes that playing Harrison will give her a little extra exposure. "Having The X-Files and West Wing on my résumé has gotten me a lot of attention in auditions. It can't hurt either, to have another episode of The X-Files coming out, and I had such a great time doing it, so it's good for my career and fun for me in the process." ●

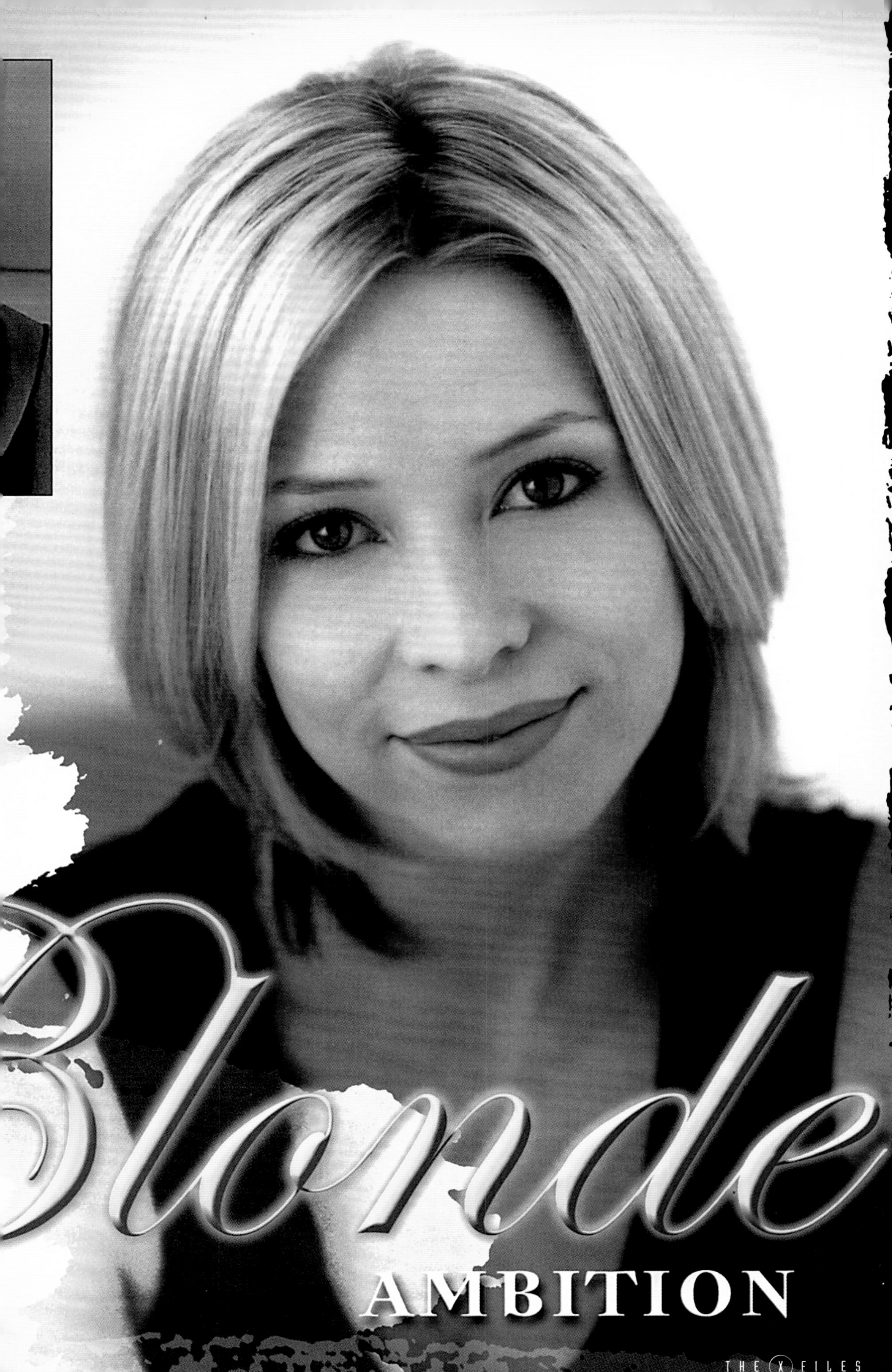

Blonde AMBITION

HOW TO BE THE NEXT MU AGE

1 Trust no one

In your eyes, everything's a conspiracy; no one can be trusted. Your harmless elderly next door neighbor is probably a spy and the man that delivers your mail secretly works for the government. Friends and family just laugh at your far-out conspiracy theories; they think you're paranoid. Some people even call you "Spooky." In your world, the only person you can really trust is yourself. After all, just because you're paranoid doesn't mean nobody's following you, does it?

2 Have an open mind

Do you believe in the existence of extraterrestrials? If the answer is a flat out no, then chances are you won't make the grade. A closed mind is a definite no-no, particularly when investigating UFO sightings, alien abductions and government cover-ups. You really must be willing to open your mind to extreme possibilities and believe in the unbelievable. The truth is out there – if you are willing to look for it.

3 Have a cast-iron constitution

This isn't a job for the squeamish; if you are faint-hearted you won't last five minutes. And passing out at the sight of blood will be the least of your worries. After all, morgues and autopsy rooms aren't exactly the most swinging places to frequent, now are they?! And what about all that weird phenomena you're guaranteed to come across: bodies with fluke worms wriggling about inside; headless corpses; corpses drained of all their body fat; and spores bursting out of peoples' throats! If I were you, I'd pack some Dramamine – just in case!

4 Have friends in high places

Let's be honest, we all need a helping hand every now and again. As the saying goes, it's not so much what you know, but rather who you know – even if you don't know their names. And having contacts in all the right places can provide a valuable source of information. For starters, a shadowy government informant type should be top of your phone-a-friend list. Then there's the well-respected senator who has access to all that highly classified information. Throw into the mix a friend in the UN

and a trio of high tech computer geeks and your contacts book is complete.

5 Have more lives than a cat

They say a cat has nine lives but you really take the biscuit. You've got to be virtually indestructible. In your line of work you have a high risk of being shot at, tortured, experimented on, injected with alien viruses, and even abducted by aliens! I mean, if the earth is going to be taken over by alien colonists, the planets' counting on you! Being one of those the-more-times-I-get-knocked-down-the-stronger-I-become types is pretty much a prerequisite.

NT LDER!

Have you ever sat there watching Agent Fox Mulder, thinking 'I could do that...'? I mean, how difficult could it be, dealing with a few sewer mutants, parasitic worms and deadly shape-changing aliens? But it's not as straightforward as you might think. Kate Anderson provides 10 handy hints on becoming one of the most famous investigators of the unknown...

6 Don't have a life

In this business the X-files must always come first. After all, investigating the paranormal and the supernatural isn't exactly a 9-to-5-with-weekends-off type job! The hours are so unsociable; so much so that you must be prepared to forgo any kind of social life. Forget a night out on the town, or a few beers with a few pals – in fact, forget about having any kind of personal life altogether.

7 Have an above-average IQ

You don't need to be a member of Mensa, have won *Who Wants to be a Millionaire* or even be a descendant of Albert Einstein to make the grade. But you do need to be smarter than average when it comes to tracking down vampires, aliens and genetic mutants. A degree in psychology would be useful, and a knowledge of witchcraft and the occult might come in handy too.

8 Have a Jerry Springer moment

You were born to appear on *Jerry Springer*. Perhaps you saw something weird and unexplainable as a kid. Perhaps your sister disappeared under strange circumstances. Perhaps you discovered your father was secretly involved in a government cover-up. One thing's for certain, candidates with a 'normal' background just wouldn't cut the mustard.

9 Have a partner

You're as different as chalk and cheese, but like Holmes and Watson you compliment one another perfectly. Of course, it makes things a bit more interesting if there's some sort of unspoken attraction between the two of you. Not that you'd dream of taking your flirtations any further; would you?

10 Have absolutely no respect for authority

No matter how many times your boss tells you to stop chasing lights in the sky and little green men, as far as you're concerned, he'd be better off talking to a brick wall! You don't really have a great deal of respect for your superiors; clashing with authority figures is part of your rebellious charm. In your book, rules are meant to be broken and that line is there to be crossed. As far as you're concerned, no one has jurisdiction over the truth – especially your boss!

How To Be The Next AGENT SCULLY!

Fancy yourself as the next Agent Scully? It might be tougher than you think. The lovely Dana after all, has been kidnapped more times than the rest of us have had roast dinners, she spends half her waking life in the morgue and she hasn't had a date in years. For those of you still determined to put the 'I' in F.B.I., Kate Anderson has 10 top tips on how to become an investigator of the paranormal – à la Dana Scully...

1 HAVE A SCIENTIFIC BACKGROUND

As far as you're concerned, science has all the answers. You're a logical thinker and you believe that there's a scientifically quantified explanation for everything – including U.F.O.s and alien abductions. And despite having witnessed some strange events in your time, you look to science to explain them. In other words, you tend to believe in something just so long as science supports those beliefs. Which sometimes makes you a little too narrow-minded for your own good. But at least these days you seem to be working on it.

2 HAVE A STRONG STOMACH

While most people feel a little squeamish at the mere thought of autopsies, morgues and dead bodies, in your opinion it's nothing to write home about. In fact, you don't know what all the fuss is about – it's all part and parcel of the day job. And poking around the insides of corpses is one of the most enjoyable aspects of your profession. It's no wonder you took such an interest in dissecting frogs during science class! Actually, when you think about it, you seem to spend so much time in morgues, they might as well be your second home!

3 DON'T HAVE A SOCIAL LIFE

When was the last time you went out on a date – the last century? Okay, so that's a little extreme, even by your standards. But it certainly seems like it at times – you don't exactly have a busy social schedule. Still, perhaps that's because in this job there's rarely time for a life, never mind a personal life. And being a workaholic doesn't help matters either. After all, who wants to play second fiddle to aliens, U.F.O.s, serial killers and liver-eating fiends?

That said, you're only human, but if you do happen to find yourself fancying the pants off some gorgeous hunk, I'd avoid men with tattoos at all costs if I were you!

4 HAVE A GOOD EDUCATION

There's no doubt about it, you need to be one smart cookie to get ahead in this career. And at least these days smart is seen as sexy! And what could be smarter than rewriting Einstein's Twin Paradox for your senior thesis? Then there's that undergraduate degree in physics and your spell in med school. You've certainly got one hell of a résumé!

5   BE SPORADIC WITH YOUR TRUST

You may not be as paranoid as some people you know, but in this game you often wish you had eyes in the back of your head. You've learned to be careful about who you trust. After all, putting your faith in the wrong person could see you wind up dead! So, if you want to stay alive and always one step ahead, you're better off trusting no one. Oh, except yourself, of course – and your partner.

6   BE OPEN TO EXTREME POSSIBILITIES

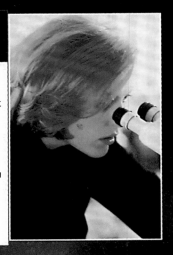

Although you still won't claim to be a believer, you're a lot more willing to believe than you used to be. But that's not to say you're prepared to take huge leaps of faith. Certainly not! However, even you have to admit your famed skepticism has somewhat eroded over time. And although seeing isn't always believing, you try to keep your eyes and your mind open to extreme possibilities. Even you have been known to take the occasional walk on the wild side, after all.

7   KNOW HOW TO KICK ASS

Okay, so you may be a woman, but in your job you have to know how to fight like a man. It's no good resorting to hair-pulling and name-calling when facing off against conspiracy assassins, alien bounty hunters, serial killers and vampires, is it? While no one's saying you've got to be able to kick ass better than Buffy or Xena, taking a few kickboxing classes definitely comes in handy. After all, they do say defense is the best form of attack.

8   HAVE A CLOSE RELATIONSHIP WITH YOUR PARTNER

Your partner is your best friend and confidant all rolled into one. You care about one another deeply, even though he can sometimes be a pain in the neck! But unfortunately your close working relationship means you're prone to idle office gossip; rumors are forever doing the rounds about you two being an item. Even you've had to admit that you share an undeniable unspoken chemistry that you can't always ignore – although not for want of trying. And then there's your constant flirtatious banter and knowing little looks!

9   BE RESPECTFUL TO YOUR PEERS

Okay, so this isn't the dark ages. But as a woman in a male-dominated environment, you know how to toe the line for the sake of your career – unlike a certain someone we could mention. In your book, respect is a two-way street – you have to give it to get it. And as far as you're concerned, the rules are there for a reason. And even though your only agenda is to get to the truth, there are ways and means, and that doesn't involve breaking those rules or crossing that line. Well, at least it doesn't nine times out of every 10!

10   BE PREPARED TO SACRIFICE EVERYTHING

Personal lives, relationships, family ties – even your own sanity – are all at risk. But they are just the tip of the iceberg: a small percentage of what's at stake. For when we say everything, we mean everything – and anything. In short, we're talking about your worst nightmares and your biggest fears. We're talking abductions, experiments, fatal diseases, and even family losses. In fact, you name it; you've been there, done that, brought the T-shirt, seen the movie and read the book!

THE MULDER & SCULLY PROJECT

SO YOU'VE MISPLACED YOUR FBI HANDBOOK? DON'T WORRY – JUST CONSULT OUR HANDY GUIDE TO SOLVING AN X-FILE

BY STEVE HOCKENSMITH AND GINA MCINTYRE

Investigating the paranormal is not for amateurs. Just look at what happened to those poor schmucks in *The Blair Witch Project*. If only they'd had a fount of supernatural lore like Mulder hiking along with them, or a sceptical scientist like Scully. No tantrums, no screaming, no standing in the corner waiting to die.

We don't want you to make the same mistake. Before you head off into the local graveyard for a midnight seance or spend the night in a supposedly haunted mansion or some other foolish thing, please – for the love of God, please! – acquaint yourself with Mulder and Scully's Eight Habits of Highly Effective Paranormal Investigators. You'll be glad you did.

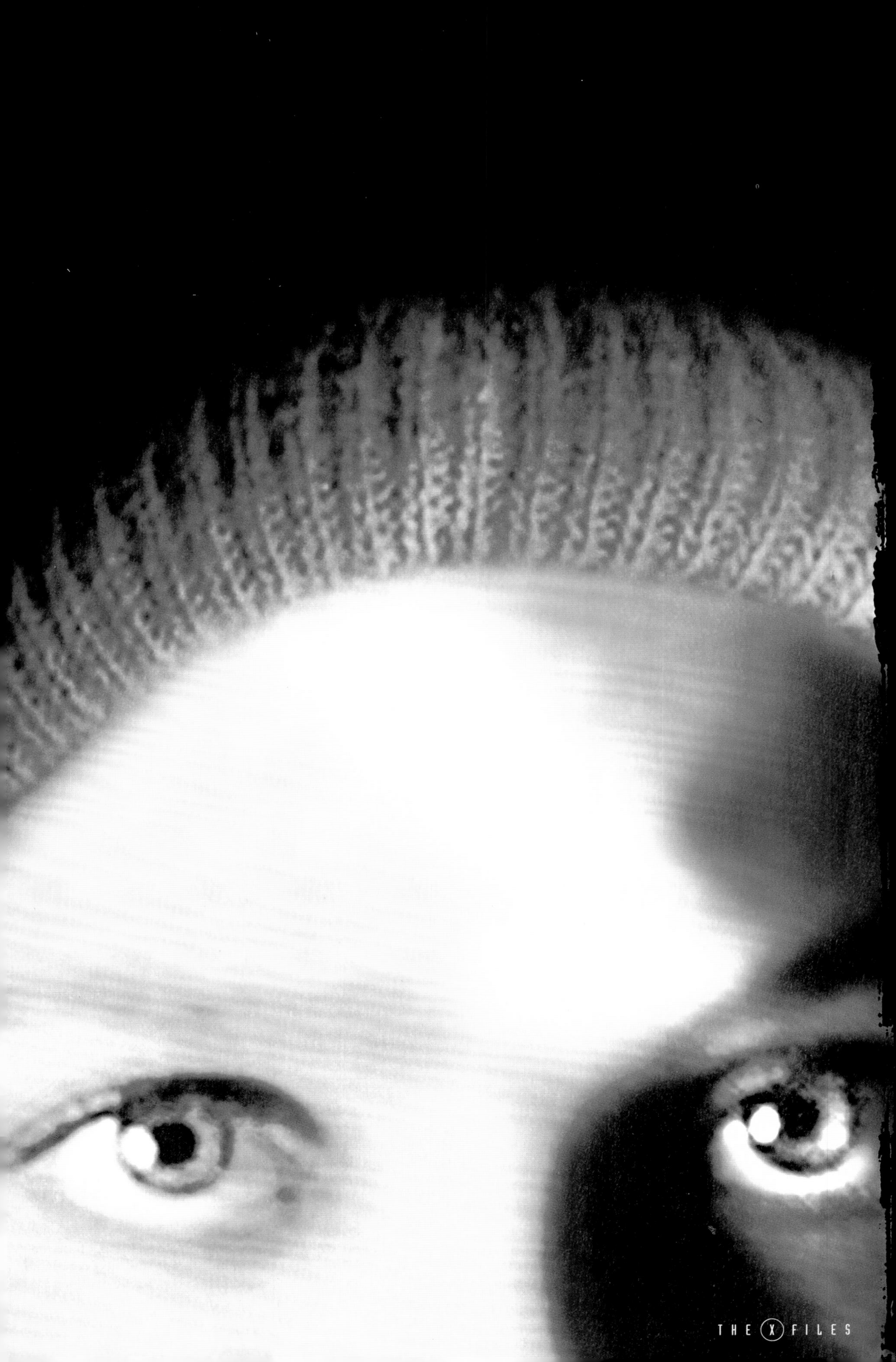

"When darkness falls, all we have left to guide

1: LOCATE THE X-FILE.

To solve an X-file, you have to know about the X-file. There are, of course, many ways to stumble onto such mysteries. You could read about it in a scientific journal. You could dig through declassified government documents looking for cases where the facts just don't add up. You could receive a desperate plea from a victim's mother or brother or spouse. Or, as is the case here, you could rent it in your local video store.

While channel surfing late one night in search of his favourite 'chatline' adverts, Mulder catches a documentary on MTV called *The Curse of the Blair Witch*. It examines the case of three annoying film school types who disappeared while hunting a legendary witch in the backwoods of rural Maryland. Apparently, they left behind a video record of their final terrifying days, which is now available at Blockbusters everywhere. The next day, Mulder rents a copy and shows it to Scully at the office. She is unimpressed. She sees either (A) three hysterical – and not terribly bright – individuals going to pieces in the woods or (B) a clever hoax. Either way, there's no proof that supernatural forces were at work. Mulder disagrees. He picks up the phone.

2: BREAK OUT THOSE FREQUENT FLYER MILES.

Nobody loves Mulder more than his travel agent, except perhaps the folks at Nokia.

"It's me," Mulder says.

"Yo, Fox, my man. Where to this time? Antarctica? Siberia? Puerto Rico? Hong Kong?" his travel agent coos, anticipating another lovely, fat commission courtesy of Uncle Sam.

"Burkittsville, Maryland."

"Uh-huh." The travel agent flips through an atlas and sees that Burkittsville is less than 50 miles from the District of Columbia. He chooses not to mention this. Instead he says, "I assume you need to fly out of D.C. immediately?"

"That's right."

Nimble fingers fly across a keyboard. "Well, I could squeeze you onto a flight out of Dulles at 11:20. That would put you into Baltimore at 11:40. You'd like a rental car, I assume."

"Of course."

"Done."

Mulder departs immediately, leaving Scully behind to keep the boys in the FBI Accounting Office off his back.

3: IRRITATE THE LOCAL AUTHORITIES BY ASKING TOO MANY QUESTIONS.

The sheriff in Burkittsville is already plenty steamed. Thanks to that danged movie, he's got tourists running roughshod over his beloved town, stealing signs and other property as "mementos" and asking a lot of durn-fool questions.

Mulder shows up, flashes his badge and begins asking questions, too. Where were the students last seen? Are you familiar with the legend of the Blair Witch? Do you believe in witchcraft? Have you noticed anyone riding a broomstick in a suspicious manner recently? Any black cats around town? Did you know that your face is turning bright red? Why are you pointing that gun at me?

Mulder eventually gets the hint and leaves the sheriff's office. Anyway, he's got things to do.

4: HEAD TO THE CRIME SCENE AND DISCOVER A PREVIOUSLY OVER-LOOKED BUT VERY USEFUL CLUE.

After getting directions from several similarly grumpy natives, Mulder finds the spot where the missing students headed into the woods. He knows exactly what he's looking

for – and it doesn't take him long to find it. Dangling from the branches of a tree not far from the road are several small stick figures. Anticipating Step Five, Mulder whips out his cell phone.

5 : CALL YOUR PARTNER TO DISCUSS WHAT YOU'VE LEARNED SO FAR.

Mulder informs Scully that he's found several "crude totems of Appalachian folk magic." He theorises that they were left there by "students of the black arts, maybe cult members" who wish to "summon a dark reckoning, a cruel spirit which feeds on the pain and confusion of the living, much like a Fox network special."

Scully rolls her eyes.

Suddenly, Mulder hears a noise in the woods. It sounds like...could it be...cackling?

"There's something out there," he says.

"Mulder, where are you?" his partner asks.

"Just a few feet from the road." He pushes through some branches, then looks around, confused. "I don't understand. I barely went a dozen steps into the woods. How can I be lost?"

Something moves in the underbrush nearby.

"Bleep," says Mulder.

6 : PULL YOUR GUN AND RUN LIKE CRAZY.

Mulder follows Step Six to the letter. Strange sounds follow him through the forest. Winded, he comes upon an old, dilapidated house. He rushes inside, aware that *something* is right behind him. He turns to confront it, his badge in one hand, his gun in the other.

"I am an FBI special agent!" he shouts. "Killing me, eating me or stealing my soul is a federal offense!"

A shape moves out of the shadows toward Mulder. As it comes closer, Mulder can see that it is an impossibly old woman. She is small and stooped, with a deeply lined face, crooked teeth and a large nose riddled with

warts. But she is dressed stylishly in jeans and a pink Oxford shirt. A white Ralph Lauren sweater is tied jauntily around her hunched shoulders.

"I don't believe it," Mulder whispers. "The Blair Witch."

The old woman cackles. "Oh, please. Just call me Blair. I'm trying to put all that witch stuff behind me."

"What do you mean?"

"I want to change my image. I've been reading *Woman's Realm* a lot." She holds up one of the little stick men. "Just look at this. Decorative stick figures are both authentically rustic and fun to make. I like to use twigs I've gathered from the backyard tied together

with hand-spun yarn soaked in a compote of fragrant cloves." She takes a step toward Mulder. "A circle of stones, a bag of teeth – it's just one of many ways to add zest to a boring old forest."

"Stay back," Mulder warns.

"Decorating a house like this poses an entirely different set of challenges." She steps closer. "But just take a look at what I've been able to do with the corners."

Mulder knows it's a trick. But there's something about the witch's voice – something he can't resist. He turns and moves toward the nearest corner, where he finds an exotic arrangement of native lichen perched atop a faux Colonial butterchurn.

"Charming," he says.

He hears a noise behind him, like the sound of rushing air.

7 : LET YOUR PARTNER SAVE YOUR BUTT.

A shot rings out.

Mulder whirls around to see Scully, her gun in her hand. Blair lies on the ground, a shovel clutched in her now lifeless hands.

"She was going to brain you, Mulder. If I'd gotten here two seconds later, you'd have that shovel sticking out of your head."

Mulder takes a cautious step toward Blair. He bends down and examines the shovel. "Lovely. Looks like an antique. Real Americana. I wonder how much she paid for it," he says. "So how'd you get here so fast?"

"I'll tell you about it later," Scully mumbles. She clears her throat loudly. "But there's one thing I don't understand. Why?"

"I've got a theory." Mulder takes the shovel in his hands and stands up. "Let's test it out."

8 : THINK DEEP THOUGHTS.

Cut to a well-manicured garden behind Blair's run-down home. Scully watches as Mulder unearths first one, then two, then three bodies from the soil beneath a bed of *American Beauty* roses.

"We are all lost in a forest of lies," Mulder thinks to himself. "Searching, circling, our maps long lost. And when darkness falls, all we have left to guide us are questions. What am I looking for? Where am I going? What did I just step in? Will I get that video back to Blockbuster before 10pm? But there are no answers, only the trail we must follow – the trail we've always followed... leading back to where we began."

There you have it. Now all you need is an understanding travel agent, a generous expense account, a partner with both a gun and a really good sense of timing and a thirst for the unknown and soon you'll be solving your own X-files the Mulder and Scully way. ●

TRUE CRIME

FEDERAL BUREAU OF INVESTIGATION CRIMINAL FILE #X909854KAT

TRUE STORIES FROM THE REAL FBI

Crime and PUNI

A hand-picked team of top-notch crime fighters is assembled to thwart the activity of a growing number of gangsters and terrorists. Only the best and the brightest are up to the task; they are the men who will save the country from every threat and found one of the most high-profile arms of the US government in the process. It's a great idea for the next Bruce Willis action flick—it's also the story of how the FBI was born.

On July 26, 1908, Attorney General Charles J. Bonaparte appointed a group of 10 former Secret Service employees and a number of Department of Justice investigators as special agents of the Department of Justice. As the new arm of the DOJ, they were to probe crimes of national importance, which with the expansion of transportation, communica-

For 90 years, the FBI has served as the government's prime instrument of justice

SHMENT

by Chandra Palermo

tion and general industry were a growing concern. In time, this force would become known as the Federal Bureau of Investigation, famous for its successful crusades and infamous for its occasional abuses of power.

The FBI's public image has evolved over the years, ranging from overwhelmingly positive to untrustworthy. The same men who stopped gangsters and spies in their tracks were also capable of violating the values of the Constitution they were sworn to protect. Allegations of corruption were levelled at the bureau even in its formative stages and resulted in the dismissal of Director William J. Burns in 1924. But the agency persevered and as a result, spent its first 40 years in a glow of great success and national pride.

The bureau's jurisdiction grew steadily throughout the first decade of its existence. During World War I, the agency came into its own, investigating matters of national security like espionage, selective service and deportation. "As the nation begins to assume a more active international role, you deal not only with the problem of espionage, but you deal with activities that can undermine the national foreign policy or military effort.

FBI Time Capsule

So here's the onset of internal security," explains Dr. Athan Theoharis, professor of history at Milwaukee's Marquette University and author of many books about the FBI. "If you have foreign policy, you need foreign intelligence, which means the CIA. The FBI comes in when you deal with counterintelligence—preventing foreign agents from stealing national secrets or undermining national unity or the war effort."

While a federal investigative force seems reasonable by today's standards, it was hard for people to swallow in the early part of the century. Many citizens assumed the FBI was established as a tool for the government to invade their privacy. "This powerful states' rights tradition and this concern about privacy rights where you see centralised government as threatening individual rights and liberties, that's going to continue after the bureau's established in 1908," Theoharis says. "So there's this real concern about if you create a federal police force, like you created a czarist police force, an autocratic dictator could use that force for political purposes to contain dissent. And that is an issue that remains very popular throughout the 20th century. You know, the fear of Big Brother is another way of saying it."

When J. Edgar Hoover was appointed as the FBI Director in 1924, he was determined to dispel the bureau's image as prying snoopers. Rather, he professionalised the agency, and it was his leadership that brought the FBI into its glory years. He fired unqualified agents, introduced regular performance evaluations and established a formal training course for new recruits, who were required to be between 25 and 35 years old, preferably with legal or accounting experience.

The crime wave that swept the country during the Prohibition era and the Great Depression couldn't have come at a better time to boost the popularity of Hoover's bureau. As the gang-busting FBI brought in larger-than-life outlaws like Al Capone and Pretty Boy Floyd, its agents enjoyed an image make-over; they also were authorised to carry guns and make arrests. The FBI's hunt for gangster John Dillinger in particular did much to trump up public support.

For 11 months, starting in September of 1933, Dillinger's gang rampaged through the Midwest, robbing banks and police arsenals and staging three jail breaks, killing as many as 10 men, including a sheriff, in the process. Dillinger seemed unstoppable, thwarting local police with relative ease. But in March of 1934, he stole a sheriff's car and drove it across the Illinois-Indiana state line, violating the federal Motor Vehicle Theft Act. The FBI set out on a manhunt, sparking numerous confrontations at Dillinger's hideouts. On July 22, 1934, on a tip from the madam of a nearby brothel, agents tracked down Dillinger at the Biograph theater in Chicago where he was catching the new Clark Gable movie, *Manhattan Melodrama*. As he exited the theatre, Dillinger was killed in a shootout.

Incidents like this helped popularise the notion of FBI agents as untouchable heroes capable of apprehending seemingly invulnerable villains. By the end of the '30s, the Identification Division, the FBI Academy and the Technical Laboratory had been established, and the notion of the "G-Man" was born.

"The G-Man always got his man. Super efficient, professional, highly disciplined," Theoharis says. "That results in this expansion for the government's law enforcement role. At the same time, there's this very powerful concern whether there's a cost to that expansion, that is, whether you're going to limit individual rights because you have a centralised agency that's not accountable. So even in the '30s, there's this very strong fear about the federalisation of crime."

As concerned as the American populace might have been about investing too much power in the FBI, their fears took a backseat to the political paranoia that erupted during World War II and the subsequent Cold War. Even if the bureau infringed on some matters of personal privacy, they also rounded up Nazi spies with speed and efficiency. In June of 1942, eight German saboteurs landed on beaches in Florida and New York, hoping to bomb and sabotage American factories involved in defence-related production. Following tips from the Coast Guard and a German informant, the FBI tracked down and arrested all of the saboteurs within 14 days of their arrival.

The FBI continued to uncover spy rings

and prevent subversive activities throughout the rest of World War II and the Cold War era. With the 1940 passage of the Smith Act, which criminalised advocating the violent overthrow of the U.S. government, the FBI was able to convict members of the Communist Party of America while riding a high tide of public approval.

The public's desire for protection might not have been the only driving force behind its acceptance of the FBI's powers, according to Dr. Gerald McKnight, head of the department of history and political science at Hood College in Frederick, Md. "One of the great talents that Hoover and his FBI honchos developed was public relations. Hoover was a public relations genius," McKnight says. "Long before we even coined the term, Hoover had made a science of public relations, largely in terms of cultivating editors, newspaper people and book writers."

Hollywood also lent a hand. In 1959, beloved all-American nice guy Jimmy Stewart starred as an FBI agent in *The FBI Story*, a movie featuring what Theoharis calls "a fairly romanticised, uncritically positive view of the FBI." And in the '60s, Efrem Zimbalist Jr. starred as FBI Inspector Lew Erskine in the heroically flavoured television programme *The FBI*.

No matter how good the government might be at putting a positive spin on its activities, however, no PR campaign is foolproof. Not surprisingly, the social unrest and political assassinations of the 1960s irreparably tarnished the FBI's spotless record. The bureau could not escape some of the widespread criticism leveled at the government during this period.

BUREAU BUSINESS: [clockwise from above] a page from Dillinger's file; the Hoover FBI building; the elder Hoover

"The erosion of Hoover and the FBI began when the Warren Commission report came out in 1964," McKnight says. "There was, in the Warren Commission report, some criticism of the FBI, and that criticism was picked up by the press. A lot of people did raise questions about the [Kennedy] investigation, and since the FBI did the investigation, the FBI took the brunt

of it. That, to my memory, is the first time in a public form the FBI had ever been criticised by a branch of the government."

The controversy surrounding the Vietnam War and the Watergate scandal further cast the government, and the FBI, as suspect. Under pressure from an increasingly mistrustful public, Congress launched investigations into corruption in the mid-'70s; the Church Committee, which conducted an extensive investigation into alleged abuses of America's investigative agencies, suggested that Hoover was something other than the picture of propriety he portrayed, arguing that the director used his position to sabotage Dr. Martin Luther King Jr. and his civil rights campaign.

"Those volumes became public, and for the first time people got a sense of the vindictiveness and the mean-spirited stuff that Hoover had countenanced and had led really," explains McKnight, who recently wrote the book *The Last Crusade* on the subject. "Basically it was his vendetta, his hatred for King that brought about this campaign to destroy King. We began to find out what Hoover and the FBI had been doing to undermine him and to undermine the whole civil rights movement. That put the FBI in the position for the first time of public scrutiny in terms of its police-state activities. And a lot of people thought

that was an unfortunate thing. Here was this great G-Man, this great legend, this great protector of American internal security, and we begin to find out that he broke laws right and left and had no respect at all for the Constitution or individual rights or civil liberties or civil rights."

The scandals continued. As recently as 1993, President Clinton removed FBI Director William Sessions from office following allegations of ethics violations. "The sense is that when the government opens up business in the morning, it starts lying and it never stops until it closes in the evening," McKnight says. "What I'm saying here is America sort of lost its innocence beginning in the '60s. I think there's a great deal of skepticism out there."

In fact, he thinks the populace might be too cynical. "Although it's understandable, I think too many Americans today feel that the government really has no answer to the problem," he says. "As a matter of fact, they feel that the government produces more problems than it does solutions and that everything that goes on in D.C. is some sort of scandal, and these are all self-centred, egotistical people without any real interest or maybe [with] just a general contempt for the American people. But the FBI will still continue, and it can do good work."

To regain some of its once-great stature, the FBI has made a number of important changes in protocol. The Director of the FBI has a limited term of office to avoid the kind of lifelong authority Hoover, who served as director for almost 50 years, held. Freedom of Information Act amendments have opened

—Information and photos courtesy of FBI

FBI records to the public. The FBI hires and promotes more women and minorities. In the wake of the lives lost in stand-offs at Ruby Ridge, Idaho, and Waco, Texas, Director Louis J. Freeh established the Critical Incident Response Group. Additionally, the bureau maintains its role as the nation's police force.

"We are responsible now for well over 200 federal violations, and that [includes] everything from kidnapping to bank robbery to cyber crime, which is certainly a new area for everybody to be involved in, and certainly it involves a national issue because of the ease with which people can access information or access other people's records through a computer system," explains Ed Cogswell, public affairs specialist for the FBI. "We have 56 field offices presently, and we have legal attaches assigned overseas in 23 countries now. And we've been doing training now with former Eastern Bloc countries of the Soviet Union. We have a training facility in Budapest where we actually are training law enforcement officers in investigative techniques and procedural matters and legal matters.

"Certainly, we have a larger concentration in counter terrorism activities," Cogswell continues. "We saw some bombings in this country – the Oklahoma City bombing, the World Trade Center in New York. We also are looking at the issue of encryption, which could significantly impair the ability of law enforcement to conduct electronic surveillance. That's really needed in racketeering investigations, corruptions

Cogswell attributes the success to current Director Freeh.

"[Freeh] really refocused the use of agent manpower, and he also developed the activity of core values and the integrity of

PHOTO COURTESY OF AP/ WIDE WORLD PHOTO

the investigative process," Cogswell says. "So I think that he's really turned it around in terms of enjoying a better public image of the FBI."

Much has changed since the agency's glory years. The FBI's had its fair share of high periods and low periods, and the balance between the need for security and the preservation of civil liberties is still a concern.

TODAY'S FBI: [top] Bill Clinton with current FBI Director Louis Freeh; [above] destruction at Waco, Texas

investigations, and organized crime investigations."

Although some of the FBI's more controversial methods, like electronic surveillance, cause people to throw a cautionary glance in the bureau's direction, most agree with Cogswell that the greater good will be served. In fact, public opinion regarding the FBI's work seems to be on the upswing these days.

But after 90 years, the bureau has been streamlined to respond to current areas of concern, like health care, domestic terrorism and fraud. Technological improvements, including advances in DNA research, are used as crime-solving tools in the FBI Laboratory to aid in violent criminal apprehension. With more than 11,000 special agents and 16,000 support personnel, the FBI is ready to tackle the challenges of the next millennium. ●

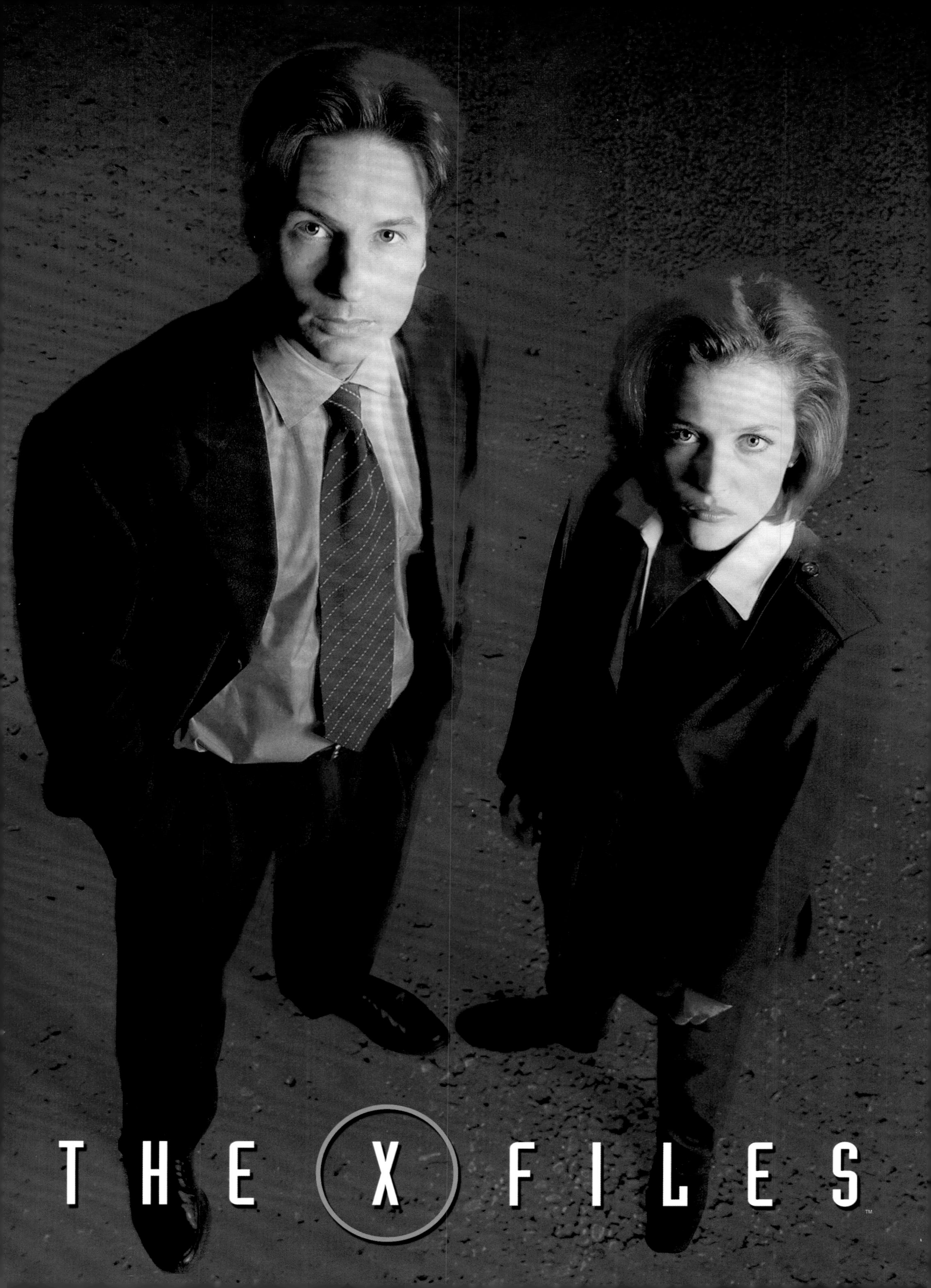
THE X FILES™

RESSLER OF MONSTERS

Dave Hughes prepares a personality profile of former FBI agent Robert K Ressler.

all the major theatres of war during his period of service – including a ten-year stint in Vietnam – earning his discharge in 1970 at the rank of Major. He immediately joined the FBI as a Special Agent, where he became involved in the investigation of interstate thefts, forgeries, frauds and other organised crime cases before being transferred to the Bureau's fledgling Behavioural Sciences Unit – where *The X-Files'* Agent Mulder cut his teeth before beginning his unofficial investigations of the paranormal – as a criminologist, instructor and counsellor.

For 20 years, Ressler worked on virtually every single one of the country's most infamous serial killer cases involving homicide, sex crimes, criminal psychology, post traumatic stress disorder, hostage negotiation and forensics, personally pioneering the procedure of criminal personality profiling that has improved the Bureau's efficiency a hundred fold in recent years. By the time he retired from active duty in 1990, Ressler had

MULDER: Scully, this is Bill Patterson. He runs the investigative support unit out of Quantico.

SCULLY: Yes, I know. Behavioural Science – you wrote the book. It's an honour, sir.

– dialogue from "Grotesque"

Robert K Ressler has spent virtually half a lifetime finding out what makes criminals tick. But as a 20 year veteran of the United States' Federal Bureau of Investigation, founder of the Bureau's Violent Criminal Apprehension Program (VICAP), active agent on such high-profile cases as the Charlie Manson, Jeffrey Dahmer and John Wayne Gacy murders and a key consultant for films like *The Silence of the Lambs* and *Copycat*, finding out what makes *him* tick may prove to be a tougher case than any he has worked on.

Born in Chicago, Illinois, in 1937, Ressler began his work in criminology while serving in the US Army, in which he enlisted twenty years later, in 1957. As a Provost Marshall, Criminal Investigation Supervisor and Military Police Operations and Intelligence Officer, Ressler saw action in

ROBERT K. RESSLER

JUSTICE IS SERVED

A TRUE STORY OF GREED, BETRAYAL AND MURDER-FOR-HIRE

"The Steele case, with elements of sex, infidelity, dogged police work and political intrigue, is a made-to-order true-crime saga." *– Joe Dirck, Cleveland Plain Dealer*

and Tom Shachtman
Authors of WHOEVER FIGHTS MONSTERS

collated the most accomplished personality profile of all – his own.

Today, Ressler runs Forensic Behavioural Services (FBS), an organisation he founded in 1990 to assist various government, military and law enforcement agencies with the kind of work he specialised in for over thirty years. Based in Spotsylvania, Virginia, a stone's throw from the FBI Academy at Quantico where he remains a consultant, researcher and lecturer, the FBS continues his work in the private sector, offering the benefit of his experience and expertise to defence and prosecution counsellors in both civil and criminal cases, and to authors, film-makers and television producers – among them Thomas Harris (*The Silence of the Lambs*) and Patricia D Cornwell (*All That Remains*) – for whom the facts are as important as the fiction.

Most recently, he has been working on his third book, *I Have Lived In The Monster*, in which he details his personal experiences working with – or rather *against* – America's Most Wanted, including his nine hour, one-to-one interview with Milwaukee mass murderer Jeffrey Dahmer.

It is seven in the morning at the FBS offices when I reach Ressler by telephone, recording our conversation in the fond tradition of an FBI wiretap. He is already working, putting the finishing touches to his book, "a sequel of sorts" to his astonishing 1992 autobiography, *Whoever Fights Monsters*, the title of which comes from Friedrich Nietzche's oft-quoted (and more often *mis*quoted) idiom that "Whoever fights monsters should see to it that, in the process, he does not become a monster, and when you look into an abyss, the abyss looks also into you.

"*Whoever Fights Monsters* left off at the time I left the FBI in 1990," he says, "whereas the new one covers cases I have worked on in the UK, Africa, Japan and the USA, and highlights interviews I did with Jeffrey Dahmer, who killed 17 young men in Milwaukee, and John Wayne Gacy, who killed 33 in Chicago." The Dahmer interview came about when the killer's attorney, Jerry Boyle, requested Ressler's assistance in compiling Dahmer's defence. "The interview was essentially to try and figure out where Dahmer fit in the serial killer 'family'. Gacy, on the other hand, I had interviewed many times while I was still with the Bureau, but I talked with him again, *after* his conviction, for purely research purposes."

Whilst all of the serial killers and sex criminals remain, ironically, far more famous than Ressler, he has also worked as a consultant on a number famous works of fiction, including Thomas Harris' Hannibal Lecter novels *Red Dragon*, filmed as *Manhunter*, and *The Silence of the Lambs*, arguably the most famous procedural novel – and film – of all time. "My life and many of my experiences were woven through those books and films," he says. "*Red Dragon*, for instance, shows Will Graham visiting a crime scene, effectively trying to get inside the mind of the killer, which is what I always tried to do because it gave me a better perspective about what the killer might have seen." In addition, he says, Clarice Starling's interview with serial killer Hannibal Lecter in *The Silence of the Lambs* echoed his own research, as described in *Whoever Fights Monsters*.

More recently, Ressler has seen his work popularised on television in *The X-Files*, particularly, he feels, in the third season episode "Grotesque", in which a serial killer turns out to be the head of the FBI's Behavioural Science Unit – a case which illustrates perfectly Nietzche's philosophy about fighting monsters.

While Ressler insists that there is no real-life 'X-Files' division of the Bureau – "if there was, I'd have known about it," – he has, nevertheless, had his fair share of the FBI's strangest cases. Most notable is his investigation of the so-called Vampire Killer of Sacramento, California. "It was a pretty frightening case – a disturbed individual whose mental disorder led him to become a human vampire who was killing people literally for their blood and internal organs, drinking and ingesting them in the belief that by doing so he would sustain his life.

"*The X-Files* would have a field day with that one."

Robert K Ressler's new book, I Have Lived in the Monster, *is published in hardcover this spring.*

For 20 years, Ressler worked on virtually every single one of the country's most infamous serial killer cases.

In Hollywood, FBI HEROES have become a rare breed

scr

by Chandra Palermo

een *idles*

Video didn't just kill the radio star— it also did a real number on the FBI.

For about 60 years after the FBI's inception in 1908, movies and TV shows portrayed its agents as the living embodiment of the bureau's motto, "fidelity, bravery, integrity." These were the same federal agents who, in the real world, kept American streets free from gangsters in the '20s and '30s and spies and subversives in the Cold War-dominated '40s and '50s.

Back in 1959, the fidelity, bravery and integrity of Jimmy Stewart's white knight of an agent in *The FBI Story* was unquestionable. Even more recently, audiences enjoyed the heroic successes of Efrem Zimbalist Jr.'s agent Lew Erskine in TV's *The FBI*, which ran from 1965 to 1974 on ABC.

"There was very little that was ambiguous in that show," says Paul Levinson, professor of communications at Fordham University in New York and author of six books on the history of the Media. "The FBI always got their man because of their superior technology and their integrity and doing the right thing. The show was so pro-FBI that [then FBI Director] J. Edgar Hoover gave it his official seal of approval. And Efrem Zimbalist Jr. would come to see Hoover and they'd be photographed together."

Today, however, FBI agents in movies and on TV are often depicted as a far cry from their valiant predecessors. The tide turned somewhere in the '70s when The Vietnam War tarnished America's invulnerable image. The Watergate scandal, which exposed President Nixon's involvement in covering up corrupt campaign practices, showed government officials as imperfect, and congressional findings charging that Hoover might have used his position to sabotage civil rights leaders

sad truth that the FBI doesn't always live up to its motto.

As the scandals erupted, Hollywood's rose-coloured lenses came off. Since then, FBI agents have appeared as inept bumblers and self-interested or potentially corrupt intruders, but they're rarely shown as infallible heroes. It would seem, the good ol' days are gone, if not entirely forgotten.

"Damn FBI don't respect nothin'."
— Sonny Corleone in *The Godfather* (1972)

One of the ways filmmakers downplay the FBI's heroic image is to make agents seem like nuisances. In the *Godfather* trilogy, which traces the rise and fall of mafia kingpins, agents aren't exactly doing anything wrong, but viewers still wish they'd just get out of the way and let things slide.

"What began to happen in the 1970s was, because of the *Godfather* movies, a glorification of organised crime to some extent," Levinson says. "With the *Godfather* movies, there was like another sort of thread of criminality – this sort of noble criminal. So Michael Corleone is a murderer in a sense, but he loves his family. He murders to protect his family. With that mixed message, the FBI becomes mixed in what their role is as well because if Michael has to deal with the FBI, then the FBI is not such a good thing."

In the late '90s, *Donnie Brasco*'s reality-based story of an FBI agent who begins to sympathise with one of the men on whom he spies provides another example of this modern convention. Not only do viewers begin to care for the bad guy along with Brasco, but they also become frustrated with the intrusive

try to either take the investigation away from the local agency or we issue orders in a very arrogant, demeaning way."

"The hero is some kind of local person, a decent person with integrity who just wants to stop the bad guy, and somehow the FBI is always coming in with red tape, making things difficult, doing things behind the back of the local police, so the FBI becomes part of the problem," says Levinson.

One of the best examples of this trend is the cartoonishly exaggerated depiction of agents in *Die Hard*. Bruce Willis wages a one-man war against hostage-taking thieves and has to work double-time when FBI agents Johnson and Johnson come in, wave off the police, dismiss all the work already done by hero Willis and play right into the criminals' hands. "Bruce Willis was doing such a fine job, and we came in and mucked it all up," says Brekke, laughing.

Brekke admits, though, that the depiction is not wholly unfounded. "The agents are always portrayed as these guys in suits, sunglasses and very arrogant, and that's not just something the media's made up," he says. "The bureau over the years has had problems with local law enforcement who felt, sometimes justifiably so, that the bureau would come in and take whatever information they had and not give anything in return."

"No, ma'am. The FBI has no sense of humour that we're aware of." —K in *Men In Black* (1997)

According to Brekke, the negative image perpetuated by movies and TV shows does have an effect on the FBI's ability to convince people to help with an investigation, and so the bureau has set out to fix the problem.

Brekke blames a long-standing lack of communication with the public. "I think that a lot of people don't understand the FBI," he explains. "And I think part of that is our fault in that over the years, we have not done a good job of really telling the public and the media and the people involved in the entertainment business really what we are."

Brekke points out regular briefings on areas of concern, like armaments, counter-terrorism tactics and cyber crime and cooperation with shows for The Learning Channel, The Discovery Channel and A&E as recent steps the FBI has taken to improve its image. He

hopes these steps will curb the growing paranoia about shadowy government conspiracies, which has gained tremendous momentum since the explosive success of *The X-Files*.

"We really haven't opened the doors to let people see what's going on in here, and that nurtures the conspiracy theorists out there and others who perceive a lack of information as something wrong going on," Brekke says. "We're trying to get the message out as to what we do, so that this perception or myth that we're either involved in a conspiracy to oppress the American people or to, in cases of local police, work to our own advantage and discredit local law enforcement can be overcome."

"Figure we take out the terrorists, lose 20, 25 per cent of the hostages."
"I can live with that." —Agents Johnson and Johnson, no relation, in *Die Hard* (1988)

Other negative depictions of the FBI are not as subtle. In *Brasco*, agents cause problems for the good guys as well as the villains. But in many other movies and TV shows, FBI agents are portrayed as downright arrogant and inept.

"That seems to be the case these days. You can never have this straight-arrow, like everything's cool, government agency," says Allan Johnson, television writer for the *Chicago Tribune*. "You've always got to fight not only the bad guys, but in many cases your own people."

Local law officers are common foils for bad agents. Rather than lend a hand with their extensive training and technology, FBI agents usurp power and ruin police investigations. "In many movies and TV shows, particularly where the focus is on local police, the FBI are perceived as being elite and often arrogant intruders who usually muck up the investigation that's being conducted by local authorities," says Tron Brekke, national spokesman for the FBI and deputy assistant director of the Office of Public and Congressional Affairs. "Stereotypically, we

"The answers are there, you just have to know where to look for them."
"That's why they put the 'I' in FBI."
—Scully and Mulder in *The X-Files* (Pilot, 1993)

Despite its influence on conspiracy theories, *The X-Files* features positive portrayals of FBI agents, according to Brekke. "It's pretty darn accurate, as to how they operate and the kind of professional demeanor that is exhibited," he says.

Brekke credits the realism on *The X-Files* to creator Chris Carter's consultation with FBI agents and experts on bureau protocol. "We'd like to see the creative people, whether it be the directors of TV or the author of a book, come to us,

FBI FACES: [clockwise from above] TV's *The FBI*, *The Silence of the Lambs*, *The FBI Story*, two scenes from *The X-Files* feature film, Tommy Lee Jones in *Men in Black*, police watch in horror as FBI agents sabotage a hostage crisis in *Die Hard*

like many of them do, and ask for our input on how the FBI would handle a particular situation," Brekke says.

The Silence of the Lambs also showcased a realistic and heroic depiction of the agency. While making this Academy Award-winning thriller about a cannibalistic serial killer helping a young agent track another killer, cast and crew members spent much time studying the bureau.

"I think the portrayal of most of the FBI people in *The Silence of the Lambs* was very, very close to reality," Brekke says. "The company spent a lot of time at the [FBI] Academy. In fact, Jodie Foster spent time with a new agent training class to learn what it's really like to be a new FBI agent. When they take the time to find out what the FBI is really like, then that usually results in a much more accurate portrayal."

"One may smile and smile and be a villain."
—Jim Garrison in *JFK* (1991)

It's true that real-life scandals caused the first dent in the stoic public image of the FBI, but since then, the negative view of the agency has been expanded and perpetuated by Hollywood fiction to a degree that is sometimes preposterous. Even if the pendulum begins to swing back towards the centre, however, the unfortunate agency may never escape frequent use as a villain.

"I think a lot of that may have to do with how it's always us against them, it's always the little person against the government," Johnson says. "And who better to personify the government cracking down on the little people than federal agents? They're the ones who crack the whip or who mete out the justice for the government."

Johnson says the depiction is an inevitable result of evolving story-telling conventions. "You tend to hiss at the bad guy more when that bad guy is supposed to be good. The FBI is obviously supposed to be the good government agency that's trying to help

the people, but if there are rogue agents within that type of government body, then you say, 'Oh man, why is he so bad? He's supposed to be the good guy.' It just helps fuel the story."

"Nature abhors normality."
—Dr. Blockhead in *The X-Files* ("Humbug," 1995)

So if a new show or movie were to portray the FBI as the epitome of fidelity, bravery and integrity, would it have even the slightest chance for success?

"Well, people ignored *C-16* big time," Johnson says.

C-16, which aired on ABC briefly in 1997, followed the adventures of an elite, maverick FBI squad that almost always got their men. It quickly failed.

"The show was hardly on at all. It was on and they pulled it off," Johnson explains. "That was probably the first show in a very long time where they branded the FBI as being this super-clean, super-cool government group."

Many heroic agents still grace our big and small screens, but those agents are often forced to deal with corrupt superiors or combat a tragic flaw. We may never see an FBI like Jimmy Stewart's again, but it doesn't mean the FBI will forever suffer humiliation at the hands of agents like Johnson and Johnson either. It just means today's audiences are looking for more complexity in their entertainment.

"With today's storytelling motivations, the hero can't be straight-arrow anymore," Johnson says. "I mean, we saw characters like Efrem Zimbalist Jr. back then, and it was OK because that's all we ever saw. But when we saw these multi-layered characters who always had some type of problem going on, or they didn't do things strictly by the book or they had their own superiors in many cases to deal with, it just became more interesting. So, no, we probably won't see another show like *The FBI*."●

WILLIAM B. DAVIS

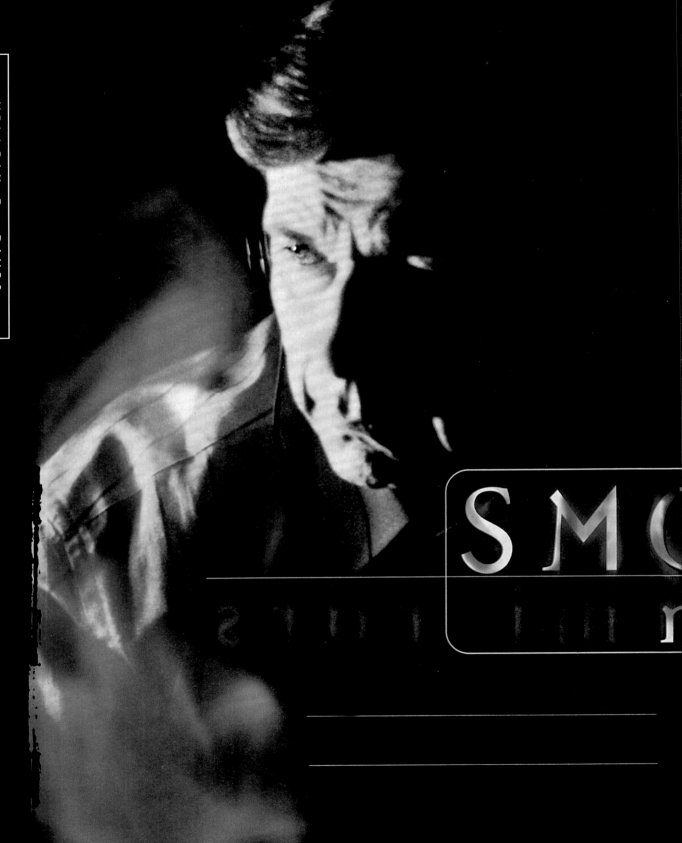

SMO

WILLIAM B. DAVIS dispels the mystery surrounding the enigmatic CIGARETTE-SMOKING MAN and his role in Season Six

SMOKE & Mirrors

THE REEDY VOICE on the telephone, until now cheerful and friendly, suddenly crackles with familiar menace. "Kill *me* off for a few weeks?" it asks petulantly, referring to the events in "Redux II." "Then I'm going to get revenge."

William B. Davis seems to enjoy playing off of his devious television persona. During interviews he frequently speaks in first person to describe the Cigarette-Smoking Man's machinations, and his tone often drops conspir-

atorially when offering caustic asides about The Project. While it's all done in good fun, it can be a little disconcerting. After all, the CSM has become the show's answer to Darth Vader—a dark, nasty arch-villain who may or may not have fathered half of the people around him. When Davis steps into character to vow retaliation against would-be assassins, he sounds pretty convincing.

It's clear he relishes the role, and with obvious reason. Despite being unceremoniously offed, reports of the

Cigarette-Smoking Man's death turned out to be greatly exaggerated. A few months later he returned with a flourish, thwarting yet another attempt on his life by The Syndicate, out-maneuvering the Well-Manicured Man and Alex Krycek, locking horns with his son, Agent Jeffrey Spender, and burning Mulder's basement office to a crisp. As the smoke from Season Five clears—literally—the CSM fittingly seems to be standing tall atop the ash heap while Mulder and Scully recuperate

"IT'S INTERESTING TO SEE how out of his depths the character gets when he has to deal with human relationships. He's better at dealing with conflicts with The Syndicate or Skinner or more political things."

—WILLIAM B. DAVIS

from recent physical and mental blows, Spender struggles to maintain his ground at the bureau and The Consortium regroups following the Well-Manicured Man's apparent death.

"I understand there are some very exciting plans for the character this year," Davis says, speaking from his hotel room after a week of filming for *The X-Files'* sixth season opener. "It's quite exciting to have [the character grow], and it's not done yet—we'll all get to find out more about him. It should be very interesting."

Of course, the CSM already has come a long way from being the morose figure puffing away on a pack of Morleys inside Section Chief Blevins' office. While he remains thoroughly enigmatic, the character's depth and substance have been amplified with each season. Mythology episodes have hinted at his past relationship with Mulder's mother, sparking suspicion that he may be the FBI agent's real father. A vast amount of (possibly) apocryphal background surfaced in "Musings of a Cigarette-Smoking Man," when the conspirator was accused of, among other things, shooting J.F.K. and being a failed crime novelist. Last year he was given the chance to interact with honest-to-goodness (or so it would seem) blood relative Spender, a plot twist Davis found refreshing. "It was fun to have something out in the open and revealed," he admits.

"I think the character is becoming increasingly complex," Davis continues. "In a way he's kind of a classic bad guy. But more and more, we're seeing hints of inner conflict

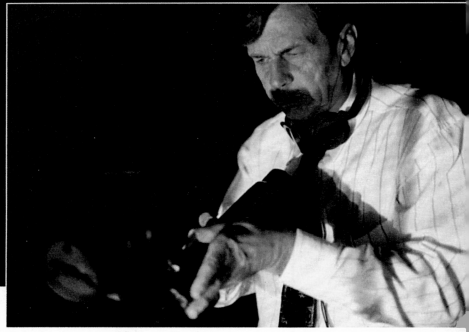

WHERE THERE'S SMOKE: William B. Davis fuels the fire of conspiracy in [clockwise from above] "Musings of a Cigarette-Smoking Man," "Talitha Cumi," "The End" and "Talitha Cumi"

[and] some personal sacrifices he's had to make. As we get involved in these personal relationships with Jeffrey Spender or Mulder and the question of his paternity, it's interesting to see how out of his depths the character gets when he has to deal with human relationships. He's better at dealing with conflicts with The Syndicate or Skinner or more political things. [In those cases], he knows his strengths, he knows where he is. But when he's with his son, it's a lot harder."

And how is this kid measuring up?

"I don't know...I'm not sure if he's going to shape up. I don't think he's got it in him—the concentration for a ruthless-type person," Davis says playfully. "It's one of those situations that my character wants him [to be one]; I want to try to correct him. And then there's the other [aspect] of it, that he doesn't want to see me. He's blocking contact."

Davis often has said that he tries to view the Cigarette-Smoking Man as a good guy, in the sense that the character believes in what he does and considers anyone who tries to stop him an enemy. That type of insight and analysis punctuates most of the actor's commentary—he discusses the role eagerly, and it soon becomes evident that he has closely dis-

says. "He has a genuine respect for Mulder; they're really similar [in] how they've dedicated themselves, [and are] almost fanatical in sacrificing their lives on opposite sides. And in 'Redux II' I try to get him to come and work for me. So I think it's a complicated relationship, and it is going to become more complicated in the future."

In typical *X-Files* fashion, it's unclear what shape that future will take; for all of Davis' personal theories and speculation, he's usually as much in the dark about the show's direction as any other fan. However, there was one instance where he did get advance warning about a particular storyline. Before his character was killed off early in Season Five, Davis knew he didn't need to be concerned about finding a new job. "They were very good at reassuring me right at that time that it wasn't going to be a lasting death," he says. Yet while Davis knew that his eventual return was virtually guaranteed (after all, he had spent a chunk of time filming scenes for *The X-Files* feature film, which was set to be released the following summer) many fans weren't so sure. The actor recalls hearing wildly differing reactions from fans following the CSM's "death."

sected *The X-Files* mythology to learn more about his alter-ego's inner workings.

But this examination isn't fueled by ego or an innate fascination with conspiracy. The 60-year-old stage and screen veteran takes his craft very seriously, as any good teacher would—when not performing, he tends to his Vancouver acting school, The William Davis Centre for Actor's Study. (The school's most famous alumna, Lucy Lawless, trained there before embarking on her future as a warrior princess). One habit Davis tries to instill in his students is the technique of deconstructing roles by forging a history for their characters. It's a suggestion he takes to heart himself, although fabricating a background for the ever-mysterious CSM is an audacious undertaking.

"What an actor basically tries to do is to try and find the life of the scene at the time they're doing it," he explains. "So I need a backstory that works for what I'm doing now. In a way it might be interesting to go back and redo my [*X-Files*] scenes from a couple years ago with what I know now, even though that, of course, is impossible. So we're always using the information that we're given and we're also always inventing things. You may later find that what you invented wasn't correct, but in a way it doesn't matter as long as it brings the scene alive. So I'm constantly reinventing and revising my story."

That supplemental creativity often requires Davis to reach independent conclusions about the character, even if the script itself doesn't offer concrete revela-

tions. For example, during a recent scene he felt he had to make a determination about a relationship that has triggered frenetic fan speculation for years.

"I just shot a scene with Agent Spender that had a couple of strange twists and

turns in it, a sort of very interesting *King Lear*-type thing, and [it] made me have to make some personal decisions about aspects of the character. Basically, I had to finally decide for myself if Mulder was my son or not," Davis says, remaining cagey about which side of the paternal fence he chose to land upon. "It was clear that it was how the scene worked for me."

Still, Davis is quick to admit that the truth remains elusive, even for him. "[The CSM's] relationship with Mulder is always ambiguous," he

UP IN SMOKE

WILLIAM B. DAVIS WAS HIRED to smoke a cigarette in *The X-Files* pilot, nothing more. When the show's writers decided to actually let the Cigarette-Smoking Man speak, it caused a now-infamous stir on the set, where some questions arose about his acting ability. "I gathered there were some discussions behind the scenes about my capabilities," Davis says, laughing. "My good friend [former producer/director] R.W. Goodwin even admitted to being one of the primary skeptics."

He need not have worried. Davis' sinister embodiment of The Syndicate's top henchman has become an *X-Files* staple, and his portrayal gains increased depth—and ambiguity—with each episode in which he appears. Here's Davis' take on some of the CSM's most notable moments:

"TALITHA CUMI": "It was exciting that it got the CSM into the field of human relationship [when he was confronted by Mulder's mother]. The other exciting thing for me was the Grand Inquisitor-like confrontation with the alien [Jeremiah Smith]. It forced me to read Dostoevsky a few times. It was interesting to try and work out the intellectual argument with the character."

"MUSINGS OF A CIGARETTE-SMOKING MAN": "In retrospect this has grown on me. It's a question of what spirit to take it in. If it's seen as putting together significant pieces of the puzzle, there obviously are things in there that are bizarre—the idea that he fixed hockey games or that he even cares—he's got a lot of things that are a lot more demanding. But if taken as a speculative take on the character, it seems to have been a popular episode. Certainly entertaining and certainly fun to do."

"REDUX II": "The scene with Samantha—I still don't know what to make of that. I took it in good coin at the time. 'Aha! So that's what's going on—he's Samantha's father.' But nothing's happened about that since then. A lot of people have said it wasn't Samantha at all, but some clone, a plant to lure Mulder over to my side. So who knows?"

"THE END": "I had a terrific workout that day. I don't know how many times I ran down that hill [fleeing would-be assassins in snowy Quebec]. It was nice to get out of that suit though. Wear something else and get into the outdoors."

"[Opinions] were very mixed," he says. "A lot of the hardcore fans were sure that he would return, the intermediate fans weren't quite sure what to make of it and the casual fans were really sympathetic. They said, 'What are you going to do now that *The X-Files* is over for you?' They were all quite sure that I was really dead."

As for himself, Davis was grateful for being resurrected by the show's writers. "It was an interesting storyline to pursue, and

I thought it was kind of cute at first to be dead, but eventually I got pretty bored with it," he admits.

While Cigarette-Smoking Man's constant evolution continues to challenge Davis, he points out that the crucial element that keeps the character fresh is the fact that he has appeared in less than a quarter of *The X-Files'* episodes. That makes the character's immense popularity even more remarkable, especially considering that the CSM's personality is as blackly corrupt as his lungs. Davis has been profiled in enough magazines and Web sites that his acting credits (including parts in *Look Who's Talking* and *The Dead Zone*), smoking habits (he quit years ago—herbal substitutes are used on camera) and athletic achievements (he's a Canadian water-skiing champion for his age division) have become X-Phile gospel. When he toured North America in *The X-Files* Expos last spring, standing ovations greeted him whenever he took the stage. Some moviegoers burst into cheers when he made his big-screen entrance in *The X-Files* motion picture. Canadian pop music group Barenaked Ladies refer to the CSM in their song "One Week," the video for which received heavy rotation on MTV. He also hit the rock 'n' roll mainstream by

"I thought it
but ev

appearing in a video for a song by the band Filter, which appeared on the movie's soundtrack. Even his negative publicity sounds pretty positive—one pro-smoking group protested that the character made nicotine addicts look bad. The consensus is clear: After Mulder and Scully,

premiere, which was sort of a weird time to see it. However objective as one would like to be, you really get wrapped up in [thinking], 'How do I look?'" he remembers with a chuckle. "Which is why I went back to see it again and look at it as a movie. I went to the most obscure matinee

I could find, with only half a dozen people in the theater. The concession people and ushers [recognized me]; it was the last day they were showing the film at that particular theater, so they gave me one of the movie posters from the wall."

Fortunately, Davis didn't spend his entire summer vacation in darkened theaters. The Vancouver resident also took the time to appear in a couple of Canadian features and a cable TV movie where he played what he calls a "very warm, friendly, caring" doctor; in more than one scene, he even got to smile. He'll be doing more of the same in *The X-Files*' new Southern California home, where he expects to make some Hollywood contacts and further expand his résumé.

"It's going to be challenging filming in Los Angeles, mostly because of the distances between the residences of the crew and the locations," he says. "But the crew is terrific and they're all very nice people." As filming continues, Davis keeps himself busy by trying to probe his character's heart of darkness and unravel the mythology's many secrets.

"I have been stumped sometimes," the actor admits, "but I always try to know what's going on." The Cigarette-Smoking Man would be proud. ●

SMOKE ON THE WATER: CSM seems to be behind it all in episodes such as [clockwise from upper left] the pilot, "Musings of a Cigarette-Smoking Man" and "F. Emasculata"

the Cigarette-Smoking Man has become *The X-Files*' best-known figure.

Although Davis has had time to get accustomed to being a pop-culture icon, he's still a little amazed at his popularity. "It's funny—sometimes I think I'm a very famous person, and other times I think I'm no more famous than I ever was," he says thoughtfully. "It is kind of strange how you'll talk to strangers and they'll treat you like someone they just met, and you'll see other people and they'll point and say, 'Look, it's the Cancer Man!' It's fun; I always enjoy meeting fans."

Appearing in *The X-Files* feature film probably won't help him retain his last scraps of anonymity. The actor, who makes a point of watching and critiquing his own work, went to see the movie twice. "The first time I saw it was at the

was KIND OF CUTE at first to be dead,
entually I got pretty bored with it."

—WILLIAM B. DAVIS

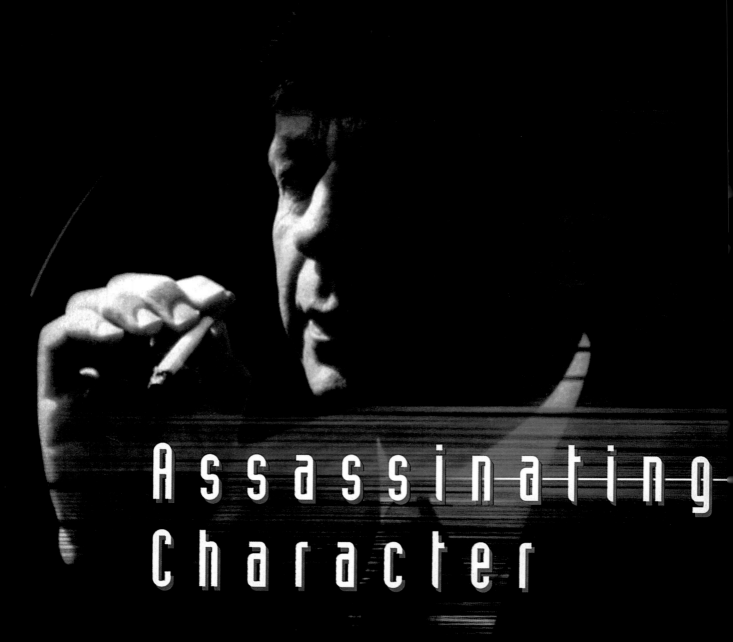

Assassinating Character

Kate Anderson tries to unpick the web of deceit around
the true nature of the Cigarette-Smoking Man

Doctor *Who* had the Master, Superman had Lex Luthor, Sherlock Holmes had Moriarty, and *The X-Files* has the Cigarette-Smoking Man. Resident bad guys, evil arch-enemies; these are the men we love to hate. And none of them come more mysterious and malevolent than Mulder and Scully's nicotine-addicted nemesis.

Always dressed in black, lurking in the shadows behind a cloud of smoke, with a seemingly limitless supply of Morley cigarettes never far from his lips, the Cigarette-Smoking Man is the ultimate man in black. He is a deceptively ordinary-looking, nameless individual, responsible for covering up government conspiracies to maintain a veil of secrecy over the covert activities that Agents

Mulder and his sister Samantha - what part do they play in the Cigarette-Smoking Man's plans?

> DON'T TRY TO
> THREATEN ME, MULDER.
> I'VE WATCHED
> PRESIDENTS DIE.
>
> The Cigarette-Smoking Man, "One Breath

Mulder and Scully seek to expose.

Our intrepid agents (and Section Chief Blevins) aside, the Cigarette-Smoking Man is the only other character to have been in *The X-Files* from the very beginning. Who can forget his chilling, silent presence way back in the pilot episode: standing in the background, puffing away on a cigarette while Blevins gave Scully the task of debunking Mulder's work on the X-Files. And what about the closing moments of that

episode, where we see him depositing evidence of a supposedly alien abduction in a huge secret vault beneath the Pentagon?

Over the course of four seasons, the man affectionately referred to as 'Cancer Man' by fans has become a pivotal player, a central figure in the show's mythology. But his developing involvement with *The X-Files'* greater story has been slow: it was 20 episodes after his first appearance before he finally got to speak,

however briefly, in "Tooms." Then in "The Erlenmeyer Flask," the season's finale, it's back to the silent treatment as we see him once again archiving evidence of a sinister government plot (this time, it seems to be an extra-terrestrial foetus) in that same Pentagon storage room.

Like most successful villains, William B. Davis' portrayal of this imposing, pernicious individual is a joy to behold. A reformed smoker (Davis puffs on herbal cigarettes whilst filming),

Behind you! The silent first appearance in the pilot episode.

> I STRONGLY ENCOURAGE
> YOU... TO DENY
> EVERYTHING.
>
> The Cigarette-Smoking Man, "Anasazi"

the Toronto-born 59-year-old actor delivers a very credible performance as the chain-smoking Devil incarnate. A former child actor, acting teacher, and director, his acting skills convinced series creator Chris Carter to hire him during production of the pilot in early 1993. There was no way of knowing then that this shadowy man, seen only in the background, would become central to the show's on-going storyline. But as the series developed, so did the character. Even Carter admits that he never anticipated the Cigarette-Smoking Man would become such an integral part of the show.

If only the character's history was as transparent as the actor's. His agenda has always been as mysterious and deceptive as his persona. At first, he appeared to be something of a silent force behind those who seemed to be in

> I WORK VERY HARD TO KEEP ANY PRESIDENT FROM
> KNOWING I EVEN EXIST.
>
> The Cigarette-Smoking Man, "Musings of a Cigarette Smoking Man"

control. But it wasn't long before he stepped out of the shadows to make his real presence felt. It later became apparent that this shadowy figure of evil was in fact just one of several other equally obscure individuals who had, over the years, been responsible for keeping the public in the dark about what appeared to be alien activity on Earth and experiments conducted on humans using alien DNA.

The character became decidedly more prominent during the second season. With the X-files division shut down and Mulder and Scully separated, he began to intervene more directly. In the season opener, "Little Green Men," the Cigarette-Smoking Man gloats to Mulder that "his time is over." In "Sleepless," he arranges for Mulder to be assigned a new partner, fresh-faced newbie Alex Krycek. Krycek claimed to be a follower of Mulder's work, but it wasn't long before we discovered that he was in fact in the employ of the Cigarette-Smoking Man and only wished to block the work which he claimed to hold so highly. In "Duane Barry" and "Ascension" (the show's first two-parter) we realize the depths of the Cigarette-Smoking Man's ruthlessness when he masterminds Scully's abduction and, in "One Breath," her return.

Perhaps season two's finest hour, "One Breath" adds another color to the Cigarette-Smoking Man's painting-by-numbers character development. Maturing as the show matured, the Cigarette-Smoking Man has been part of some of the show's most revealing and important scenes. Here, in one of the most riveting and powerful, he is confronted by a distraught, gun-wielding Mulder. We ascertain that, as well as having watched "presidents die," the Cigarette-Smoking Man is "in the game because I believe that what I'm doing is right… If people were to know of the things I know, it would all fall apart." Ultimately, the Cigarette-Smoking Man and Mulder are a lot alike. Like opposite sides of a coin, both are fanatics willing to sacrifice everything – even their own lives – for what they are committed to, what they perceive to be right.

Season two's finale, "Anasazi," and its continuing parts "The Blessing Way" and "Paper Clip," open wide the conspiracy and the Cigarette-Smoking Man's place within the shadowy syndicate behind it. Far from being the almighty figure depicted in the first two seasons, we discover that he is in fact more of a middle manager, answerable to the higher powers within the syndicate, such as the Elder and the Well-Manicured Man.

"Anasazi" also revealed the first of two major revelations tying him closely to the Mulder family – that at one time he had a professional relationship with Mulder's father. The second was to come a whole season later, with his coded references to a friendship with Mrs Mulder. This sparked fan rumors that the Cigarette-Smoking Man would turn out to be Mulder's biological father – but the truth was much more shocking, as revealed in season five's "Redux" and "Redux II."

Towards the close of the second season, the Cigarette-Smoking Man's agenda seemed relatively clear. As an instigator in a government cover-up, he was a constant presence, responsible for

> YOU LIVE IN FEAR. THAT'S
> YOUR WHOLE LIFE.
>
> Jeremiah Smith to the Cigarette-Smoking Man,
> "Talitha Cumi"

undermining Mulder's investigations, preventing the wayward agent from uncovering evidence that would enable him to go public and expose the truth. However, killing Mulder and Scully was never an option because, if he did, he risked turning one man's mission into a crusade. Besides, the Cigarette-Smoking Man had the perfect weapon to use against Mulder – his readiness to believe. But by the end of "Anasazi," it had all changed. By attempting to destroy both the evidence and Mulder by burning the buried boxcar full of mutated corpses, it became a whole new ball game.

Up until then, the Cigarette-Smoking Man had always appeared to be in control. However, when Mulder gained possession of top-secret government files that provided evidence of

Old friends - but how deep does that friendship go?

Above and left: How far will the Cigarette-Smoking Man go to cover up his secrets?

'flying saucers,' it signalled a decisive shift in his agenda. That data the original tape contained – albeit encrypted – could expose everything that he had worked so hard to keep under wraps. His policy and promise to Bill Mulder not to harm his son gets thrown out of the window, with the Cigarette-Smoking Man doing everything in his power to retrieve the data and protect himself. But early into season three, he is forced to compromise when the contents of the tape are memorized by a tribe of American Navajo Indians and Skinner forces him to cease meddling in Mulder's work.

Third season episodes like "731" and "Apocrypha" continue the show's on-going mythology arc but only serve to cloud our perception of the Cigarette-Smoking Man's current agenda. While he is a member of the consortium, his position in the group still isn't crystal clear. He readily disobeys their orders, and lies to them to cover his own back. Often he is more than willing to act unilaterally: such as in "Apocrypha," when he moves a salvaged UFO to another secret location. "Wetwired" adds yet another twist to the conspiracy, when we discover that Mulder's current informant X (who so far has proved hard to trust) is an employee of the Cigarette-Smoking Man. Even if X's actions are more those of a double agent – and not, like Krycek, a collaborator – it's still chilling to know that someone Mulder receives information from is working closely with his nemesis.

Season four blew clouds of smoke around 'Cancer Man's' background with the intriguing but ultimately troubling "Musings of a Cigarette Smoking Man." For four years, the Cigarette-Smoking Man's history was tantalisingly unclear, now it's completely obscure. In an episode littered with contradictions and uncertainties, the nicotine addict (born, we are told, on 20 August 1940 to a communist father who was executed for passing on information about America's plan to end WWII, and a mother who dies of lung cancer) is characterized as a failed, frustrated adventure writer. He was also an assassin, given a secret assignment to kill President John F. Kennedy and later Martin Luther King.

> I CAN KILL YOU WHENEVER I PLEASE... BUT NOT TODAY.
>
> The Cigarette-Smoking Man, "Musings"

Regardless as to the credibility of this amusing and unusual episode, the Cigarette-Smoking Man remains as mysterious, nameless and dangerous as ever. He is one of the men responsible for Scully's terminal cancer. We know too that he is Scully's best hope of a cure. With this power over the series central characters, as well as his sway over the conspiracy as a whole, his role in *The X-Files* is almost as fundamental as those of Mulder and Scully themselves… even though a cloud of smoke continues to cloak the truth about him.

> AS ALWAYS, MAINTAIN PLAUSIBLE DENIAL.
>
> The Cigarette-Smoking Man, "Anasazi"

Year of the RAT

Nicholas Lea reveals what it's like to bring to life treacherous "Ratboy" Alex Krycek

PHOTO BY KHAREN HILL

And behold, the death of a traitor to the dark cause shall lead to the ascendence of the rat.—*The Gospel According to Carter, Chapter 6, Verses 12-13*

With the alien colonization of Earth close at hand and no living son to assume his legacy, the Cigarette-Smoking Man must take on a new apprentice. It's the opportunity of a lifetime for renegade agent Alex Krycek, who, in the last four years, has murdered Bill Mulder and Melissa Scully, betrayed U.N. operative Marita Covarrubias and schemed with and against the now immolated power brokers of The Syndicate. Given his credentials, Ratboy seems like the perfect candidate for the job.

Nicholas Lea, who plays the dash-ing rogue, is prepared to tackle the assignment, should it come his way. Not only would the promotion be a boon to his character's scandalous résumé, it would finally nail down Krycek's mysterious motivations. Since his debut in Season Two's "Sleepless," the rebel agent has remained true only to his duplicitous nature. He originally portrayed him-self as a man who shared Mulder's passion for the paranormal, later admitting his ties to the nefarious CSM. Krycek then defied his fellow conspirators' orders in many of the key mythology episodes—"The Blessing Way," "Tunguska," "Terma," "Patient X"—his actions underscoring his shifty nature and earning him an unflattering, rodent-inspired nickname.

Now, Krycek might have discovered

by Gina McIntyre

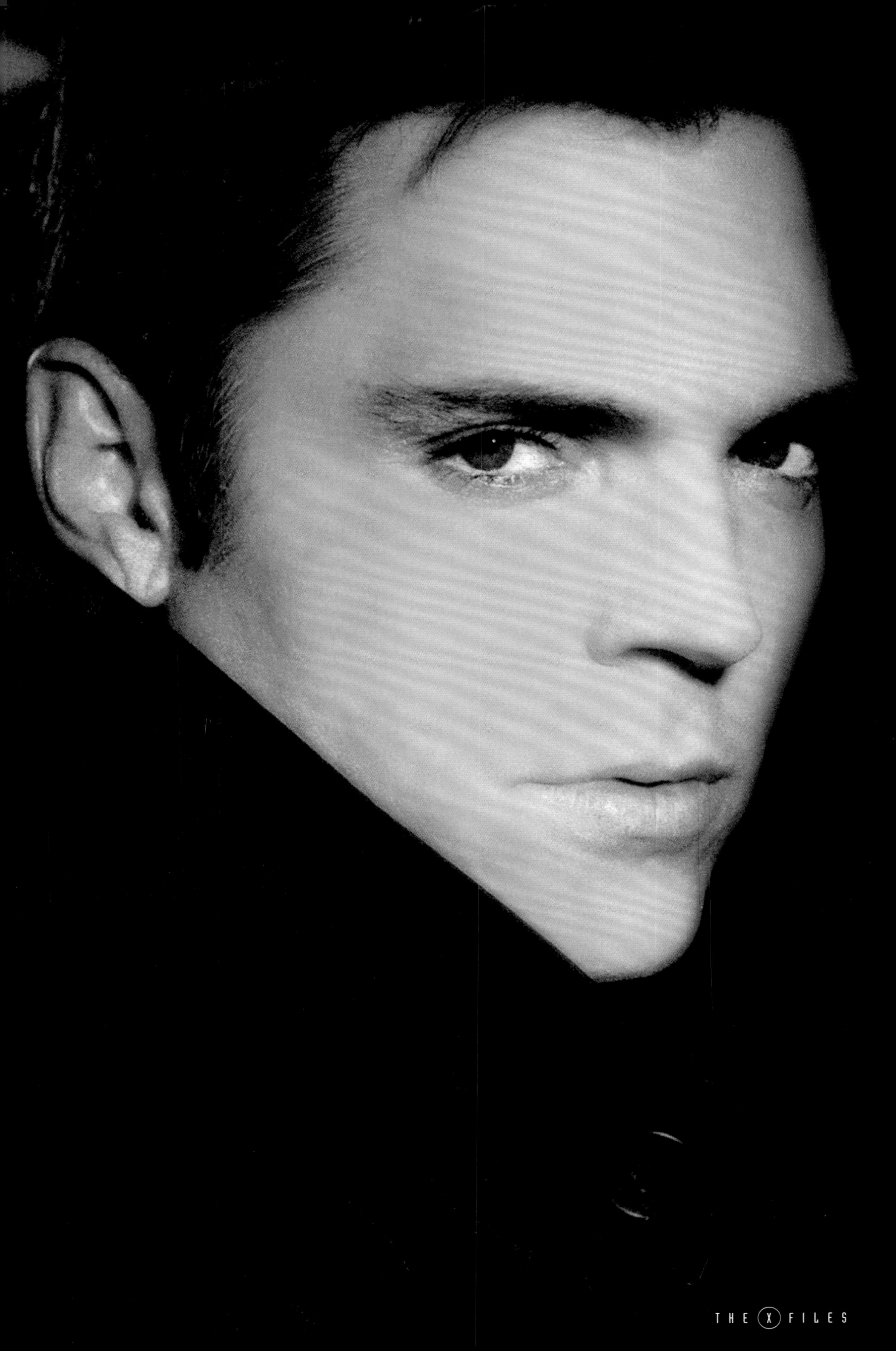

NICHOLAS LEA

his true calling. In the wake of the tumultuous events of epic mythology two-parter "Two Fathers"/"One Son," he certainly seems to be gunning for the position of second-in-command. And with Spender conveniently out of the way, Krycek's chances to succeed the CSM are better than ever before. Lea wisely cautions, however, that only Chris Carter can accurately forecast what will happen in the series' dark world. Placing bets on Krycek's future is an exercise in futility.

"There's some big changes," Lea says, referring to the Season Six episodes. "I would say there's certainly changes in the environment, changes in what appears outwardly to be allegiances. What appears

changed, motivations for the character are pretty much the same."

In other words, Krycek is just as underhanded as he's been all along. As sneaky as he is, though, the character brings a unique dynamic to the series' chemistry. While Mulder and Scully remain the heroes and the CSM the chief villain, Krycek is somewhere in the middle, treading the fine line between good and evil.

"All I know is that he's pretty much a free agent and he really is just trying to further his own success or his own livelihood," Lea offers. "That's sort of what I like about this character is that he's not the good guy, he's not truly the bad guy. He fills that void in between and there isn't really another character on the show that does that, be it the Cigarette-Smoking Man or The Syndicate or Mulder and Scully, Skinner and Spender. I like the fact that I sort of play both sides. I really enjoy the ambiguity of what appear to be his motives."

Lea's feelings toward Krycek are not so unclear; the character has put him on the fast-track toward international celebrity. Born in New Westminister, British Columbia, June 22, 1962, Lea was a relative

"[The fans] don't know whether to like me or hate me and

on the surface is not really what's going on underneath, which is in keeping with what I've been doing all along—false motives, trying to win over people's trust in order to further my own means. It's hard to tell when he's telling the truth and when he's lying. Although the environment's

late-comer to acting; his first ambition had been to work as a professional illustrator. After a brief stint in the Canadian Navy, Lea enrolled in art school, but his interest in performing spurred him toward the stage. He served as frontman and guitarist for an alternative rock outfit called Beau Monde (French for "beautiful world") for five years before realising that his real passion was acting.

Lea's big break came in 1983 in the Dorothy Stratten biopic *Star 80*, but as luck would have it, the young actor's scenes found a permanent home on the editing room floor. Undaunted, he worked steadily in a number of lesser-known television series and films before landing the role of Officer Enrico "Ricky" Caruso on *The Commish* in 1991. The show turned into a three-year gig for Lea and earned him some valuable on-screen experience, which translated into guest-star spots on other series— including *The X-Files*. Yes, the handsome clubgoer who meets an untimely demise in Season One stand-alone "Genderbender" is none other than Lea. Rob Bowman, who directed the episode, was so impressed with Lea's performance that he recommended the actor for the part of Krycek. Chris Carter agreed to allow Lea to audition, and he was cast the same day.

Since that time, Lea has enjoyed ever-increasing celebrity stature. Turns on *Highlander, The Outer Limits, Sliders* and *Lonesome Dove*, not to mention a leading role in the Canadian syndicated series *Once a Thief*, have elevated him to stardom, but it is his recurring appearances on *The X-Files* that have won him a loyal following. Search the Internet for "Alex Krycek" and you'll find dozens of Web sites devoted to the man behind the rat.

Not that his years on the show have been easy. Krycek has suffered more abuse than almost any other character at the pens of Carter and his league of sinister scribes: He's been repeatedly pummelled, possessed by the black oil, suspended from a 20-storey building. He's even lost an arm to an angry, axe-wielding Russian mob. Given that Lea performs a majority of his own stunt work, the physical demands of the role are often exhausting.

"Nick Lea loves to do everything," says former *X-Files* Vancouver stunt coordinator Tony Morelli. "It's bad as a stunt man; it's great as a stunt coordinator because the cameras can be right there as he's doing it. [When the dailies] come back the next day, everyone says, 'He did that! I can't believe it.' I say, 'I made it as safe as I

I love that. That's what I'm trying to accomplish."

could and told him what could happen and he pulled it off.' When we hung him [over the side of a building for 'Terma'] he was gung ho. It was a little nerve-racking to see him. He was cabled, didn't bother him. I knew he was going to be OK, but it's just that nervous feeling."

Of course, his most famous physical feat had nothing to do with hanging from Walter Skinner's balcony or any other stunt. For "Patient X," Lea tackled the awesome responsibility of filming *The X-Files'* first love scene, as Krycek and Uniblonder Marita Covarrubias engage in an amorous tryst on board the agent's battleship hide-out. Between the prosthetic limb the actor wears as part of his costume and the various crew members watching as Lea and co-star Laurie Holden repeated the action for multiple takes, filming the sequence became something of a surreal experience. Still, the scene confirmed Lea's status as television's first one-armed heartthrob.

FROM BRAT TO RAT: Introduced as Mulder's unwanted sidekick in "Sleepless" [above left], Krycek's nasty nature has since reared its ugly head in [clockwise from above] "S.R. 819," "The Red and the Black" and "Terma."

"When I read the script where Covarrubias and I make-out I was as shocked as anybody," Lea says. "That's another good thing about playing this character is they can almost do anything with him as long as he maintains that kind of personal integrity. You can throw him almost into any situation. One of the things I was really happy about was that you really did get to see a different side of that character in those couple of episodes with the kid in Russia and all that.

"A lot of people saw that as being really evil, but I tried to inject into those scenes, especially when we were on the ship, some true empathy for the kid," Lea continues. "I'm not sure how many people really caught that. It was written so that I was doing these things, and I said, 'I think it's really important that we see a side of this guy that he doesn't want to do this to the kid but he has to in order to get things done, which is still a double-edged sword.'"

Additionally, the episode called for Lea to memorise lengthy passages of Russian, which demanded hours of extensive training. Before his *X-Files* tenure, Lea had never studied the language; on camera, however, he effortlessly spouts off Russian lines as though he were a native speaker.

"It's a great challenge and I enjoy that challenge," Lea says. "But it's really hard work and it takes a lot of time. There is a tremendous amount of pressure to make it really believable. On set even, I feel like I'm under pressure. I don't care what TV show you work on, even a movie for that matter, it's all about time and money eventually. It's also about giving the best performance and producing the best product possible but that inevitably relates to cash. You don't want to go wasting a lot of time on set trying to get your Russian right. I enjoyed it while it happened. I thought it was a great idea."

That unbridled enthusiasm toward his craft is perhaps why Lea is so well-suited for the series. He speaks passionately about the work he has done for the show over the years, always careful to pledge his devotion to his dubious alter ego. Although Lea plans to pursue a wider variety of projects now that the series has relocated to Los Angeles, he

says he will never be too busy to bring Krycek to the screen. For the time being, *The X-Files* is his top priority.

While the actor has benefited from the series' enormous popularity worldwide, the show, too, has prospered from its choice in Lea. No small thanks to Lea's screen presence, his tremendous ability to work under pressure and his singular performances, the diabolical Krycek remains one of the series' most popular and enduring characters.

RAT ATTACK: Not willing to settle for merely harassing Mulder and Scully, Ratboy's dastardly deeds include the murder of Melissa Scully in "The Blessing Way" [above] and Bill Mulder in "Anasazi" [below].

"I fulfill a purpose on this show and hopefully my character continues to fulfill a purpose," Lea says. "[Executive producer] Frank Spotnitz likes to call my character an event character, which means that every time I'm on, something tends to happen, which is good.

"I see him as very slippery and really smart, while others see him as a real backstabber and an opportunist," Lea continues. "I see him as somebody who's really clever. I enjoy the ambiguity of what and who he is. That's one thing I get from the fans is that they don't know whether to like me or hate me and I love that. That's what I'm trying to accomplish."

Now we know. ●

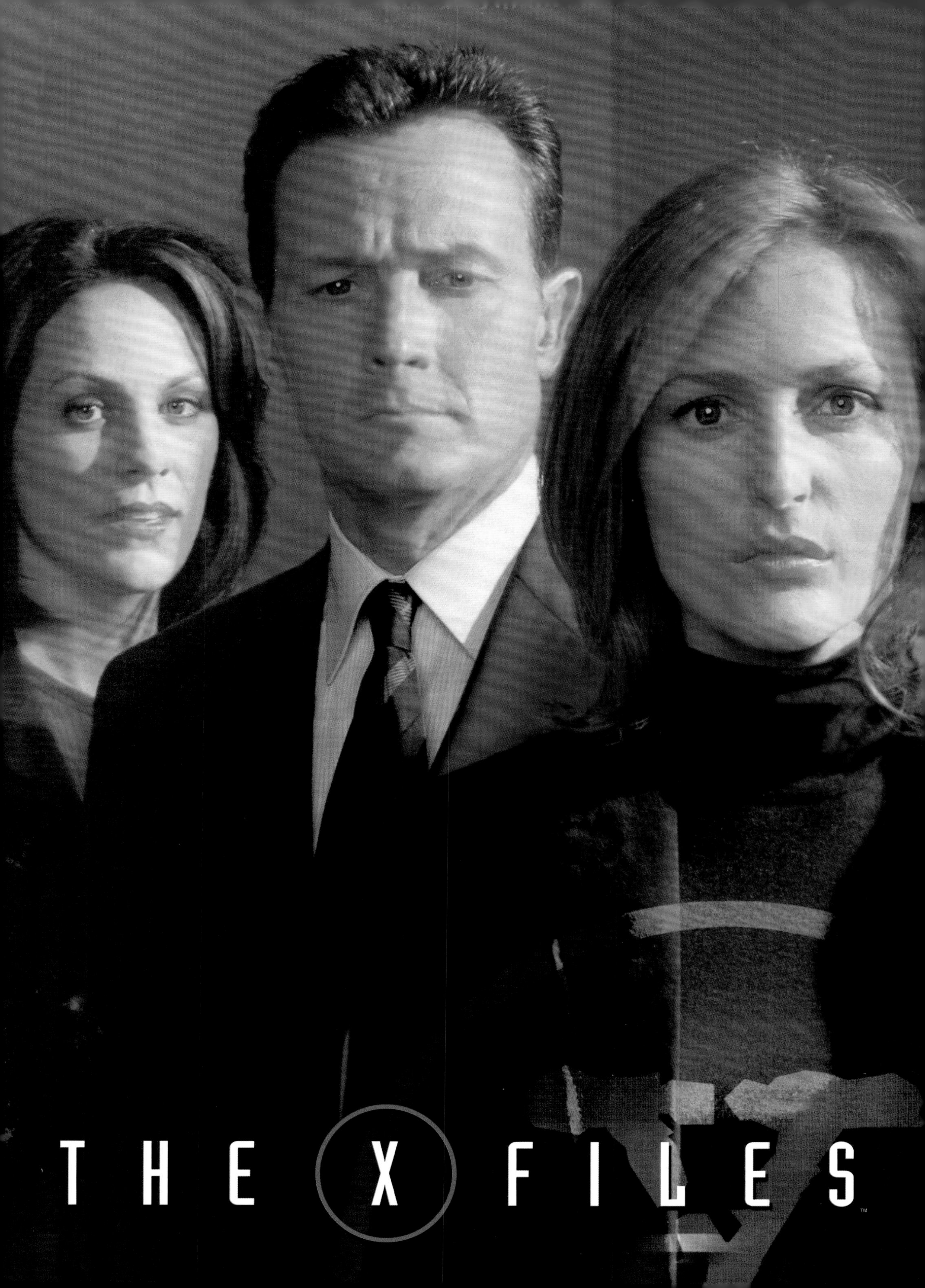
THE X FILES™

KRYCEK PROFILE

You Dirty Rat!

K. STODDARD HAYES EXAMINES THE CHARACTER OF ALEX KRYCEK, ONE OF MULDER AND SCULLY'S NASTIEST, DEADLIEST AND MOST PERSISTENT ENEMIES

Alex Krycek is a liar and a murderer. Everyone says so, usually to his face – everyone being Skinner, Mulder, Scully, and even Doggett, who only met him twice. However, they have left out an important element in their description. More than a liar and murderer, he is also the most cunning player in the game of alien colonization.

Throughout his seven year career as a rogue F.B.I. agent, Syndicate trigger man, and wanted malefactor (by both sides), Krycek is always the wild card, his loyalties doubtful, his purposes hidden, even his actions most often a mystery.

Krycek didn't start out as the king of murder and double dealing. When he reports to his F.B.I. superiors at the end of "Sleepless," he is just an ambitious young man putting his feet on the lowest rungs of power. He's eager to prove his abilities and his loyalties to this shadow bureaucracy, which he senses is the real power in the Bureau. No doubt he's also hoping to become one of them as soon as he can.

When he sets out to stop Mulder from rescuing Scully at Skyland Mountain, his methods are crude – he simply kills the tram operator and strands Mulder in the tram high up the mountain. And the only way he can think to silence Duane Barry is to murder him. These acts accomplish his goals, but they also incriminate him beyond question, since Mulder and others know that he was the only one who could have killed Barry or the operator. He confirms his guilt by disappearing immediately afterward.

Though his crimes in "Ascension" make Krycek an outlaw to Mulder and to Skinner, they apparently make him a trusted agent for the Syndicate. The next time we see Krycek, he's been charged with two assignments that are crucial to protecting the Syndicate's secret conspiracy: the murder of Bill Mulder and the recovery of the digital tape that contains conspiracy records. It's pure bad luck that he botches a third job, the assassination of Scully, when he and his fellow assassin mistake Melissa Scully for her sister in the dark of Scully's apartment ("Anasazi,"

"REQUIEM"

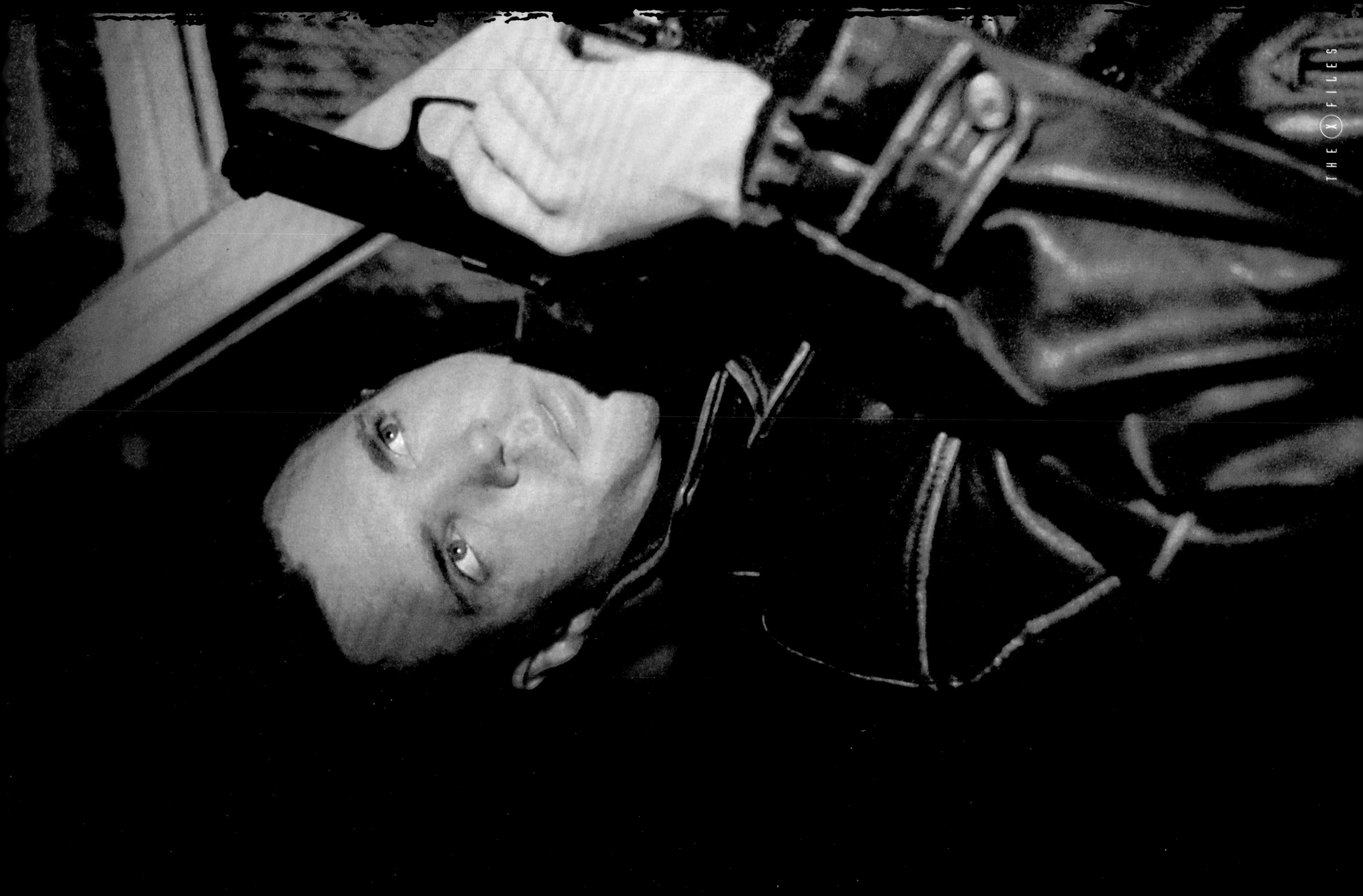

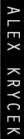

"PIPER MARU"

"The Blessing Way," "Paper Clip").

For Krycek, his possession by the Black Oil entity is a critical turning point. The entity uses Krycek as a host, to get it to the Cigarette-Smoking Man, who has its ship. The Cigarette-Smoking Man lets the Krycek entity get to the missile silo where the ship is stored, knowing the entity will leave Krycek and re-enter its ship. But then, instead of freeing Krycek, his own associate, the CSM leaves Krycek trapped in the silo ("Piper Maru"/"Apocrypha").

"PATIENT X"

Whether it's the possession or the betrayal that changes Krycek is impossible to say. But from then on, Krycek becomes an independent agent. He works with the Syndicate as an ally not a servant – often enough, an unreliable ally, who is just as likely to betray vital information to Mulder, Scully or Skinner, as to try to kill the X-files agents on the Syndicate's orders.

The two-part story "Tunguska" and "Terma" shows just how far Krycek has gone from the callow, ambitious young agent of "Sleepless." Two years later, Krycek is at the top of his game. He knows exactly how to get Mulder to trust him – not completely, Krycek knows that's impossible – but just enough to do what Krycek needs him to do. He joins a terrorist militia, then secretly betrays their plans to Mulder and allows himself to be arrested. And he allows Mulder to have just enough information about a mysterious diplomatic pouch whose contents, a black meteor fragment, he needs to make disappear. He lures Mulder to Siberia to make him disappear, by telling Mulder the rock was found near the Tunguska impact site – a name he knows Mulder will recognize, but which he himself pretends not to know.

These episodes show how much Krycek will risk when something important is on the line. While the

Cigarette-Smoking Man rarely puts his own person in danger or hardship, Krycek has more guts. He's willing to put himself in Mulder's hands if its necessary to accomplish his purposes, even though he knows that Mulder needs very little excuse to kill him for the murder of his father. He can be certain that at the very least he'll endure some very uncomfortable days as Mulder's prisoner (how uncomfortable he may not have realized until Skinner handcuffs him to an outdoor balcony, and Mulder threatens to leave him handcuffed in a car at the airport).

None of this deters Krycek from his plans, which go off just as he intends – almost. The one thing Krycek doesn't count on is the result of his lie to the local Siberian peasants, that he's a gulag escapee. Believing the lie, they save him from the gulag experiments in the only way they know – by cutting off his left arm, without anesthesia. Yet even this doesn't seem to throw Krycek off his stride. Through all that happens he continues to run the game, engineering the murder of the doctor who might identify the black oil, and the final destruction of the space rock.

As a human being, Krycek is the sort of man you would never want to have as your enemy – nor indeed, to have in

(Continued overleaf)

THE KRYCEK FILES

A FEW OF THE UNRESOLVED AND DEBATABLE QUESTIONS
SURROUNDING KRYCEK:

WHY DID THE BLACK OIL ENTITY SEEK OUT KRYCEK AS A HOST? ("PIPER MARU")

THE ENTITY POSSESSED JOAN GAUTHIER IN SAN
FRANCISCO, THEN USED HER TO TRAVEL ALL THE WAY TO
HONG KONG, WHERE IT CORNERED KRYCEK IN AN AIRPORT
MEN'S ROOM TO TRANSFER ITSELF TO HIM. COULDN'T IT
FIND SOMEONE IN THE US TO GET IT TO THE CIGARETTE-
SMOKING MAN AND ITS SHIP?

HOW DID KRYCEK ESCAPE FROM THE MISSILE SILO? ("TUNGUSKA", 'TERMA')

KRYCEK TELLS MULDER THAT THE TERRORIST MILITIA
FOUND HIM AND FREED HIM WHEN THEY WERE SCAVENG-
ING FOR WEAPONS TECHNOLOGY. BUT THE MILITIA
LEADER TELLS MULDER THAT KRYCEK CAME TO HIM AND
HIS GROUP AND ENLISTED THEM IN HIS PLANS.

DID KRYCEK KILL BILL MULDER? ("ANASAZI")

HE'S THE ONLY ONE WE SEE IN THE BATHROOM WITH
MULDER'S FATHER JUST BEFORE THE FATAL SHOT. BUT
KRYCEK HAS ALWAYS DENIED THAT HE KILLED MULDER'S
FATHER AND EVEN SPEAKS TO MULDER AND SCULLY OF "THE
MAN WHO KILLED YOUR FATHER, AND YOUR SISTER" AS THE
CIGARETTE-SMOKING MAN. AND IF HE WAS THE KILLER,
WHY DID HE WAIT UNTIL MULDER ARRIVED BEFORE PULLING
THE TRIGGER? WHY NOT DO THE JOB AND ESCAPE BEFORE
MULDER ARRIVES?

HOW DID KRYCEK GET AN ALIEN VACCINE, TWO DIFFERENT TIMES? ("THE RED AND THE BLACK," "DEADALIVE")

KRYCEK MAKES A DEAL WITH THE WELL-MANICURED MAN,
FOR HIS OWN FREEDOM IN EXCHANGE FOR THE BLACK OIL
VACCINE. THE WELL-MANICURED MAN TELLS THE SYNDICATE
THAT KRYCEK GOT THE VACCINE FROM THE RUSSIANS, WHO
DEVELOPED IT. HOW DID KRYCEK GET SUCH HIGH-UP
CONNECTIONS IN RUSSIA, TO HAVE ACCESS TO THE VAC-
CINE? MORE PUZZLING STILL, WHY DOES KRYCEK HAVE THE
REPLICANT VACCINE FOR MULDER? WE NEVER LEARN WHO
MADE THIS VACCINE NOR HOW KRYCEK GOT IT.

WHY DOES KRYCEK DECIDE TO KILL MULDER? ("DEADALIVE")

BY HIS OWN ACCOUNT, KRYCEK HAS PROTECTED MULDER FOR
YEARS, FEEDING HIM INFORMATION, ALWAYS HOPING
MULDER WOULD WIN THE ALIEN WAR. THEN SUDDENLY,
AFTER HELPING SCULLY ESCAPE THE REPLICANTS, KRYCEK
AMBUSHES MULDER WITH THE DECLARED INTENTION OF
KILLING HIM. HIS EXPLANATION, THAT IT'S TOO LATE TO
STOP "THEM" AND THAT MULDER KNOWS TOO MUCH, IS NO
DIFFERENT THAN THE CIRCUMSTANCES OF MANY PAST
SITUATIONS, INCLUDING SOME WHEN KRYCEK HELPS THE
AGENTS. IT'S CERTAINLY NOT ENOUGH TO ACCOUNT FOR
KRYCEK DECIDING HE HAS TO KILL THE ONE MAN HE FEELS
SOME SORT OF KINSHIP WITH.

"S.R. 819"

"THE END"

your life at all. As a character in a complex, conspiracy-driven TV series, he's indispensable. Conspiracy stories derive much of their suspense from complex plotting that keeps the audience guessing about what the characters know, who they are allied with and what they intend. In this dramatic setting, Krycek is the ultimate adversary, a bad guy whose loyalties and motivations are always in question. Sometimes he is clearly an agent of the Syndicate, other times he seems to be working for no one but himself, and at still other times, he seems actually to be trying to help the good guys.

And how does he know what he knows, or get the items that he gets, such as the alien vaccine, or the nanotechnology infesting Skinner's blood? Many of Krycek's actions remain mysterious, creating the kind of plot puzzles that fans can debate endlessly on web sites and message boards [see *The Krycek Files* boxout] These mysteries, as well as his close association with the alien colonization storyline, create a kind of anticipation surrounding the character. Whenever Krycek appears, we expect surprises.

Krycek also makes an important contribution to the character mythology of the *X-Files*, through his relationships with the Syndicate and with Mulder. Krycek, more than any other character, shows us that the Syndicate is not as omnipotent as it first appears. He double-crosses them, and sometimes even holds power over them; as they in turn double cross him and argue among themselves over what he might be offering. Krycek shows us that the Syndicate's members are just mortal men, after all.

More important, Krycek builds up Mulder's personal mythology. In the world of the *X-Files*, it's a given that Mulder is the one man who can expose the conspiracy and save the world from the alien colonization, just by his determination to find the truth. Krycek consistently treats Mulder as the most important person involved in this war. True to Krycek's ambivalent nature, he does this sometimes by trying to stop Mulder, and sometimes by trying to help him. He underlines this in "The Red and the Black," when he ambushes

Mulder in his apartment. Mulder is in the height of his unbeliever phase, and Krycek's intent is to snap him out of it, and make him join the fight again.

"There is a war raging, and unless you pull your head out of the sand, you and I and about five billion other people are going to go the way of the dinosaur," he says, implying both by his words and by his urgency, that Mulder is essential to victory.

Krycek's relationship with Mulder is one of the most intimate in the whole series. Mulder consistently shows more violence to Krycek, in his language and his words, than to almost anyone else. Aside from the liar and traitor aspects of Krycek's career, Mulder is certain that Krycek murdered his father. And yet when Krycek talks, Mulder can't

help listening, and even, in spite of himself, believing Krycek and going where he leads.

For his part, Krycek usually talks to Mulder as if Mulder is the only person who can handle the game as well as Krycek himself. The success of his scheme in "Tunguska" shows how well he understands Mulder. Their final encounter in "Existence" shows how much Mulder means to him. Krycek would shoot anyone else from ambush. When he decides he has to kill Mulder, he needs to meet him face to face, so he can explain.

"I could have killed you so many times, Mulder, you gotta know that. I'm the one that kept you alive, praying you'd win somehow... You think I'm bad, I'm a killer. We wanted the same

thing," says Krycek, and then he calls Mulder "brother."

"I wanted to stop them. All you wanted was to save your own ass," Mulder retorts, but then he affirms their intimacy by using Krycek's first name. "If you want to kill me, Alex, then kill me. Just don't insult me trying to make me understand."

Krycek, who has killed many people without a second's hesitation, aims his pistol at Mulder, puts his finger on the trigger – and hesitates. He hesitates so long that Skinner has time to get there and stop him. And even though Krycek begs Skinner to kill Mulder, he knows, and we know, that it's not going to happen. Not killing Mulder is the last choice Krycek ever makes. ●

PASSION WITH MARITA IN "PATIENT X"

THE KRYCEK EPISODES

SEASON TWO
"Sleepless"
"Duane Barry"
"Ascension"
"Anasazi"

SEASON THREE
"The Blessing Way"
"Paper Clip"
"Piper Maru"
"Apocrypha"

SEASON FOUR
"Tunguska"
"Terma"

SEASON FIVE
"Patient X"
"The Red and the Black"
"The End"

SEASON SIX
"S.R. 819"
"Two Fathers"
"One Son"
"Biogenesis"

SEASON SEVEN
"The Sixth Extinction II: Amor Fati"
"Requiem"

SEASON EIGHT
"DeadAlive"
"Essence"
"Existence"

"REQUIEM"

Actor John Neville
oozes refined menace
as the Well-Manicured Man

Dapper and Deadly

by Annabelle Villanueva

A young man approached John Neville last year at Canada's Stratford Festival, a world-renowned Shakespearean theater series.

"You're an actor, aren't you?" the man asked.

Neville responded in the affirmative—as a veteran stage and film actor who served as the Stratford's artistic director from 1986 to 1989, being recognized at a playhouse wasn't unusual.

"I said 'yes,' thinking he's going to compliment me on my playing of Shylock, which I had done," Neville remembers. "And he says, 'Yes! *X-Files.*'"

The London-born thespian should have known better. Although a stage turn in *The Merchant of Venice* is every stage-trained actor's dream, it has nothing on the splash Neville's made with just a few nattily trimmed fingernails. Ever since his debut as the Well-Manicured Man in Season Three's "The Blessing Way," he's slinked to the top of *The X-Files*' nefarious Syndicate, the mysterious cabal that meets in a plush New York City club and plots a far-reaching conspiracy.

"It's a very interesting character," Neville says. "There's some kind of mystery about him, and you're not quite sure [what his motivations are]. People on the street ask me, 'Is he a goodie or a baddie?' and I say, 'I don't know yet.'"

Though that ambiguity might leave

SCREEN PRESENCE: Neville in *The X-Files* [right] and *Munchausen*

performances are slightly more refined: He played Henry Higgins in an American tour of *My Fair Lady* and appeared on Broadway in *Ghosts*. Now a resident of Toronto, he landed his *X-Files* gig after being approached by one of the show's casting directors. Though he didn't know much about the *The X-Files* when he joined the large cast of supporting characters, Neville has since learned to appreciate the show for the unique creation it is.

"The first thing one has to say is that it's good writing. I think this is universally recognized now, not just by me," he says. "Chris Carter really knows what he's doing...I think *The X-Files* started [the current interest in aliens and conspiracies.] It's to his credit that he thought of this, invented it and helped to make it a success along with his team of people."

Neville also is quick to shower praise on the series' stars, David Duchovny and Gillian Anderson. "I have to say I admire them both as actors, because what they've done over four years is carry this series and it's a lot of very hard work indeed. I think credit is due to them for maintaining that high standard of devotion and integrity in their work."

Part of the Well-Manicured Man's mystery lies in the infrequency of his appearances—unlike the Cigarette-Smoking Man, Neville's character's only been seen in a small handful of episodes over the past two years. However, he's slated to turn up in some Season Five episodes and *The X-Files* feature film. Although excited about the big-screen project, Neville recognizes that his enthusiasm pales in comparison to the frenzied anticipation X-Philes are experiencing. "I had lunch with my bank manager the other day, who's an absolute fanatic," he says. "I mean, he cannot wait for for the movie." Neville adds that he's been taken aback by the fan response.

"I went to England last summer to do a play with Peter Ustinov, who's an old friend, and I discovered to my amazement that the series is a cult [hit] in England," Neville explains. "I mean, I knew it was a cult in California, for instance, and Canada, but finding it was a cult [hit] in England...I was somewhat surprised."

Ultimately, Neville is pleased to be a part of *The X-Files'* success not just for the worldwide fame but also for the recognition it brings him in his own family. "I said to Chris Carter that after all the things I've done in my career, all the plays of Shakespeare, *The Adventures of Baron Munchausen* and a lot of movies, finally I've made it with my grandchildren." ●

Neville scratching his head, the Well-Manicured Man himself seems to relish shades of gray. In "The Blessing Way," he approaches Scully at William Mulder's funeral, telling her he's from a "consortium representing global interests...that would be extremely threatened" if a digital tape containing information about the government's knowledge of alien life were leaked. Dressed in a dapper dark suit and striped shirt, the distinguished-looking gentleman is a picture of urbanity, but his crisp British accent sounds oddly ominous. Still, he warns Scully about the death sentence hanging over her head—she's scheduled to be killed either at her home or at an impromptu meeting with someone she knows—and tells her some members of the consortium are acting impulsively. When asked the nature of his business, he gives a characteristically enigmatic reply: "We predict the future. And the best way to predict the future is to invent it."

Perhaps the Well-Manicured Man's most mysterious quality is the tight-lipped grip he holds over *The X-Files'* other sinister conspirator, the Cigarette-Smoking Man. The duo spend most of their joint scenes glaring at one another, and in Season Three's "Paper Clip," the Cigarette-Smoking Man gets berated by his superior for accidentally killing Scully's sister. But after the Well-Manicured Man set up a meeting with Mulder and started to flirt with being a not-so-"baddie" in the third season's "Apocrypha," he disappeared until Season Four's epic two-parter "Tunguska"/"Terma," when he returned to bump heads with the Cigarette-Smoking Man once again.

Though his character's goals aren't always clear, Neville has some ideas about his alter-ego's opinions of Agents Mulder and Scully. "He's not exactly on their side, but I think he admires them," he says. "He admires the work they do."

The Well-Manicured Man's shifty variegations probably come easily to the 72-year-old Neville, whose lengthy acting career has included playing characters ranging from Hamlet in the 1950s to Isaac Newton in a 1987 episode of *Star Trek: The Next Generation*. In addition to heading the Stratford Festival, he's also served as the artistic director of theaters in Alberta, London and Nottingham, England. His stage distinctions, including directing *Twelfth Night* and *Henry V* for London's storied Old Vic Theatre, earned him the Order of the British Empire in 1965, but screen stardom didn't come until more than 20 years later, when Terry Gilliam cast Neville in the lead role of his magnificent-

ly over-budgeted curiosity, *The Adventures of Baron Munchausen*.

Since *Munchausen*, Neville has worked steadily and eclectically in film and television, with small roles in *The Fifth Element*, *Dangerous Minds* and *Little Women*, as well as a spot on the 1990 NBC series *Grand*. In the recent comedy *High School High*, he had one of his biggest stretches of all—playing Jon Lovitz's father. His stage

THE X FILES™

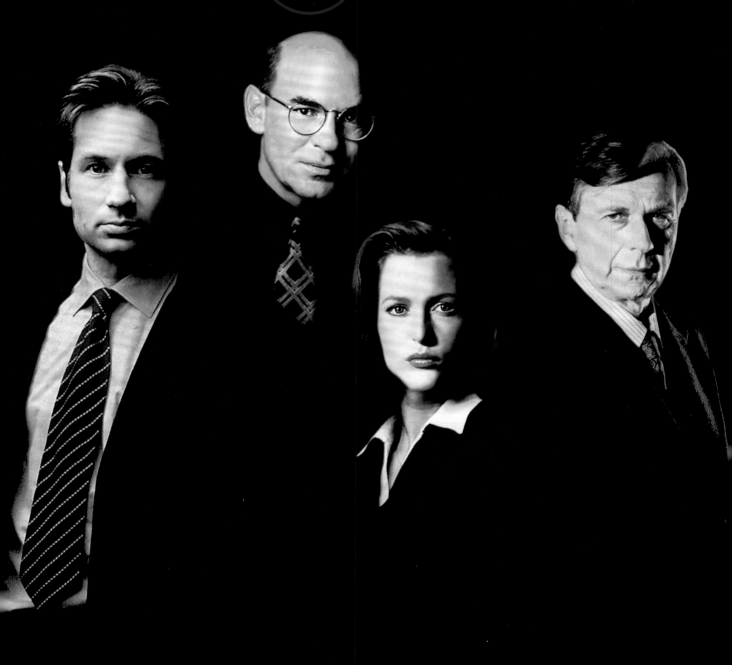

Out of the SHADOWS

DON S. WILLIAMS - THE CONSPIRACY'S

ELUSIVE "ELDER" - FINALLY STEPS

INTO THE SPOTLIGHT IN SEASON FIVE

Of all the Syndicate's shadowy movers and shakers

he just might be the most shadowy of them all. We know he is a man of great stature who belongs to a Consortium of nameless cohorts. We know he plots and plans with these sinister men in darkly lit rooms where the air is heavy with the smell of cigarette smoke. He wears expensive suits and speaks in husky tones. He is ambiguous and formidable, pondering undiscovered secrets and the havoc they will wreak when revealed.

But who the heck is he?

The answer: venerable Canadian actor Don S. Williams. Determining what sort of business the enigmatic character, known only as the First Elder, conducts is another matter. Williams says not even his friends or family are able to decipher the character's true nature or whether he is motivated by altruism or acrimony.

"The first couple of times I appeared, people who knew me always asked me, 'Are you a good guy or a bad guy?' And I quite honestly said, 'I don't know.' Then they would start their speculations as to who I really was and what I was up to, which usually was pretty dark," Williams explains.

And what does the actor think about his television alter-ego? Well, he's a tad more optimistic about the Elder's secret agenda. "I think that I have some objectives and that I have a mission, and people who are working toward a mission aren't necessarily bad guys. They're usually good

BY GINA MCINTYRE

ILLUSTRATION BY BRIAN TROST

THE ⓧ FILES

guys, so maybe I'm a good guy," he reasons.

One can always hope.

Williams, though, is unquestionably a good guy. He reflects on his prolific 42-year career in the entertainment industry with astonishing humility. Having produced and directed 278 television shows and feature films, acted on stage and screen, authored screenplays and taught workshops, the 60-year-old actor now has his most famous role on his hands.

Since making his series debut in Season Three's premiere episode, "The Blessing Way," the First Elder has firmly entrenched himself in *X-Files* mythology. Whether locking horns with Cigarette-Smoking Man ("Redux II") or explaining to a horrified Agent Scully that bizarre experiments were conducted on the homeless and insane ("731"), the character is never uncomfortable with the authority he wields. And whenever he appears—"Paper Clip," "Apocrypha," "Herrenvolk" and "Zero Sum"— he usually knows more than anyone else.

No matter how serious the situation, the Elder seldom gets angry, preferring to voice his views in a deliberate, cool fashion. But Williams is much more enthusiastic than the stone-faced man he portrays, especially when discussing the notoriety the character has brought him. Some of the nicest benefits of celebrity, he explains, are the least expected.

"About a year ago, I went into my favorite deli to buy some salami. While the server was slicing it, she said,

ILLEGAL ALIENS: THE FIRST ELDER
BUTTED HEADS WITH THE CIGARETTE-
SMOKING MAN IN THE CONSPIRACY-
LADEN "REDUX II" [ABOVE]

'There's something familiar about your voice.' And I said, 'Oh, really?' 'It's an unusual voice. It's a nice voice, but it's unusual,' she said. Then she suddenly looked up from the salami and said, 'You're not on *The X-Files*, by any chance?' It was the voice she recognized. I guess that's because at that time, most of my appearances were in very contrasted, heavy, dark lighting. But that was kind of fun. I suspect she threw an extra slice of salami on the pile," Williams speculates.

And bigger and better sandwiches are just the beginning. Williams says he's even being asked for his John Hancock these days. "I had to go into an office connected with volunteer work that I do, and the receptionist, who turned out to be a big-time X-er, asked me rather shyly for my autograph. It's been a long, long time since I was asked for an autograph. It was quite pleasant," Williams says.

More impromptu autograph sessions might indeed be in store for the actor, thanks to his more prominent scenes during *The X-Files* fifth season. Yes, the mystery man seems to have traded his traditional dark havens for sunnier climes, conducting meetings with Cigarette-Smoking Man at outdoor stadiums rather than stuffy offices ("Redux II"). The change of scenery pleases Williams.

"It indicated to me that somebody felt their original choice to put me in that role was a good investment, and

they were now interested in developing the role and the position of the character in the scheme of things," Williams explains. "I guess I didn't screw up."

That's putting it mildly. By the conclusion of the show's fifth season, Williams will have a total of nine episodes of *The X-Files* and a big screen credit in the upcoming feature film to add to his résumé. Not that his list of credits wasn't already quite lengthy: There have been starring roles in countless Canadian television shows, a turn in the 1992 NBC-TV movie *Fatal Memories*, guest-starring stints on *The Commish* and a host of performances on the Canadian stage (among them playing Bottom in *A Midsummer Night's Dream*, directing productions of *Our Town*, *Heaven Can Wait* and *The Merchant of Venice* and founding his own Moodyville Theatre Company). Yet Williams' work on *The X-Files* remains separate and distinct, the actor says, primarily because unlike his other professional gigs, he has no clue what could happen next.

"As an actor, there's not much chance of giving anything away because I don't know anything to give away. That's what I like about the show—never quite being sure what's going on or who's doing what to whom. Everything is very underplayed, understated, and I like that," he says.

And just how does an actor approach a character when he doesn't really know who that character could turn out to be? The seasoned thespian has that covered, too. "Basically, I follow the advice of Spencer Tracy and do whatever the director tells me.

I have to do that because I'm not totally sure what's really going on," he explains.

After two years as the First Elder, Williams is accustomed to the uncertainty that accompanies his role on *The X-Files*, a show that piqued his curiosity even before the pilot aired. You see, the actor's North Vancouver home is, rather conveniently, just down the street from North Shore Studios where *The X-Files* is filmed, making Williams privy to industry buzz about the then-brand-spanking-new project.

"[When] I first heard about [*The X-Files*], I thought, 'Well, it's another cop show.' Once it came out, [I] realized it wasn't. I was, frankly, curious to see whether it would [be successful] because it did have a different quality to it. It was interesting to watch and see if it would work," he says.

Obviously, things ultimately worked out pretty well for the show. In the course of Williams' *X-Files* tenure, a lot of things have changed. *The X-Files* has grown from a well-kept secret to a multi-million dollar phenomenon, capturing the imaginations of countless fans and earning its rightful place in pop culture iconography. And Williams has happily ridden its wave of success, which most recently took him to Los Angeles for one week to film a hush-hush part in the top-secret big-screen project.

The experience, he says, was not unlike a regular set visit. "It just had a feeling of being bigger. It was like a comparison between a live performance at a studio theater and a live performance at an opera hall," Williams says. "I was a little overwhelmed at the treatment I got. My wife and I flew down first class. The only thing that I was upset about [was] when the limousine pulled up to the door here, it was too early in the morning. None of the neighbors were up to see it!"

So would Williams perhaps be willing to drop a few hints about what X-Philes will see when the film hits theaters this summer? It's not exactly pertinent to the movie's storyline, but he did let slip the details of one behind-the-scenes incident. "When I was in my dressing trailer, the wardrobe attendant brought my clothes. She introduced herself, and said, 'You're Canadian, eh?' And I said, 'Yeah.' And she said, 'Do something for me. Say *about*.' So I said it. And she looked at me kind of strangely and said, 'Okay, good point.' She was a little disappointed that I said it the way she said it. You [Americans] always claim that we say 'ooot' and 'abooot.' Well, we don't," he quips.

If Williams sounds proud of his Canadian heritage, he is. Quick to describe his love for the crisp, natural beauty of the city of North Vancouver, which is situated on the shore of

an inlet on the Pacific Ocean, the part-time environmentalist lovingly paints an image of a shoreline which immediately rises into mountains overrun with cedar trees, an outdoor refuge where peace dwells just outside the day-to-day machinations of the city below.

A profound respect for the Canadian wilderness is something Williams has cultivated for years. In the late '60s, long before thinking green was

THE TWO FACES OF DON: DON S. WILLIAMS ISN'T ALWAYS SO SINISTER

trendy, Williams produced and directed an award-winning television documentary on the plight of the Canada goose, titled "Nis'ku." To bring attention to the endangered species, Williams spent an entire year traipsing though parts of Canada and the United States to complete the film, which was named best Canadian television film of 1970.

"[It was] very meaningful in that it was a departure from what I usually did," Williams explains. "It was basically a wildlife documentary, which was a long ways away from the dramatic work I had been doing."

It more closely resembled Williams' political endeavors, which have become something akin to a second career for him, an ideal occupation for a patriot. He first began working with Canada's Liberal Party as an

idealistic teenager and, for more than four decades, has devoted countless hours and incalculable energy to his volunteer efforts. The man who plays a mafioso-style member of *The X-Files'* seemingly corrupt Syndicate is a busy, well-connected politico in his spare time? Williams downplays the ironic coincidence as merely that—a coincidence.

"I got involved [in politics] because somebody told me that if you're not willing to change things, you can't complain about the way they are. And that's why I'm still involved," he says. "I find that change that I work for is within the party as well as within the government system. Being liberals, we don't always agree on everything, so we have to work some things out internally, too. I

sometimes find myself at odds with the powers that be, but so what?"

Williams latest political challenge, serving as the chair of the North Shore Arts Commission, is keeping him quite busy when not on *The X-Files* time clock or entertaining his two grandchildren. "What I'm working towards is turning North Vancouver into a tourist destination based on the arts. We have several world-renowned painters and sculptors living here so we have a good base to start with," he explains.

Rumor has it they have one or two hit TV shows, too. ●

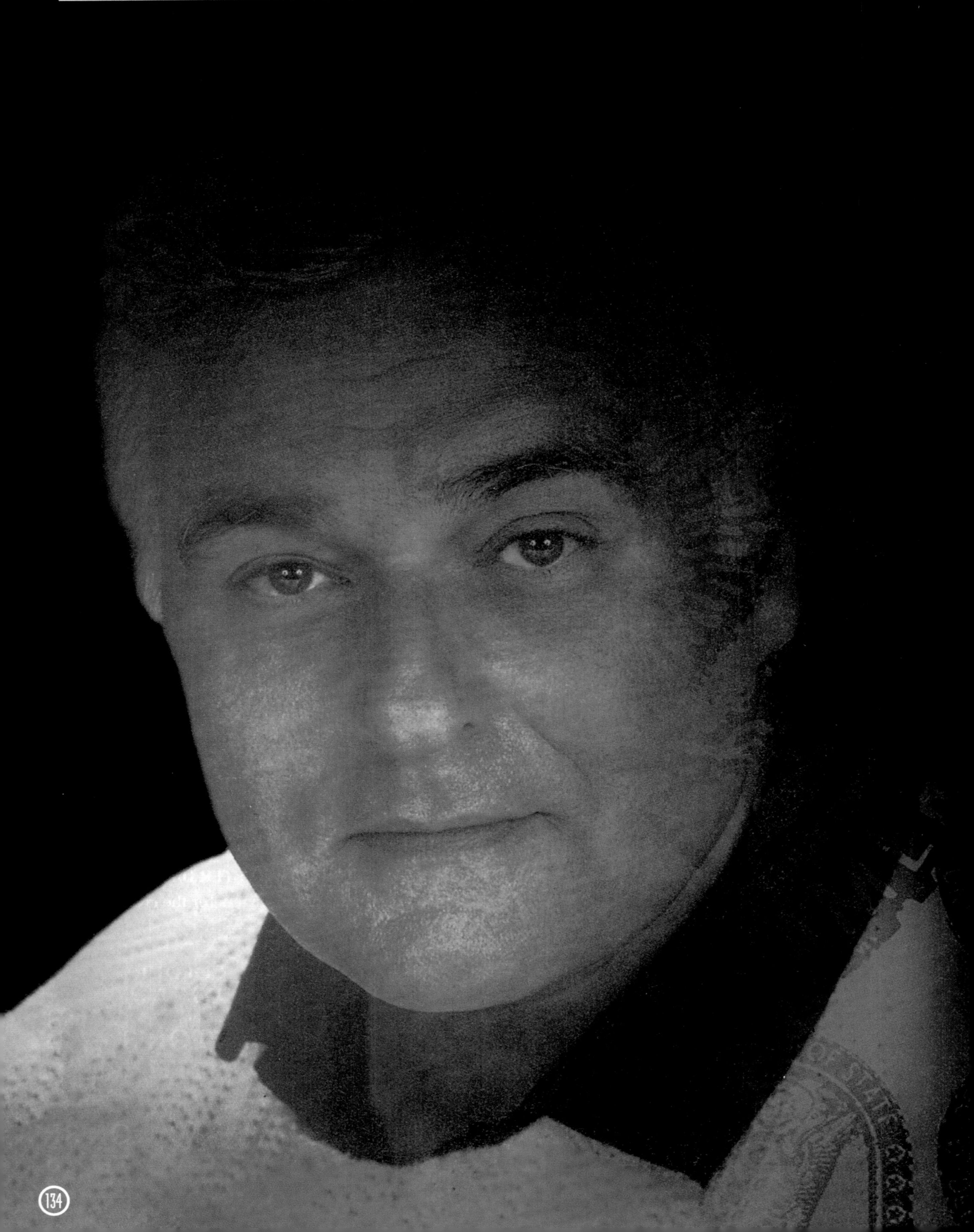

Knockin' on Blevins Door

Dave Hughes talks with Charles Cioffi, aka Division Chief Blevins – the man responsible for the partnership of Mulder and Scully

SPOILER ALERT 5 SEASON

"**A**in't that fun?" The deep New York Italian accent thunders down the transatlantic wires from Santa Monica, California. The 62-year-old actor Charles Cioffi (pronounced Choffee) is chuckling about the apparent demise of his character, Division Chief Scott Blevins, in "Redux II" the extraordinary one hundredth episode of *The X-Files*.

Those who have followed the show since the first episode will remember Blevins. He is the FBI Division Chief who, at the very beginning of the pilot show, assigns Special Agent Scully to work with Mulder on the unsolved FBI cases known unofficially as the X-Files. Initially, Blevins keeps a close eye on the new partnership's activities, with Scully reporting her observations about Mulder's methods back to her superior. But slowly, the silent, smoking presence in Blevins' office in those early episodes begins to take over as the series' principal malignant force. Blevins recedes into the background...

Until, nearly four years later, he reappears in the final episode of season four, "Gethsemane". Here, he listens patiently to a more mature Agent Scully as she reports on the illegitimacy of Mulder's investigations – and reports his apparent suicide. By the end of the three-part story arc, Blevins has been lied to, threatened, implicated in a government-wide conspiracy, accused of accepting illegal payments from a biological research group – and shot in cold blood by his right hand man. No wonder Charles Cioffi is chuckling.

"Yes, they never really included him that much in the storyline since the beginning of

the show," he says. "When we did the pilot and the first two episodes, he was more involved – recruiting [Scully], questioning her and things like that. Then all of a sudden, for four years, he just dropped out of the picture, and then came back in at the end to wrap up this particular storyline." Does he know the reason for Blevins' return? "They just seemed to want to say, 'Okay, this was the first four years, and now we want to be off doing something else.'"

Unfortunately, the summary execution of Cioffi's character came at precisely the point when he had begun to get really interesting. "I know," Cioffi agrees. "They get him away from the sitting behind a desk and feeding lines to Gillian... They had set up Blevins as being a villain, but if you look at the last episode, you'll see that he may not necessarily have been a villain – he may have been a pawn." In other words, the look of horror on Blevins' face when Mulder effectively accuses him of treason might be the shock of being wrongfully accused, rather than of being found out. Cioffi embraces this theory wholeheartedly (see boxout).

Of course, everyone has their opinions about the climactic events of the "Gethsemane"/"Redux"/"Redux II" three-parter, and Cioffi is no exception. "They dangled too many carrots in front of the audience," he states. "This is not like a French Opera, where you wrap everything up with a pink ribbon at the end. No, they have to carry on and carry out some of those storylines. I mean, that was such an emotional thing, that for four years we have been confronted, almost every episode, with this [subplot] about Mulder's sister. And then to actually [have him] confront his sister and have the Cigarette-Smoking Man as her foster father, and she doesn't want to see her real mother?"

> "THEY HAD SET UP BLEVINS AS BEING A VILLAIN, BUT IF YOU LOOK AT "REDUX II", YOU'LL SEE THAT HE MAY HAVE BEEN A PAWN."

Above: Mulder plans the ultimate deception; Left: Trouble for Mulder (both photos from "Redux")

> "I DON'T EVEN REMEMBER GOING IN AND MEETING CHRIS CARTER OR ANY OF THOSE PEOPLE; THEY JUST CALLED UP AND SAID, 'HERE'S THE JOB.'"

He whistles appreciatively. "I mean, that's an awful lot of stuff, you know?

"If you look at 'Redux', there was an awful lot of re-introducing people and sitting behind desks and walking down corridors... The dialogue I remember as being especially difficult because it was so stilted: everything was exposition. So you're continually telling a story, but you don't show anybody anything – it's like an hour-long narration. And then finally, in the last episode, everything happens. It really moves: two people get shot, and she almost dies, and he comes back, and Mulder meets his sister and – Holy Jesus! How can they keep this up? Well, they can't keep this up, but they're going to end it and try to move on in another direction."

Having worked on the first three *X-Files* episodes, and three of the most recent ones, Cioffi is perhaps in a unique position to comment on the changes behind the scenes from season one to season five. How were things different the second time around? "I did six shows altogether: three, and then three," he says, "and the last three shows I did, everybody was so relaxed. The first three episodes, everybody was

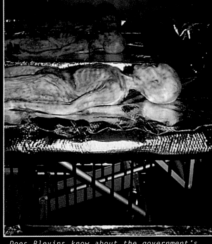

Does Blevins know about the government's secrets?

> "PACINO HAD EVERY ACTOR IN AMERICA TO CHOOSE FROM AND HE ASKED ME... I MEAN, HOW COULD YOU SAY NO TO SOMETHING LIKE THAT?"

very touchy, and they were flying by the seat of their pants. First of all, they were shooting an American show in Vancouver, and things were being operated by remote control from Los Angeles; and Chris [Carter was in charge of this new show], and I don't know what kind of a track record he had. I think the people were a little nervous and edgy.

"And now, four years later, you go back, and everybody is so sweet – they can't do enough for you, you know? The largesse has really gotten to be considerable. And consequently, it was a much easier set to work on." Considering that television success often brings with it inflated egos and exaggerated senses of self-importance, it's refreshing to hear that *The X-Files* has become more relaxed over the years. So what else does Cioffi remember about the pilot show? Did he have an audition? "They just called up and they said, 'There's this thing, it's called *X-Files*.' I don't even remember going in and meeting Chris Carter or any of those people:

Scully investigates the cause of her cancer

This page: Is this the result of the Rousch corporation's secret work?

SCOTT FREE?

So, was Blevins the mole? Or was he, like Mulder and Scully, merely part of a grander game in which he was not a major player? Cioffi has his own theories about whether Blevins was to blame; but are they the rational explanations of an innocent man, or the desperate blatherings of the guilty?

"In 'Redux II', you see [that] the big heavy man [the First Elder, a high-up member of the Syndicate] who was giving orders to the Cigarette-Smoking Man [First Elder] wants to get rid of all these people for his own nefarious reasons. And then we see the character that Ken Camroux played [the First Agent] sitting at my desk, talking on my telephone. He reaches into the desk and shoots me. And you realise that, no, it's not Blevins, it's the First Agent who has been the bad guy all along," he theorises, referring to the mysterious higher-up who appeared in Blevins' office in the pilot episode, and returned almost two full seasons later in "Anasazi".

And you see the panic on Blevins' face, and you realise that maybe Blevins was not the guy who was in charge of this whole thing, and he was not the leak on the inside. Skinner does say that he was on the take from the Roush corporation," he concedes, "but then they could have doctored the books. Or maybe he was kept a hostage for some reason; maybe they had some J Edgar Hoover-type, hanky panky stuff on him in order to keep him quiet."

they just called up and said, 'Here's the job.' I think they just made the offer because of the kind of characters I generally play in motion pictures, which are usually dark and sombre, and not too many lines, but more of a presence. And that's kind of what they wanted Scott Blevins to be."

In more than 30 years since his career began,

> "WE SEE (BLEVINS) GET SHOT AND FALL ON THE GROUND, BUT WE DON'T NECESSARILY KNOW THAT HE IS DEAD..."

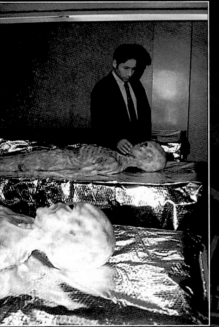

Cioffi has racked up an impressive résumé of stage and television appearances, and co-starred in such feature films as *Klute*, *Shaft*, *Missing*, and the recent *Shadow Conspiracy*. And in the summer of 1992, Cioffi's long-time friend Al Pacino invited him to co-star in the two-man play *Chinese Coffee* at Broadway's Circle in the Square theatre. "He had every actor in America to choose from and he asked me to do it with him," Cioffi says proudly. "I mean, how could you say no to something like that?"

Cioffi has been taking it easy since filming "Redux II" last autumn. "Right now I'm doing a guest spot on an Aaron Spelling pilot called *Odd Jobs*. Other than that, I'm just enjoying being here looking at the Pacific, and my wife of 38 years and I have a great time."

The same cannot be said for Cioffi's *X-Files* character. Is Blevins really gone for good? "You know, they never actually say [he's been killed]... We see him get shot and fall on the ground, but we don't necessarily know that he is dead – we don't know what has happened to his body.

"I had a great time working with these people – they're just the loveliest bunch of people, and Gillian and David are just the sweetest things – and I wouldn't be a bit surprised if Blevins came back. You know," he adds conspiratorially, "I was talking to one of the producers, Kim Manners, who also directed the episode, and I said, 'So I guess that's it for me,' and he just looked at me with a very Mona Lisa smile and said, 'You know, in *The X-Files* nothing is as it appears. Don't be surprised if you come back, just because it looks like you've died.'"

DOUBLED AGENT

He may have been one of John Doggett's most trusted agents, but maybe Doggett should have paid more attention to those telltale alien marks on the back of Agent Crane's neck.

Ian Spelling chats to actor Kirk B. R. Woller.

K irk B.R. Woller had no idea when he signed on to play Special Agent Gene Crane in "Within" and "Without" that it was to be the beginning of a recurring gig that would see him return for "Via Negativa," "Essence" and "Existence."

"I did the first two episodes," Woller recalls, "and then the story I heard was that Frank Spotnitz said, 'Let's get that Agent Crane guy back.' I guess that's what got me back in 'Via Negativa.' Then, at the end of the year they were writing the last two episodes. From what I heard, Kim Manners said, 'I'm not going to do it unless we have Kirk.' So he's my hero."

Agent Crane, of course, is probably no one's hero. On the other hand, no one's quite certain who or what he is... "I think that what makes Agent Crane interesting for me as an actor is that he was second-in-command of the task force, to Agent Doggett (Robert Patrick)," Woller says. "My first day on set as a guest star in that two-part episode was Robert Patrick's first day as a regular. I had all these ideas and I just knocked on Robert's trailer, and he welcomed me with open arms. We sat there and discussed our opinions about a lot of different things. Crane was honored to be working with Doggett. And I determined that Crane always respected Mulder as an FBI agent. Robert and I played it that Doggett was very tentative and suspicious about the possibilities of there being UFOs, and I decided that Crane's point of view was that maybe there was some possibility of that. That meant Robert and I could both approach our scenes from a Ying and Yang perspective, so Robert and I and Doggett and Crane could kind of play good cop-bad cop.

"WITHOUT"

"As it went on," Woller continues, "in the last two episodes of Season Eight, Crane suddenly switched. I made a choice as an actor that Crane was fully cognizant of what had happened to him, that he was a human replacement. I played the last two episodes as an FBI agent who agreed to involve himself with something that was of a higher calling."

Woller, who considers himself a "huge" X-Files fan, was born in Olympia, Washington, and has appeared in episodes of NYPD Blue, Dark Skies, Sliders, and ER, as well as such films as Mercury Rising, The Day Lincoln Was Shot (a telemovie with Lance Henriksen), Swordfish, A.I. Artificial Intelligence and Hometown Legend (co-starring Terry O'Quinn of Millennium, The X-Files and Harsh Realm). Woller's role in A.I. was that of a cop in the Rouge City sequences, but director Steven Spielberg was forced to cut his scenes for time purposes. However, Spielberg was impressed enough to cast Woller as one of the eight cops – the others include some guy named Tom Cruise and Millennium's Klea Scott – in his bigbudget film version of Philip K. Dick's classic sci fi epic Minority Report. In fact,

Woller spent a month shuttling back and forth between the sets of The X-Files, where he filmed "Essence" and "Existence," and those of Minority Report.

Though he's clearly an actor on the rise – and just began production on Path to War, a John Frankenheimer-directed drama starring Alec Baldwin, Tom Skerritt, Michael Gambon and Donald Sutherland – Woller would welcome a return visit to The X-Files. "I haven't heard anything yet," concludes the actor, who now calls Los Angeles home. "Chris Carter said to me when we did the last two episodes, 'Kirk, you'll definitely be back because you're kind of the antagonist now.' So I'm waiting with bated breath to be asked to come back." ●

"WITHOUT"

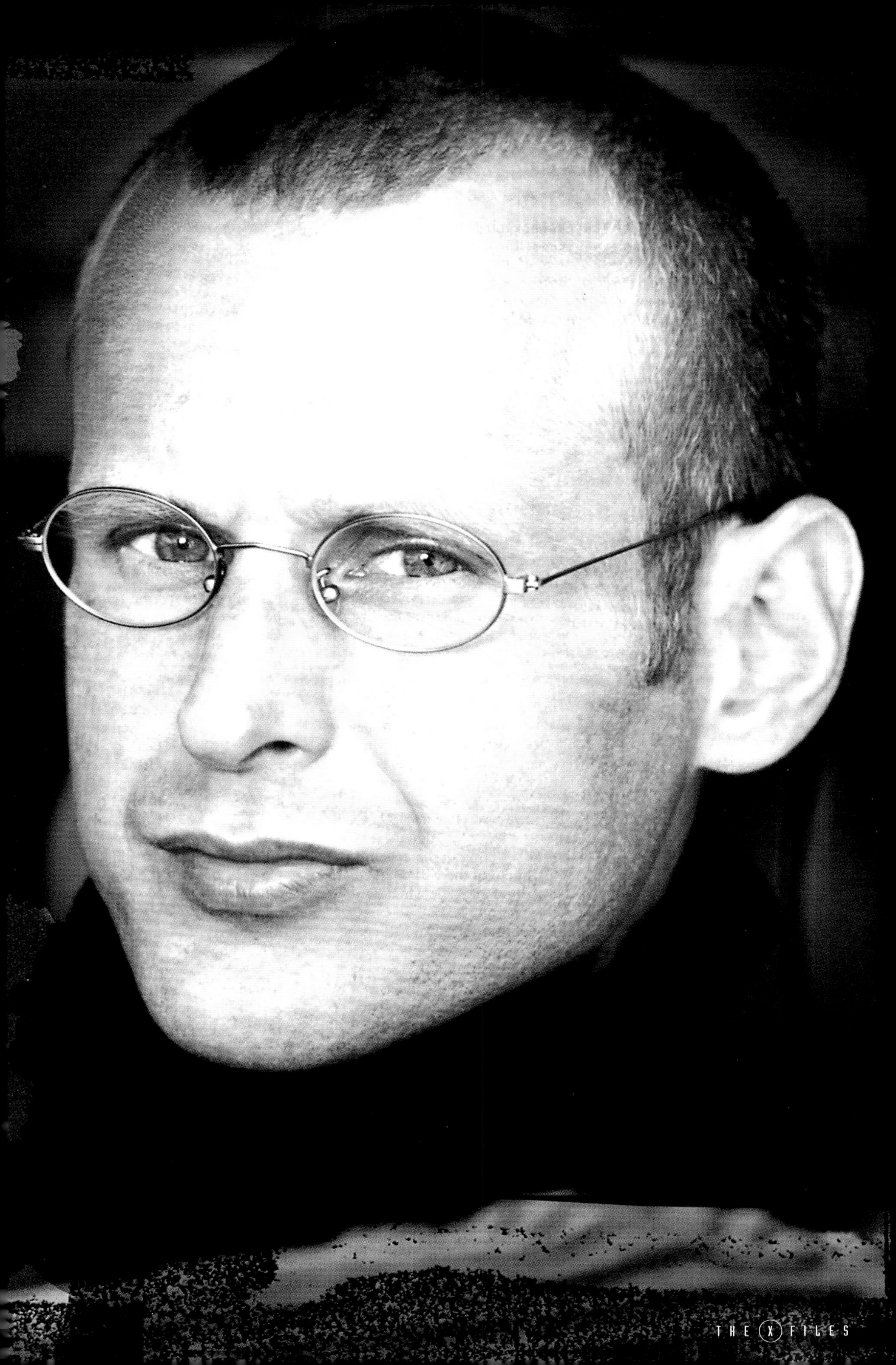

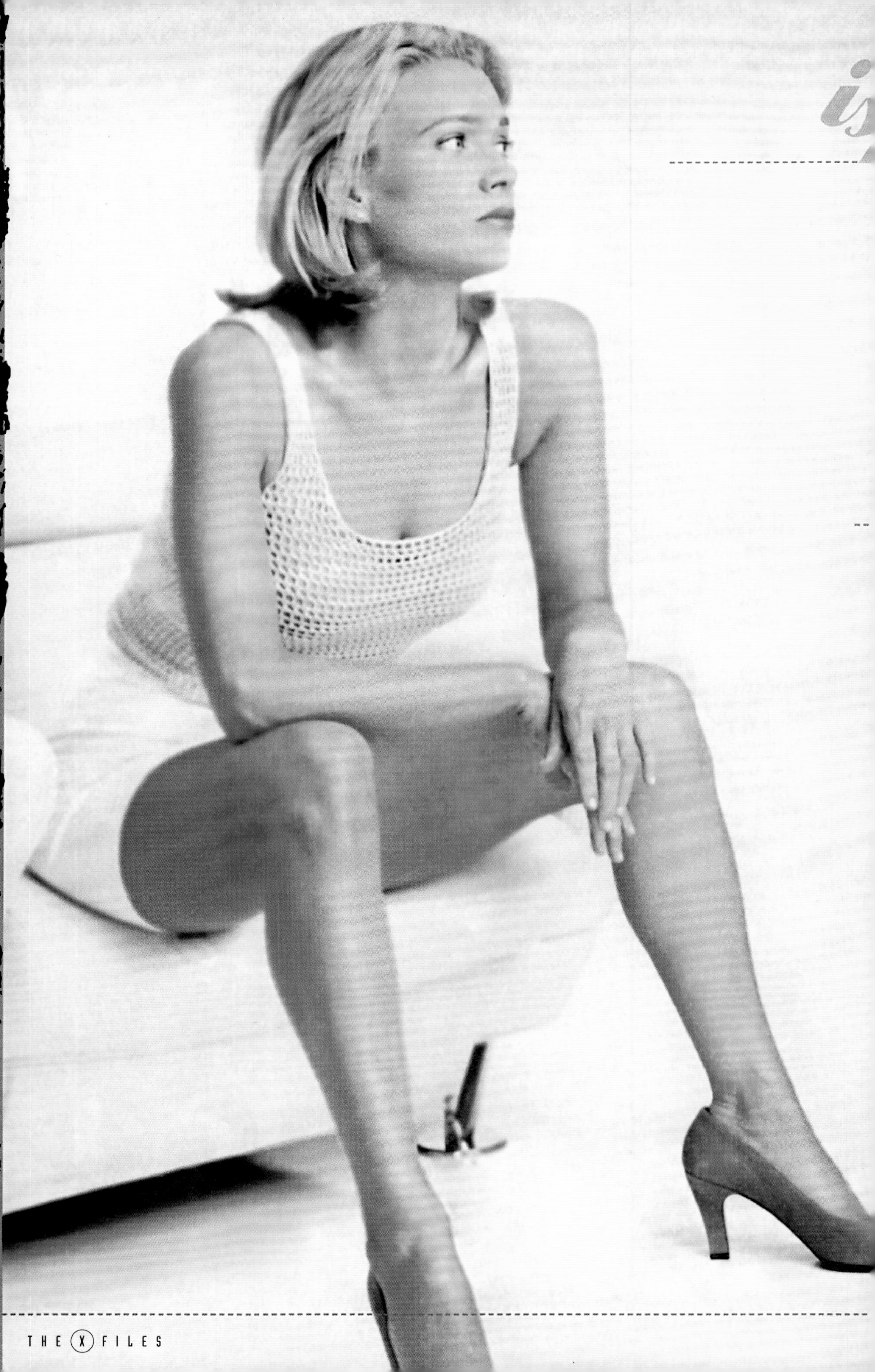

i, SPY

Laurie Holden reveals what it's like to play sexy U.N. operative Marita Covarrubias

by GINA MCINTYRE

Marita Covarrubias has had a pretty rough time on *The X-Files*. In Season Five's "Patient X"/ "The Red and The Black," the vampy U.N. operative became the subject of some sinister experiments, and when she next reappeared, in Season Six's "One Son", she was looking, shall we say, a bit worse for wear.

Her condition though, has since improved dramatically. The team of attending physicians known as *The X-Files* creative genius made it clear to the actress who plays Covarrubias, Laurie Holden,

that a recovery was definitely on the horizon. "I knew that I would eventually be coming out of my coma," Holden explains. "Usually, they give the actors the courtesy of letting them know if they're going to be killed, so I knew that if this was it someone would have told me. I was told by some of the powers that be that they had big plans for my character."

Marita Covarrubias made her mark as the third in a series of ill-fated informants to the intrepid Agent Mulder. In fact, the death of her conspiracy predecessor, the mysterious X, paved the way for

Covarrubias' first foray into the mythology. As X lay dying from an assassin's bullet in the Season Four premiere "Herrenvolk," he scrawled a cryptic message to Mulder in his own blood, guiding him to the office of the Special Representative to the Secretary General of the United Nations. There, the agent encounters a cool Covarrubias.

Since then, the actress has appeared in several of the key conspiracy episodes and even a stand-alone (Season Four's "Teliko"), but in typical *X-Files* fashion, her character's real motivations and loyalties remain a mystery. In "Tunguska," for example, she is more than willing to call in some favours to help Mulder trace a diplomatic pouch containing the oily substance to which she later falls prey. But just a few episodes later, in "Zero Sum," she pledges to follow the dastardly Cigarette-Smoking Man's directive to block Mulder's quest for the truth. That ambiguity, though, is one of the things Holden finds so appealing about the role. "What I like the most about my character is that she's so cool and evasive and that because she's such an enigma you can't define her," she says. "There are so many ways of reading into what she says and what she does. There are forever questions surrounding that character."

Unlike her character, Holden exudes a down-to-earth charm. She speaks in comfortable, pleasant tones, sometimes pausing before the end of a sentence to consider a point she is making. More often, though, her comments are interrupted by a grin or a good-natured laugh that implies all is well

Black" among Season Five's standout offerings. "They really gave me the opportunity to spread my wings as an actress [through] the twists and turns that came out of 'Patient X,'" she says. "With every script I've received, there are so many ways of reading into what it means, who I'm really working for and this, that and the other. I just get excited whenever a script arrives regardless of what script that may be."

When the "Patient X" script called for Marita to begin spouting a foreign

SECRET AGENT WOMAN: Holden in [clockwise from above] *The Magnificent Seven*, "The Red and The Black," "Patient X" and at *The X-Files* feature film premiere

with the world. After all, in terms of career advancement, a recurring guest spot on *The X-Files* is a feather in the cap of any actor, particularly when he or she is as much of a fan of the series as Holden is. "I think the writing on this show is beyond brilliant. I have never come across such intelligent, thought-provoking material before. In terms of artists collaborating and putting this together, I feel very privileged to be involved with that storytelling," she says.

During Season Five, Holden had the chance to take her performance to another level. Searing scenes between the Uniblonder and rogue Alex Krycek, played by co-star Nicholas Lea, helped place "Patient X"/ "The Red and The language, Holden admits that she was more apprehensive than excited, though; speaking Russian was a requirement she had not anticipated. Determined not to let a language barrier hinder her performance, she and Lea huddled together for some intensive study sessions with a Russian dialect coach. "That was such a feat, I can't even tell you," she remembers. "They were so patient and so wonderful, but there were many hours spent going over every word and inflection. The ultimate test was that my dialect

coach in Vancouver had me call a friend of his who was Russian. Over the cell phone, I said my lines. I knew if I passed the test or not by whether or not this person on the other end could understand me, and he could so I figured I was alright."

Luckily, Russian was familiar territory for Lea, who had already had some training with the language for other *X-Files* episodes, and he readily passed along a few valuable pointers to Holden. "It was easier for him because he'd done it before, but it was my first time doing it," she says. "He

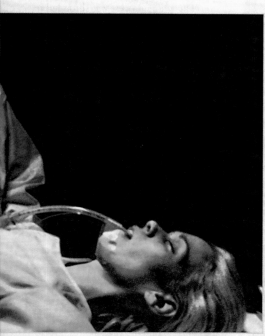

was very sweet. He would just say, 'Laurie, relax. It will come. Just keep working at it, and the second time you do it it will be easier.' Now I know that if they throw any more Russian at me, I've got it covered."

Of course, the real fire between Covarrubias and Krycek happens after the first act. In some respects, the infamous love scene, the first in the history of the show, presented the actors with an even greater challenge than learning a new language; both knew that the scene would forever become a part of the show's lore. "It was exciting because we knew that it was the first love scene on *The X-Files*, so it was just kind of like a part of *X-Files* history we knew we were creating. Nick and I are friends so we had a real sense of humour about it. For actors, whenever you do a love scene, it's not always the most comfortable experience, but everyone

had a wonderful sense of humour about it. We just had so much fun," Holden says.

In television, it's fairly standard that scenes have to be shot and re-shot multiple times to get just the right take, and the amorous battleship embrace was no exception. "We did it a few times," Holden continues. "The irony is that [Nick and I] came together very quickly with our passion, and it was quite a feat in itself. Every time our lips touched we were actually knocking teeth, so every time we came together it was like two quarterbacks coming together, like, 'Wham!' It actually appears a lot more passionate than it really was."

Given everything that has happened in the course of the episodes in which she's appeared, it's not surprising that Holden feels as though she really is ready for anything. "I know that anything that Chris Carter writes is going to be so interesting and thought-provoking. He always has this wonderful way of coming up with things that you would never expect. I'm sure that he has something interesting and fascinating up his sleeve. I find the mythology episodes to be the most fascinating just because I love the subject matter of aliens and conspiracies and what's out there. I really couldn't be happier with my part on the show and being part of the overall mythology."

*C*asting Holden as Covarrubias couldn't have been a better move, either. Not that the 30-year-old actress is an aloof politico in real life, nor does she have a fetish for one-armed renegades like Krycek.

> *"I find the mythology episodes to be the most fascinating just because I love the subject matter of aliens and conspiracies and what's out there."*

She is, however, profoundly interested in the unexplained and has some impressive hands-on experience in the science fiction realm, including guest star spots on *Poltergeist: The Legacy* and *Highlander: The Series*. In fact, her very first role was as the young daughter of late screen legend Rock Hudson in 1980's TV mini-series *The Martian Chronicles*.

"My step-father [Michael Anderson] is a director. This is kind of how I came into acting," she explains. "He was directing a mini-series in Malta called *The Martian Chronicles*, and there was an actress who at the last moment had to bail out of the role. I was in Malta, and they all looked at me and said, 'Can you act?' The next thing I knew they dyed my hair

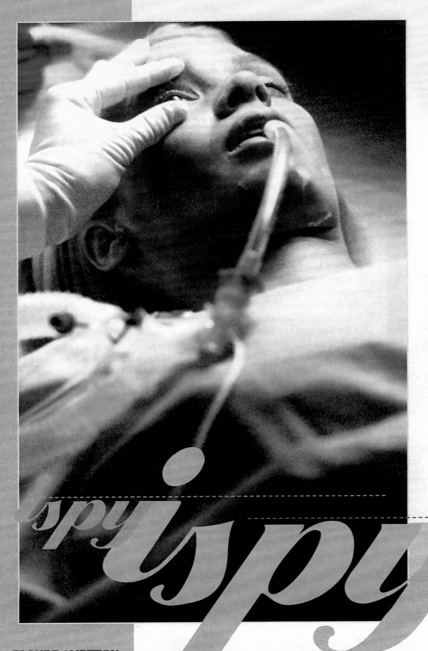

spy spy

BLONDE AMBITION:
Holden in "The Red
and the Black" [above]
and *The Magnificent
Seven* [above right]

true passion for.' So I transferred to
UCLA and the rest is history."

Landing the part of Covarrubias was
equally historic for Holden, and she reflects
on her casting coup with a similar kind of
matter-of-factness. The story goes something like this: Coreen Mayrs, former
Vancouver casting director for *The X-Files*,
cast the actress in a movie of the week, then
contacted her to set up an audition for the
series. As one might expect, trying out for
the show was unlike any professional experience Holden had previously encountered.

"The whole process was shrouded in
secrecy," she remembers. "I didn't receive
a script. I was given no information regarding the character. All I was told was that it
was a woman of intelligent seriousness
who worked at the United Nations. That
was it. I went and I met with Chris Carter.
It was a 10-minute meeting. I read twice. I
read once standing and once sitting. I
remember that it just happened so fast.
This was probably one of the most painless
auditioning experiences of my life in terms
of going and having a meeting and finding
out right away that you got the part. There
were no call backs. There was no network
approval. It was a meeting with the great
man himself, and the rest is history."

About the same time, Holden became
an X-Phile. "I started watching when I
signed on for the show because I needed to
have a better understanding of what I had
become a part of, and I got hooked," she
says. "I've always been fascinated with that

subject matter, the unknown and all it
entails. We've all heard so many things
over time about all the different conspiracies. It makes you think."

*W*hen not participating in high-
level government cover-ups,
Holden stars alongside Michael Biehn and
Ron Perlman on the CBS western *The
Magnificent Seven*. Holden portrays fron-
tier woman Mary Travis, whom she
describes as "spunky, vivacious, a woman
who knows who she is." It's a fitting
description of Holden herself, and the
actress says she has been trying to bring a
touch of her own personality to the character, namely more humour. Travis had been
mourning the loss of her husband and
dealing with single parenthood during the
Old West, well before alternative family
structures were recognised. Holden says
she enjoyed showcasing the character's

black and I'm playing Rock Hudson's
daughter. I kind of got thrown into it. So
that's when I started. I think I was seven."

Despite her young start in the business
and a family connection to the industry,
acting was not always Holden's primary
pursuit. While growing up in Toronto, she
periodically dabbled in the craft, but when
the time came for college, Holden set her
sights on something a bit more practical.
"I initially wanted to be an investment
banker or a lawyer," she confesses. "I went
to McGill University [an English-language
university in Montreal], and I studied eco-
nomics and political science. I thought
that was what I wanted to pursue. Then, I
just got bit again by that bug, and I was
like, 'OK, I think acting is what I have a

independence and strength in the series. "She's a very different person," explains Holden. "We've done a 180 [degree turn] on this character."

While starring in one prime-time series and guest starring on another sounds complicated, things became much easier once *The X-Files* had comfortably settled into its new Los Angeles home. "I think now that *The X-Files* is in Los Angeles it will be easier for me to do both," Holden surmises. "During Season Five it was more hectic shooting schedule wise only because they were shot in different countries. There were a lot of late night flights, travelling back and forth every couple of days. On the days I have off from *Mag Seven*, I'll be able to zip over to *The X-Files*. It's really a great situation."

At some point, Holden adds, she would like to try her hand with some lighter roles for the silver screen. Playing devious double agents and pioneering feminists can become more than a little daunting after a while, even for the most professional thespian. "I would, down the line, love to pursue feature films and romantic comedy in general," she says. "I just love farce and humour, all of that fun stuff. Maybe it's because I've been playing such serious roles that I'm ready to break out and be a goofball."

What would she say to a role in the next *X-Files* feature film? "Definitely would love to do that," she quickly offers. "That's a given." ◆

PHOTO COURTESY OF CBS

"Maybe it's because I've been playing such serious roles that I'm ready to break out and be a goofball."

CREDITS CARD

LAURIE HOLDEN

X-Philes all know Laurie Holden as icy Marita Covarrubias, but the actress has brought a number of other roles to life on the big and small screens since making her debut at the tender age of seven in the 1980 TV movie, *The Martian Chronicles*.

TELEVISION
The Magnificent Seven (1998) "Mary Travis"
Poltergeist: The Legacy (1996) "Cora Jennings/ Sarah Browning"
Due South (1995) "Jill Kennedy"
Highlander (1992) "Debra Campbell"
Murder, She Wrote (1984) "Sherri Simpson"

FILM
The Man Who Used to Be Me (2000) "Amy Ryan"
Past Perfect (1996) "Ally Marsey"
The Pathfinder (1996) "Mabel Dunham"
Expect No Mercy (1995) "Vicki"
Physical Evidence (1989) "Matt's Girl"
Separate Vacations (1986) "Karen"

Pilot
Agent Scully joins Agent Mulder in the F.B.I.'s X-files division, and the two head off to investigate cases of alien abduction.

"Deep Throat"
The agents investigate the disappearance of an air force pilot and Mulder meets the mysterious informant Deep Throat.

"Squeeze"
Mulder and Scully encounter Eugene Victor Tooms, a homicidal, limb-stretching mutant.

"Conduit"
The agents investigate an abduction case bearing similarities to the disappearance of Mulder's sister, Samantha.

"The Jersey Devil"
On the trail of a seemingly cannibalistic murderer, the agents come across a beast woman.

"Shadows"
Mulder and Scully investigate ghostly incidents involving a secretary named Lauren Kyte.

"Ghost in the Machine"
The agents investigate murders in a building under the control of a sentient computer.

"Ice"
In the Arctic, Mulder and Scully come under threat from parasitic ice worms.

"Space"
Mulder and Scully investigate mysterious incidents at N.A.S.A..

"Fallen Angel"
Deep Throat informs Mulder of a crashed spacecraft and that Mulder has 24 hours to investigate before the government cover up the whole thing.

"Eve"
The agents come across two deadly, identical young girls.

"Fire"
On the trail of a mutant killer with fire-controlling powers, Mulder must face his fear of fire as well as old flame Phoebe Green.

Series Guide

by Kate Lloyd

"Beyond the Sea"
Shortly after the death of her father, Scully encounters a man on Death Row who claims to be able to contact him.

"Genderbender"
A religious sect member capable of changing sex becomes the prime suspect in a murder spree.

"Lazarus"
The consciousness of a dangerous criminal possesses an F.B.I. agent who happens to be Scully's ex-boyfriend.

"Young at Heart"
The agents investigate a violent bank robbery, which seems to have been carried out by Johnny Barnett, a psychopath Mulder once helped convict, and who apparently died years ago.

"E.B.E."
The agents track a U.F.O. being transported across the countryside in a truck.

"Miracle Man"
Mulder and Scully investigate deaths involving a young healer.

"Shapes"
The agents visit a Native American reservation where a deadly creature - perhaps linked to the legend of the Manitou - is on the prowl.

"Darkness Falls"
Mulder and Scully become trapped in the woods, surrounded by deadly insects.

"Tooms"
Mr Eugene Victor Tooms is back!

"Born Again"
The agents investigate mysterious deaths surrounding young Michelle Bishop, who may be the reincarnation of a murder victim back for revenge.

"Roland"
The agents come across the case of an autistic janitor, who may be being directed by the deadly will of his dead brother.

"The Erlenmeyer Flask"
Deep Throat tips Mulder to a critically important case involving a missing fugitive and the cloning of extraterrestrial viruses.

THE X FILES

Season Two

"Little Green Men"
Mulder, separated from Scully, investigates possible alien transmissions in Puerto Rico.

"The Host"
Mulder and Scully discover a horrific flukeworm-like mutant lurking in the sewers.

"Blood"
The agents investigate a succession of 'spree killings', which may have been caused by an experimental insecticide.

"Sleepless"
Mulder and his new partner Agent Krycek investigate murders involving a group of elite Vietnam veterans.

"Duane Barry"
A crazed ex-F.B.I. agent and alleged former alien abductee kidnaps Scully.

"Ascension"
Mulder searches for Scully, but is his new partner, Agent Krycek, a help or a hindrance?

"3"
Mulder meets a woman named Kristen, who is involved with a group of vampire fetishists.

"One Breath"
Scully returns, but in a comatose state.

"Firewalker"
At a volcanic research base, Mulder and Scully face the threat of deadly spores, which cause a horrific death.

"Red Museum"
Mulder and Scully investigate the Church of the Red Museum, and Deep Throat's murder is avenged.

"Excelsis Dei"
The agents investigate bizarre, ghostly incidents at an old folks' home.

"Aubrey"
A female police officer has visions of a 50-year-old murder, and appears to be becoming possessed by the spirit of her murderous grandfather.

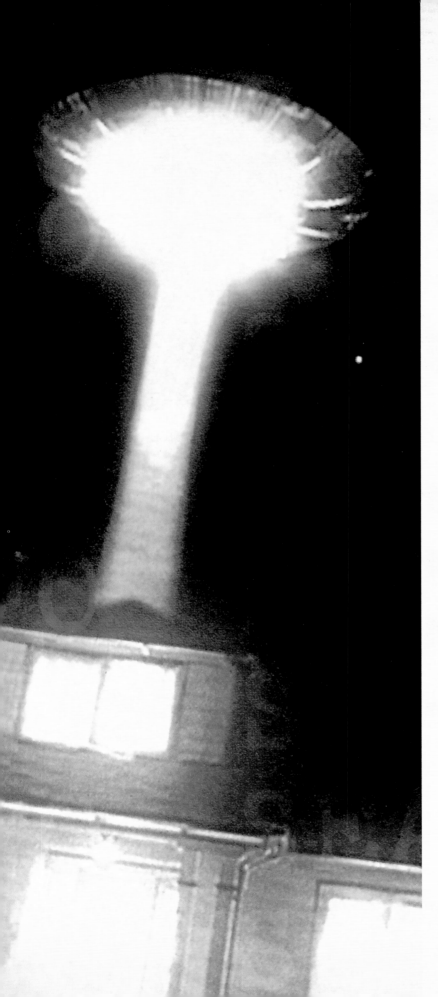

"Irresistible"
Scully is kidnapped by a psychotic death fetishist called Donnie Pfaster.

"Die Hand Die Verletzt"
Mulder and Scully face teachers who are practicing dark magic. Enter mysterious substitute teacher, Mrs Paddock...

"Fresh Bones"
Mulder and Scully face incidents involving voodoo.

"Colony"
Mulder meets a woman who claims to be his sister, Samantha, but an Alien Bounty Hunter is hot on her trail.

"End Game"
After the apparent death of Samantha, Mulder tracks the Alien Bounty Hunter to a submarine in the Arctic.

"Fearful Symmetry"
Mulder and Scully face the possibility that aliens are experimenting with animals.

"Død Kalm"
Stuck on a ship in the Norwegian Sea, infected water causes the agents to age rapidly.

"Humbug"
Mulder and Scully investigate murders amongst the inhabitants of a freakshow community.

"The Calusari"
A family faces a series of tragedies, which may be linked to the murderous ghost of the young son's stillborn brother.

"F. Emasculata"
Mulder must track an escapee from the infected prison.

"Soft Light"
Mulder and Scully are on the trail of a scientist whose shadow is a deadly black hole.

"Our Town"
The agents almost fall foul of a group of cannibals.

"Anasazi"
The agents discover a disk containing top secret information, Mulder's father is murdered, apparently by Krycek, and the CSM leaves Mulder for dead in a burning boxcar.

Season Three

"The Blessing Way"
Albert Hosteen sets about
healing an injured Mulder.
Meanwhile, Scully discovers an
implant in her neck and is
warned by the Well-Manicured-
Man that she is to be the target
of assassins. However, her sister
is shot by mistake.

"Paper Clip"
Mulder and Scully discover a
disused mine full of thousands
of files.

"D.P.O."
Mulder and Scully investigate
the case of a teenager who can
apparently conduct lightening.

**"Clyde Bruckman's
Final Repose"**
The agents meet Clyde Bruckman,
a man who is apparently cursed
with the ability to know how
others are going to die.

"The List"
A killer is executed, and
exacts a deadly revenge on his
enemies from beyond the grave.

"2Shy"
The agents tackle a mutant who
sucks the fat out of women.

"The Walk"
An amputee at an army veterans'
hospital is using telekinetic
powers to commit murder.

"Oubliette"
A woman forms a psychic connection with a kidnap victim, but
only Mulder believes her story.

"Nisei"
Mulder gets his hands on a
video showing an alien autopsy,
while Scully meets up with some
fellow abductees.

"731"
Mulder is trapped on board a
train with an alien, a deadly
assassin and a ticking bomb.

"Revelations"
Mulder and Scully try to protect a young stigmatic from a
crazed religious serial killer.

"War of the Coprophages"
Mulder and Scully face killer

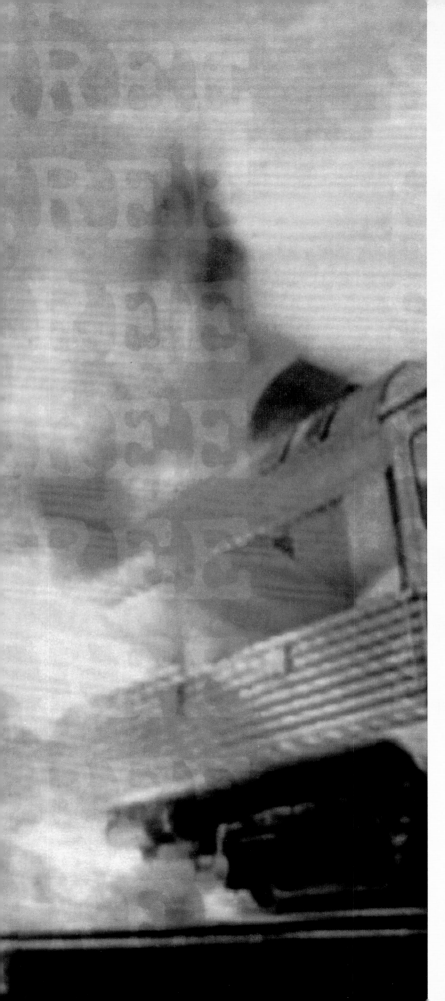

cockroaches, and an attractive
entomologist called Bambi.

"Syzygy"
The agents face two teenage
girls who demonstrate violent
powers with astrological links.

"Grotesque"
On the trail of a grisly serial
killer, Mulder faces a terrifying trip into the dark side.

"Piper Maru"
An alien entity from a crashed
aircraft is possessing people's
bodies, and ends up in Krycek's.
Meanwhile, Skinner is shot by
Melissa Scully's killer.

"Apocrypha"
Scully protects an endangered
Skinner, while a possessed
Krycek deposits the alien oil in
a missile silo.

"Pusher"
A man with a mind-controlling
ability proves a deadly enemy
for Mulder and Scully.

"Teso dos Bichos"
People begin to vanish soon
after an Ecuadorian urn containing a female shaman's body
is brought to a Boston museum.

"Hell Money"
Mulder and Scully become
embroiled in a deadly lottery
in San Francisco's Chinatown.

"Jose Chung's 'From Outer Space'"
Author Jose Chung interviews
Agent Scully about a recent
U.F.O. abductee case.

"Avatar"
Skinner becomes a murder
suspect and experiences strange
visions of an old woman.

"Quagmire"
Mulder and Scully investigate a
mysterious lake monster, and
Scully's dog Queequeg is killed.

"Wetwired"
Mulder must stop a paranoid and
violent Scully as she becomes a
victim of strange television
signals.

"Talitha Cumi" (1 of 2)
Mulder tries to track down a
healer known as Jeremiah Smith
to cure his dying mother.

"Herrenvolk" (2 of 2)
As Jeremiah Smith and Mulder go on the run from the Alien Bounty Hunter, the Syndicate lays a trap for X.

"Home"
A dead and deformed baby leads Mulder and Scully into an encounter with the horrific Peacock family.

"Teliko"
Mulder seeks the truth behind an African folk tale involving men having their skin pigmentation drained.

"Unruhe"
A man appears to have the ability to place his dark fantasies onto photographic film.

"The Field Where I Died"
Mulder meets a woman with apparent multiple personalities who belongs to a religious cult and claims to have known Mulder in a previous life.

"Sanguinarium"
When a patient dies during an operation, the clues lead to witchcraft rituals.

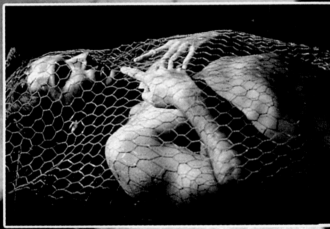

"Musings of a Cigarette-Smoking Man"
Frohike relates what he believes are key moments from the life of the enigmatic Cigarette-Smoking Man.

"Tunguska" (1 of 2)
A piece of Martian rock leads Mulder on a dangerous journey to Russia where tests with the alien black oil are occurring.

"Terma" (2 of 2)
Captured in Russia and infected with the black oil, Mulder learns that he has been betrayed — by Krycek.

"Paper Hearts"
Mulder experiences strange dreams about a killer who preys on little girls, and who may have been responsible for Samantha's abduction.

"El Mundo Gira"
A Mexican family blames mysterious yellow rain for the disappearance of their son.

"Leonard Betts"
A hospital worker can regenerate himself, including lost body parts, but needs to ingest cancerous tumors to do so.

"Never Again"

With Mulder on holiday Scully gets too close to the subject of her solo assignment: a man who believes his tattoo talks to him.

"Memento Mori"

Scully learns she has a potentially fatal brain tumor, a condition afflicting many former alien abductees.

"Kaddish"

A Jewish man has allegedly returned from the grave to take revenge on the racist teenagers who attacked him.

"Unrequited"

Prominent military personnel are inexplicably murdered. Is a Vietnam vet with extraordinary mental abilities to blame?

"Tempus Fugit" (1 of 2)

Mulder is told that a passenger plane carrying Max Fenig (last seen in "Fallen Angel") has crashed after a possible U.F.O. interception.

"Max" (2 of 2)

Mulder tries to get to the bottom of why Max was on the downed plane and whether he had been in possession of alien technology.

"Synchrony"

A scientist from the future visits a younger version of himself to prevent a calamitous discovery from happening.

"Small Potatoes"

A meek man who can seemingly assume any human form is accused of fathering five babies, all with tails, to five mothers in the same town.

"Zero Sum"

Skinner acts in an apparently underhand manner: is he secretly working for the Cigarette-Smoking Man or is he trying to save Scully?

"Elegy"

Mulder and Scully investigate a mysterious death at a bowling alley.

"Demons"

Mulder submits himself to radical hypnotherapy to delve into memories of his sister's abduction but the procedure goes wrong — with terrible consequences.

"Gethsemane" (1 of 3)

Mulder is told by Michael Kritschgau that everything he has come to believe about aliens is all part of an elaborate ruse.

"Redux" (2 of 3)
Mulder has faked suicide to infiltrate the Department of Defense and find answers about the alien conspiracy.

"Redux II" (3 of 3)
Mulder is offered a role in the Syndicate by the CSM in return for seeing the 'real' Samantha and getting a cure for Scully's cancer.

"Unusual Suspects"
In a flashback to 1989, the events which led to the formation of conspiracy watchdogs The Lone Gunmen are revealed.

"Detour"
Mulder and Scully are waylaid en route to an F.B.I. seminar by a case of three missing persons in a Florida forest.

"Post-Modern Prometheus"
A black and white retelling of the Frankenstein story featuring a hideous mutant, a mad scientist and Jerry Springer!

"Christmas Carol" (1 of 2)
Scully learns of Emily, a three-year-old girl who she believes is the secret daughter of Melissa, her sister.

"Emily" (2 of 2)
Tests show that Emily, seriously ill with anemia, carries Dana's D.N.A., not Melissa's. Mulder aids Scully in finding out how this could have happened.

"Kitsunegari"
Psychic-killer Robert Modell (Pusher) escapes from a mental hospital and hunts for Mulder.

"Schizogeny"
Troubled children suffer from false memory syndrome planted by their therapist, who seems to be passing on memories of her own abuse as a child.

"Chinga"
A doll belonging to an autistic girl which apparently has supernatural powers threatens residents of a small coastal town in Maine.

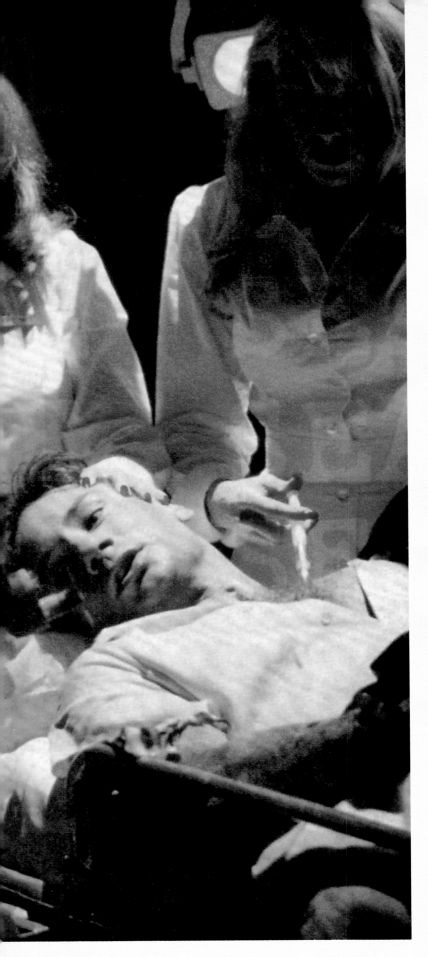

"Kill Switch"
A computer virus goes out of
control and leads to the death
of its creator.

"Bad Blood"
A strange case of small-town
vampirism is told from both
Mulder and Scully's wildly
different perspectives.

"Patient X" (1 of 2)
Cassandra Spender tests
Mulder's growing skepticism in
alien abductions, and Scully
soon discovers she has a lot
more common with the woman
than she at first thought.

**"The Red and the Black"
(2 of 2)**
When Cassandra is again abducted by aliens, Mulder runs into
conflict with her son, young
over-zealous F.B.I. agent Jeffrey
Spender.

"Travelers"
Mulder consults a retired FBI
agent, Arthur Dales, to find
out what he knows about his
father William Mulder's involvement in a Cold War X-files type
of case.

"Mind's Eye"
The agents come into contact
with a young blind woman who
can apparently visualize what a
vicious killer is doing.

"All Souls"
Scully goes to the assistance of
a family whose adopted daughter
died as a result of alleged
divine intervention.

"The Pine Bluff Variant"
Mulder goes undercover to
expose a terrorist group that
plans to release a deadly flesh-
eating biological weapon.

"Folie a Deux"
A man takes Mulder hostage in
an office, where he claims that
his co-workers are zombies and
that his boss is literally a
monster.

"The End" (1 of 2)
Mulder discovers that the
answers he has been seeking for
many years may lie in the form
of a young boy with amazing
psychic powers.

Season Six

"The Beginning"
Mulder and Scully fail to be
reassigned to the X-files and
are sent on different missions.
But when Gibson Praise returns,
they secretly work in unison.

"Drive"
Mulder is kidnapped by a man
afflicted with a condition
which will cause his head to
explode – unless he keeps
moving at high speed.

"Triangle"
When a British liner that vanished just before World War II
reportedly returns near the
Bermuda Triangle, Mulder apparently goes back in time.

"Dreamland" (1 of 2)
Mulder's identity is switched
with that of an Area 51
employee, Morris Fletcher.

"Dreamland" (2 of 2)
Fletcher, relishing his time in
Mulder's body, has Mulder (as
Fletcher) arrested.

"Terms of Endearment"
A demon impregnates women
in the hope of having a
'normal' child.

"The Rain King"
A weatherman's unrequited love
for a colleague manifests itself
through climate changes.

**"How the Ghosts
Stole Christmas"**
Mulder and Scully are driven to
the brink of a murder-suicide
pact while investigating a
house haunted by a couple who
met that exact fate.

"Tithonus"
Scully meets a crime-scene
photographer who turns up when
homicides take place; is he the
perpetrator or a psychic?

"S.R. 819"
Skinner has 24 hours to live
unless Mulder finds an anti-
dote to the virus infecting him.

"Two Fathers" (1 of 2)
The agents uncover secrets
involving Samantha, and the
CSM's relationships with Mrs
Mulder and Cassandra Spender.

"One Son" (2 of 2)
Mulder and Scully are reassigned to the X-files in the wake of their discoveries about the Syndicate's alien conspiracy; but it costs Spender his life.

"Arcadia"
Mulder and Scully pose as a married couple to investigate a series of strange deaths in an exclusive picture-book suburb.

"Agua Mala"
Retired F.B.I. agent Arthur Dales suspects there's something in the water at a Florida town, causing the disappearance of several inhabitants.

"Monday"
The agents face death in a bank robbery - time and time again. Can they escape the loop?

"Alpha"
An animal expert brings a wild wolf-like creature, thought to be extinct, to California, but it escapes and runs amok.

"Trevor"
A violent inmate escapes from solitary confinement during a tornado and appears to be able to walk through solid matter.

"Milagro"
Scully is attracted to Mulder's neighbor, a writer whose words hold a strange, deadly power.

"Three of a Kind"
The Lone Gunmen crash a Government defense convention in Las Vegas and are reunited with Susanne Modeski.

"The Unnatural"
Dales' brother tells Mulder of a gifted black baseball player in Roswell in the 1940s who may have been an alien in disguise.

"Field Trip"
The agents investigate a case of rapid decomposition at a mountain site but become trapped in a cave and start to hallucinate.

"Biogenesis"
Scientists analyzing artifacts in Africa conclude that life on Earth originated elsewhere in space. Mulder investigates one of the scientists' death and is affected by the artifacts.

THE (X) FILES

Season Seven

"The Sixth Extinction"
(2 of 3)
Skinner and Kritschgau
investigate Mulder's catatonic
state while Scully is in Africa
deciphering the alien symbols.

"The Sixth Extinction II:
Amor Fati" (3 of 3)
Scully becomes Mulder's only
hope as his grip on reality
becomes weaker.

"Hungry"
The agents track down a man who
has an insatiable appetite for
human brains.

"Millennium"
Mulder and Scully consult
Frank Black to prevent the
Millennium Group from instigat-
ing the end of the world on
December 31, 1999.

"Rush"
A rebellious teenager develops
the ability to move so fast that
his murderous actions cannot be
seen by the naked eye.

"The Goldberg Variation"
Henry Weems appears to be the
most fortunate man in the
world, except that with every
stroke of good luck comes
calamity for someone else.

"Orison"
A preacher tries to save the
soul of death fetishist Donnie
Pfaster by helping him escape
from prison. The killer then
renews his acquaintance with
Scully...

"The Amazing Maleeni"
A sideshow magician's head-
turning trick turns out to be
his last - but what was his link
with a bank robbery?

"Signs and Wonders"
A Tennessee priest is apparently using snakes to dispense
divine retribution.

"Sein und Zeit" (1 of 2)
Mulder gets closely involved in
the case of a girl's abduction
and it seems to Scully that it's
due to similarities with
Samantha's disappearance.

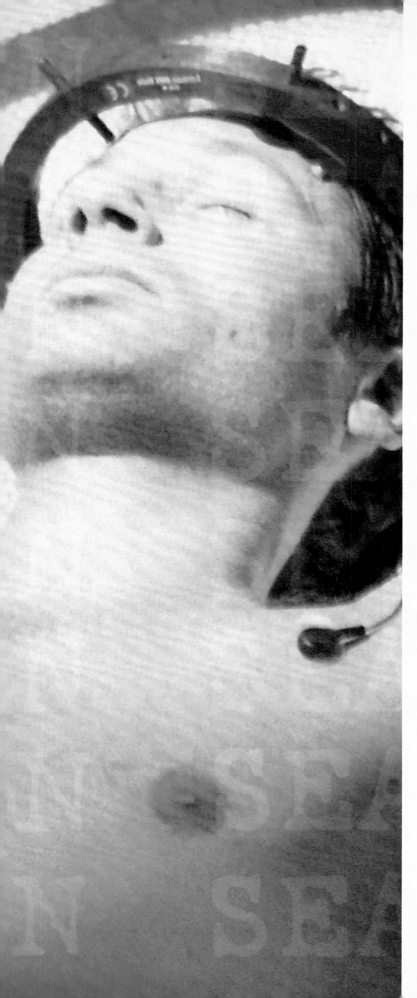

"Closure" (2 of 2)
The arrest of a child murderer leads Mulder to the truth about his sister's disappearance.

"X-COPS"
The agents become inadvertent TV stars as a camera crew follows the cops - and the F.B.I. - on the trail of a mysterious series of deaths.

"First Person Shooter"
The agents delve into virtual reality when a software programmer dies while testing a new game.

"Theef"
A doctor and his family are menaced by a spell-weaving murderer.

"En Ami"
The CSM offers Scully a cure for diseases such as cancer if she agrees to travel with him without Mulder's knowledge.

"Chimera"
Mulder takes on a case involving ravens and missing people while Scully is stuck in a difficult stakeout.

"all things"
Scully learns that a former lover is dying, and takes stock of her life.

"Brand X"
Cigarette company Morley engages in experiments that result in horrific deaths.

"Hollywood A.D."
Mulder and Scully look on in horror as Garry Shandling and Tea Leoni portray them in a fictional Hollywood version of their exploits.

"Fight Club"
Two volatile lookalike women create chaos as they encounter each other across the US.

"Je Souhaite"
Mulder receives three wishes from a world-weary genia.

"Requiem" (1 of 3)
Mulder and Scully investigate a U.F.O. crash at the site of their first X-files case seven years ago, and come into contact with old adversaries.

THE X FILES

"Within" (2 of 3)
Following Mulder's disappear-
ance, new F.B.I. Deputy
Director Kersh assigns Agent
John Doggett to head the
manhunt. Meanwhile, the now
pregnant Scully must protect
Gibson Praise.

"Without" (3 of 3)
Scully believes she is closer to
Mulder's whereabouts as she
encounters the Alien Bounty
Hunter in Arizona.

"Patience"
Newly assigned to the X-files, a
skeptical Doggett must help
Scully solve a series of attacks
by a bat-like creature.

"Roadrunners"
Scully tries to go it alone in
remote Utah where a religious
cult worships a parasitic slug.

"Invocation"
A ten-year-old boy who inexplicably vanished in 1990 mysteriously returns - but he hasn't
aged a single day.

"Redrum"
A lawyer charged with murdering
his wife finds time rolling
back, with each day becoming the
day before, possibly offering a
chance to prove his innocence.

"Via Negativa"
Skinner and Doggett must
unravel the cause of a murder
spree conducted by a religious
cult leader, whose mind-alter-
ing drug-taking means he can
enter people's nightmares.

"Surekill"
Scully and Doggett look into
the case of an assassin with
seemingly impossible powers of
sight.

"Salvage"
A man who seems to be made of
metal enacts revenge on those
who created him.

"Badlaa"
A mystic smuggles himself out of
India and plagues two families

"The Gift"
Doggett finds a possible clue to Mulder's disappearance in a file that was kept secret from Scully.

"Medusa"
A lethal contagion spreads through the subways of Boston.

"Per Manum"
The case of a woman allegedly murdered after giving birth to an alien baby leads Scully to doubt the nature of her ensuing pregnancy.

"This Is Not Happening (1 of 3)
Doggett brings in another agent to assist the Mulder case, but Scully's fears about finding him come to a head with the sudden recovery of abductees seized at the same time.

"DeadAlive" (2 of 3)
When a former abductee awakens from the dead, Scully pins her hopes on resurrecting the recently buried Mulder.

"Three Words" (3 of 3)
A White House shooting prompts Mulder and the Lone Gunmen to investigate a twist in the alien colonization conspiracy.

"Empedocles"
Agent Reyes asks for Mulder's help in finding a killer who may have a supernatural connection to the unsolved murder of Agent Doggett's son.

"Vienen"
Reluctant partners Mulder and Doggett investigate several deaths aboard an oil rig.

"Alone"
Doggett, teamed with an eager new partner while Scully's on maternity leave, investigates the mysterious disappearance of two men.

"Essence" (1 of 2)
The alien conspiracy resurfaces as a threat to Scully and her baby emerges.

"Existence" (2 of 2)
Reyes takes charge of guarding Scully, as Skinner, Mulder and Doggett struggle to head off the alien replicants who are pursuing her.

Season Nine

"Nothing Important Happened Today" (1 of 2)
Mulder flees from aliens, while the arrival of a deadly SuperSoldier called Shannon McMahon spells trouble for Doggett, Reyes and Scully.

"Nothing Important Happened Today" (2 of 2)
New mum Scully searches frantically for the truth behind the origins of her baby, William, who is exhibiting strange powers of telepathy.

"Daemonicus"
Doggett and Reyes seek Scully's help in solving a mysterious case which appears to involve Satanic rituals.

"4-D"
Agent Doggett and Agent Reyes are murdered while investigating a case - or are they? Meanwhile, another Reyes suspects the existence of a parallel universe killer.

"Lord of the Flies"
As a series of young people die in strange insect-related incidents, it's down to Doggett, Reyes and Scully to unearth the real killer.

"Trust No 1"
Scully attempts to arrange a secret meeting with Mulder, but a deadly killer is on his trail, and Scully has to put her trust and Mulder's safety in the hands of a stranger.

"John Doe"
John Doggett wakes up in a nondescript Mexican town with no memory of who he is or how he got there. Meanwhile, Scully and Reyes attempt to locate the missing agent.

"Hellbound"
The agents investigate a grisly case in which the victims are skinned alive, which turns out to be more then just a copycat murder case.

"Provenance" (1 of 2)
Scully must defend her gifted young son, William, from a suc-

"Providence" (2 of 2)
The agents set off on the trail of Scully's baby William, who has been kidnapped by a religious cult.

"Audrey Pauley"
As Doggett and Scully watch a dying Agent Reyes slips away in hospital after a car crash, Reyes finds herself somewhere very strange indeed.

"Underneath"
An old enemy of Agent Doggett's - notoriously known as the 'Screwdriver killer' - is released from jail.

"Improbable"
Burt Reynolds guest stars, as Reyes, Scully and Doggett investigate crimes which seem to involve numerology.

"Scary Monsters"
Reyes, Doggett and Leyla Harrison head out to help a young boy who appears to be in danger - although not everything is as it appears.

"Jump the Shark"
The Lone Gunmen are reunited with Jimmy Bond and Yves Adele Harlow, but they may have to make the ultimate sacrifice to prevent disaster.

"William"
A disfigured man is discovered in the X-files office - and tests reveal that he has Mulder's DNA. Has Mulder finally returned to Scully?

"Release"
One of Scully's students displays an inordinate ability to profile serial killers, and his insights re-open the murder case of Doggett's son.

'Sunshine Days'
One man's obsession with the 1970s sitcom *The Brady Bunch* combined with his remarkable telekinetic ability lead the agents to believe that they have discovered proof for the ultimate X-file.

"The Truth"
Mulder's return leads to his being tried before a military tribunal that seeks to justify and prove the very existence of an alien conspiracy - and the X-files themselves.

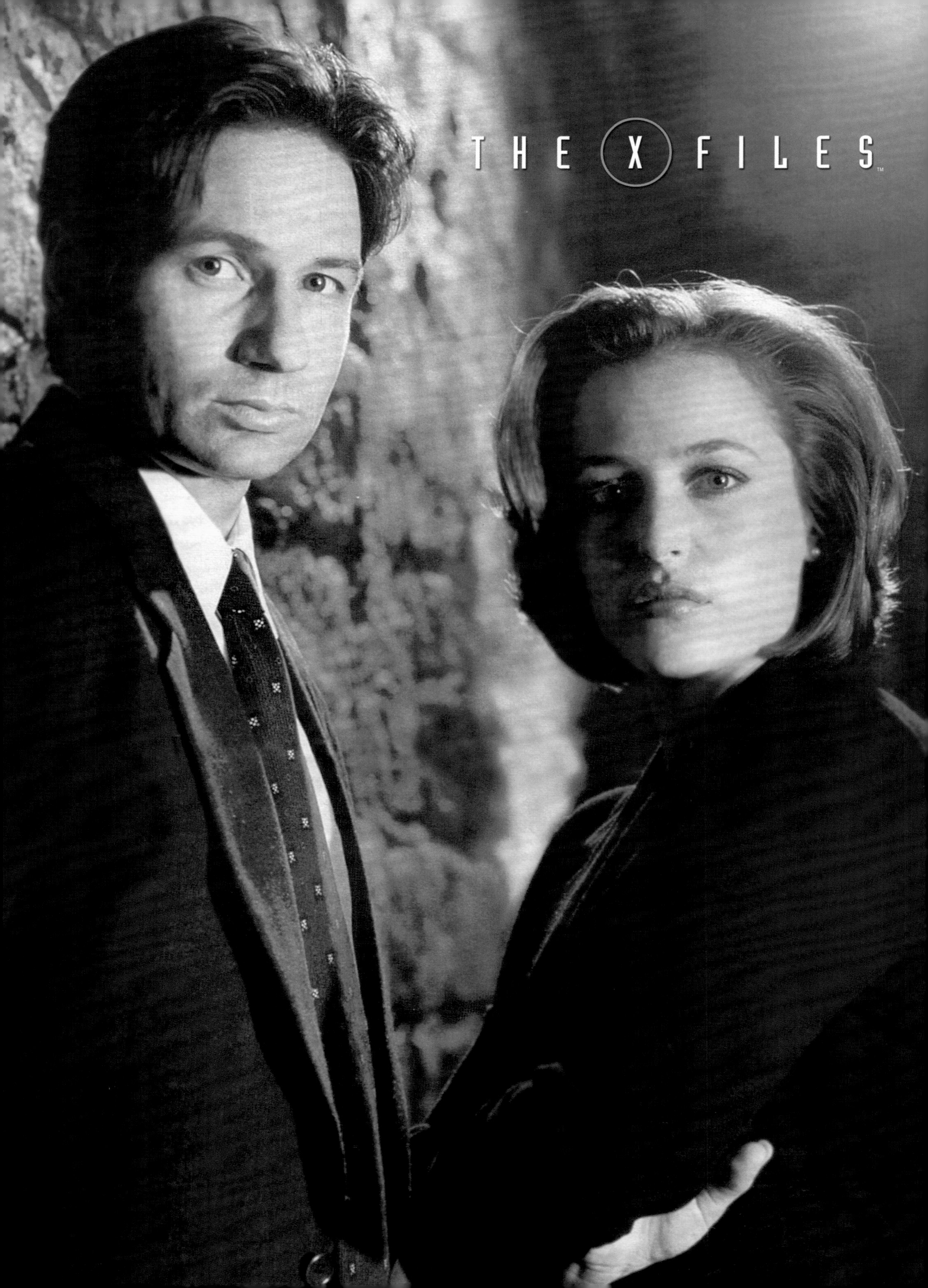
THE X FILES

THE SHIPPER NEWS

IT MAY HAVE TAKEN THEM YEARS TO GET TOGETHER, BUT THE SEXUAL TENSION BETWEEN MULDER AND SCULLY CRACKLED THROUGHOUT THE SERIES. WE TRACE SOME OF THE SHOW'S MOST ROMANTIC MOMENTS

BY KATE ANDERSON

What place does love and romance have in a sci-fi series? Well, much more than you'd think. At least in *The X-Files* universe. Cast your mind back to the Pilot episode; remember that scene where a scantily clad Scully bursts into Mulder's room and asks him to examine the strange marks on her back? Talk about sexual tension. It seemed inevitable that Mulder and Scully – two of the youngest and most attractive F.B.I. agents in TV history – would become involved. And from that moment onwards, some fans became very vocal in their desire to have the agents 'get it together' – romantically speaking. They would head straight to the Internet and numerous online groups to share their comments with other likeminded fans. Of course, Mulder and Scully didn't initially get it on. Instead we had to endure year after year, season after season of teasing and flirting. And let's be honest, we couldn't get enough! And so we begin our look at the best, most memorable 'Shipper' moments starting where it all began, with the Pilot…

PILOT (SEASON ONE)
Having discovered some strange marks on her back, similar to the two small marks found on the bodies of the four dead teenagers they are investigating, Scully rushes to Mulder's motel room and asks him to check them out. She drops her dressing gown and even though she is only wearing her underwear, Scully allows her partner (whom she only met a few hours ago!) to get up close and personal. Mulder reassures her that they are just mosquito bites. A very relieved Scully pulls up her dressing gown and embraces him.

"ICE" (SEASON ONE)
Fearing that Mulder may have been infected by the paranoia-inducing alien parasite that was responsible for turning a team of geophysicists into psychotic killers, Scully examines Mulder for signs of the worm-like parasite. She begins to explore his back, and then pulls down the back of his shirt, massaging his shoulders for any presence of the alien parasite. As Scully turns to leave, Mulder grabs her. For a brief moment, Scully thinks he's about to attack her. But Mulder reassures her before pulling down the collar of her shirt and examining her neck.

"E.B.E." (SEASON ONE)
Mulder and Scully investigate a government cover-up of a U.F.O. shot down over Iraq and transported to the U.S.. Seeking help, Mulder takes Scully to meet the Lone Gunmen – an extreme government watchdog group. Back at their office, she tells her partner that they were the most paranoid people she has ever met. Referring to Frohike's observation, Mulder rather coyly replies that he

thinks it's remotely plausible that someone might think she was hot.

"TOOMS" (SEASON ONE)
Eugene Tooms is released from Druid Hill Sanatorium. Convinced it's only a matter of time before he will kill again, Mulder conducts an unauthorized surveillance of the liver-loving fiend. Scully arrives (with provisions: root beer and a sandwich) to take over the stakeout from Mulder.
Mulder is worried she could get in trouble; he doesn't want her risking her own career. But Scully tells him that she wouldn't put herself on the line for anyone but him. Mulder tells her it could be love if she's brought him an iced tea. But Scully tells him it must be fate – it's root beer.

"LITTLE GREEN MEN" (SEASON TWO)
Mulder returns to Washington and gets a ticking off from Skinner for traveling to an alien contact site in Puerto Rico and abandoning a routine assignment. To make matters worse, he discovers the tape he made as evidence of extraterrestrial contact is blank. He tells Scully that although he doesn't have the X-files anymore, he still has his work; and he has her and he has himself.

"RED MUSEUM" (SEASON TWO)
The agents take time out during their investigations into a religious cult that may be linked to the disappearance of several teenagers, to enjoy a meal at a local restaurant. Scully comments on the food – they're eating spare ribs – and Mulder notices a smear of sauce on her cheek. Without saying a word, he leans over and dabs it away with his napkin. Scully appears to be a little

embarrassed but then she smiles wryly, enjoying his attention.

"PUSHER" (SEASON THREE)
A deadly game of Russian roulette between Mulder, Scully and Pusher – a man who has the ability to bend people's minds – ends with Pusher's hospitalization. Mulder and Scully stand by his bedside. Pusher is in a coma. Mulder tells Scully that her opinion of Pusher was correct; he was always a little man and this was something that made him feel big. Scully tells Mulder that they shouldn't let him take up anymore of their time. And she gently slips her hand into his fingers.

"QUAGMIRE" (SEASON THREE)
The agents take a boat out to search for a lake monster called Big Blue to whom locals attribute a series of deaths. But something crashes into their boat and they have to abandon the sinking boat. Stranded on a large rock, they begin to open up to each other and when Mulder coyly asks Scully if she's recently lost weight, his partner thanks him for noticing. But then she realizes that he was just teasing her. Their conversation gets even more deep and meaningful, and Scully compares Mulder's obsession for the truth to Captain Ahab's hunt for Moby Dick. Afterwards, Mulder grins ands asks Scully if she's coming on to him!

"THE FIELD WHERE I DIED" (SEASON FOUR)
Mulder and Scully investigate a fanatical religious cult and meet a woman who may have been Mulder's soul mate in a past life. Mulder asks Scully if early in the four years they've been together, someone told her that they'd been friends together always, would it

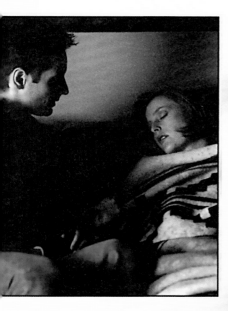

have changed the way they look at each other. Scully tenderly replies that even if she'd known for certain, she wouldn't have changed a day, except for "that flukeman thing"– she could have lived without that just fine.

"MEMENTO MORI" (SEASON FOUR)
Scully is diagnosed with having cancer. She admits herself to a special clinic to undergo radical treatment for the disease. Arriving at the hospital, Mulder panics when he discovers Scully's room empty. He finds her comforting a dying friend. He tells Scully he was scared something had happened to her. But she tells him that she is not going to let the cancer beat her; she's got things to prove. Mulder smiles and they fall into each other's arms. He tells her the truth will save her; it will save them both. He then cups her face in his hands and tenderly kisses her on the forehead.

"DETOUR" (SEASON FIVE)
On the trail of semi-human creatures that have the ability to turn invisible, Mulder and Scully become separated from the other two members of their group that presumably have been attacked by the invisible predators. Scully and an injured Mulder take shelter overnight. A slightly feverish Mulder flirts outrageously with Scully, telling her that the best way to regenerate body heat is to share a sleeping bag with somebody else who's preferably naked! Scully replies that if it rains sleeping bags he might get lucky!

"POST-MODERN PROMETHEUS" (SEASON FIVE)
Mulder and Scully's investigation into the bizarre genetic experiments of an amoral scientist leads them to the Great

Mutato – a modern day Frankenstein's monster. Discovering that he isn't a monster at all, they take the Cher-loving Mutato to see her in concert. As Cher belts out *Walking in Memphis*, Mulder suddenly leaps to his feet. He holds out his hand and invites Scully to dance. No words are needed and they dance happily, beaming at each other, until the music ends.

THE X-FILES MOVIE (1998)

A weary-looking Scully turns up at Mulder's apartment. She informs him that she has given her resignation to Skinner. She's quitting. Mulder tells her that he can't carry on without her. He can't do it alone; he doesn't want to do it without her. Touched by his honesty and vulnerability, Scully walks towards Mulder and embraces him. They pull apart slightly and Scully kisses his fore-head. They gaze at one another briefly and slowly, Mulder leans closer; his lips slightly apart, he puts a hand behind Scully's neck to draw her to him. But just as they are about to kiss, Scully gets stung by a bee!

"TRIANGLE" (SEASON SIX)

A trip to the Bermuda Triangle causes a time warp and lands Mulder in hot water on a British luxury liner that disappeared just prior to World War II. Onboard, he meets many familiar faces, including a Scully look-alike. Mulder tries to make her believe that the ship they are on has been caught up in a time warp and that if she doesn't convince the crew to turn the ship around the course of history will be changed forever. Realizing that he may never get a better chance, he grabs her and kisses her on the lips. Her response being a right hook to his jaw!

"TRIANGLE" (SEASON SIX)

In hospital after his bizarre encounter with a 1930s Scully look-alike and a bunch of Nazis on board the *Queen Anne* luxury cruise liner, Mulder tries to convince Scully, Skinner and the Lone Gunmen that it wasn't just a dream. As Scully starts to leave, Mulder calls her back. He props himself up on one elbow and as Scully leans in close, he tells her that he loves her. To which Scully replies "Oh brother" and walks away. Mulder then feels the bruise on his jaw; maybe it wasn't a dream after all!

"ARCADIA" (SEASON SIX)

Mulder and Scully go undercover, posing as a married couple to investigate the mysterious disappearance of several residents of an upscale, uptight suburb. Under the guise of Rob and Laura Petrie, they move into the house that was occu-pied by David and Nancy Kline – the most recent inhabitants who disappeared without a trace. Once inside the house, Scully pulls out a camcorder and begins to film the interior as she narrates her case notes. An unusually flirty Mulder steps in front of Scully's lens and teasing-ly asks if she wants to make their honey-moon video.

"THE UNNATURAL" (SEASON SIX)

A tale about a talented alien baseball player who hid amongst an all African American team in Roswell, New Mexico during the 1940s prompts Mulder to show Scully the finer points of the game. As an early – or late – birthday present, Mulder offers to teach Scully how to play baseball. She meets him at a Washington public park. He asks her if she's ever hit a baseball. Scully says she's found more necessary things to do in her spare time. They stand together in the batting cage; Mulder puts his arms around Scully and together they hit ball after ball into the night sky.

"MILLENNIUM" (SEASON SEVEN)

Mulder and Scully team up with Frank Black to prevent members of the Millennium Group bringing forth the apocalypse before the new Millennium. Minutes before midnight, the agents watch the celebrations in Times Square on TV. Mulder glances over at Scully, then he leans in close and their lips meet in a kiss. When they pull away, they share a knowing smile and Mulder com-ments that the world didn't end. "No it didn't," replies Scully.

"PER MANUM" (SEASON EIGHT)

After hearing reports of alien fertilization on humans, Scully begins to question her own pregnancy and more importantly, its conception. In flashback, Scully recalls the previous year. She finds Mulder in her apartment and tells him that her last chance of getting pregnant through artifi-cial insemination has failed. Mulder tries to comfort her; he places his hands on her shoulders and tells her to never give up on a miracle. He then leans forward and gently kisses her on the forehead.

"EXISTENCE" (SEASON EIGHT)

Mulder, Doggett and Reyes team up to safeguard a pregnant Scully from aliens intent on harming her and her unborn child. Agent Reyes manages to get Scully to safety but as she prepares to give birth, they are surrounded by aliens. Scully gives birth to a healthy baby boy and the aliens silently leave. Back at her apart-ment, a glowing Scully introduces Mulder properly to her baby – their baby. She's named him William in memory of Mulder's father. As Mulder cradles their son, he leans over and kisses Scully ten-derly on the lips. ●

THE X FILES

20 COOLEST MOMENTS

For the past eight years. *The X-Files* has enthralled us with more than 130 hours of exceptional, intelligent and entertaining television. Cleverly conceived and beautifully executed, whether dealing with government conspiracies. aliens or freaks of nature. *The X-Files* is without doubt one of the greatest ever TV shows. So to celebrate this and to help kick off a brand new era for *The Official X-Files Magazine*, we've looked back over all the episodes to present what we consider to be the 20 coolest *X-Files* moments of all time. These are the moments which have shocked, amazed and inspired us over the past eight years; moments which mark out important events; moments which stick in the mind and have you rewinding the video again and again. They all have that certain 'something' that just makes them quintessential *X-Files* moments. In short. they're all pretty darn cool...

by Kate Anderson

20 SCULLY AND DOGGETT'S FIRST MEETING

EPISODE: "Within" (8x01)
WHAT HAPPENS: Mulder is missing, and the FBI is investigating his disappearance. A fuming Scully throws water into the face of her soon-to-be new partner, John Doggett.
WHY IT'S SO COOL: With Mulder gone, we all knew that Scully would be getting a new partner, but we didn't expect it to start off so disastrously!
X-TRA: So they didn't hit it off initially, but after a few tense moments their relationship endured and *The X-Files* was given a whole new lease of life.
AND: Check out other cool first meetings: Mulder and Scully in "Pilot"; Mulder greeting new partner Krycek in "Sleepless".

19 BLACK OIL EXPERIMENTAION... ON MULDER!

EPISODE: "Tunguska" (4x09)
WHAT HAPPENS: Mulder is used as a human guinea pig when Russians try to develop their own vaccine against the black oil virus.
WHY IT'S SO COOL: One of the most unforgettable images in *X-Files* history. This really is the stuff of nightmares; trapped, unable to move and on the verge of suffocation – Mulder has never looked more helpless or scared. In a grim Russian gulag, no one can hear you scream...
X-TRA: The black oil is a sentient viral extraterrestrial life form that gestates an alien being in its human victims. The Syndicate began developing a vaccine in the 1970s. Aliens plan to take over the universe by infecting all other lifeforms with the virus.

18 SCULLY BREAKS DOWN

EPISODE: "Badlaa" (8x12)
WHAT HAPPENS: After the weirdest Season Eight case of all (involving a perception-altering killer), Scully finally breaks down in front of Doggett, confessing to him that it's all been an act: she's been pretending to be a believer all along, making such huge leaps because it's what Mulder would do. But she can't do it any more.
WHY IT'S SO COOL: It breaks your heart to see Scully so shaken by her recent experiences. She has been desperate to try and see things through Mulder's eyes. His absence has forced her to become the believer, and she finally admits that she's not comfortable with it.
X-TRA: If you like this you'll also like Scully's beautifully-acted confessions in "Revelations" and "All Souls".

17 SCULLY MEETS OTHER FEMALE ABDUCTEES

EPISODE: "Nisei" (3x09)
WHAT HAPPENS: Scully encounters a group of female abductees who recognise her from the 'tests'.
WHY IT'S SO COOL: The scene where a room full of women produce bottles and containers with their implants is one of the most haunting and shocking X-Files moments – ever. In short, unforgettable.
X-TRA: Scully discovered her implant whilst passing through a metal detector in "The Blessing Way". More light was shed on the chip in "Memento Mori", where she learned that she was dying from cancer. She was close to death in "Redux II" but miraculously her illness went into remission.

16 THE MURDER OF MULDER'S DAD

EPISODE: "Anasazi" (2x25)
WHAT HAPPENS: Bill Mulder is murdered in his own house by Alex Krycek. He dies in his son's arms, begging forgiveness.
WHY IT'S SO COOL: So close to the truth, this is yet more pain for Mulder to endure. Just how much more heartache can one man take?
X-TRA: Let's face it, you really wouldn't want to be related to Mulder and Scully. Mulder's sister disappeared, his dad was murdered and Scully's sister was also murdered (in a case of mistaken identity).

16

15 MULDER AND SCULLY'S ICY CONFRONTATION

15

EPISODE: "Ice" (1x07)
WHAT HAPPENS: Paranoid over who may have been infected by an alien parasite, Mulder and Scully draw their weapons on each other.
WHY IT'S SO COOL: Dramatic, intense and riveting, this is the first moment where we see their faith in one another really tested – and their trust.
X-TRA: It's not the only time Mulder and Scully have drawn their guns on one another. Scully shot Mulder in "Anasazi", and they repeatedly shot one another (sort of) in "How the Ghosts Stole Christmas".

14 SCULLY'S SOLILOQUY

EPISODE: "Max" (4x18)
WHAT HAPPENS: Toying with the Apollo 11 keyring Mulder gave her for her birthday, Scully takes a moment to reflect on recent events; their personal repercussions and the meaning of life.
WHY IT'S SO COOL: While some mythology episodes tend to lack a sense of closure, "Max" features a truly powerful conclusion. Scully delivers a truly breathtaking, exquisitely written soliloquy about life, sacrifices and dreams. One of those moments that really brings a lump to your throat.
X-TRA: "... that what can be imagined can be achieved... that you must dare to dream... but that there's no substitute for perseverance and hard work... and teamwork... because no one gets there alone...."

13 THE DEATH OF SCULLY'S FATHER

EPISODE: "Beyond the Sea" (1x12)
WHAT HAPPENS: Scully wakes up to see her father sitting opposite her in her living room – and then he disappears. Moments later, her mother rings to tell her that her father has died of a massive heart attack.
WHY IT'S SO COOL: An extremely eerie moment in what turns out to be a seminal episode for Scully. Really the first opportunity we got to see Gillian Anderson completely act her socks off!
X-TRA: As much a sceptic as Mulder is a believer, "Beyond the Sea" is an interesting and inspired reversal of roles as the show continues to experiment with its formula. The closing scene, with Scully seeking solace at Mulder's hospital bedside, telling him that she can't believe because she is afraid to, is beautiful and touching.

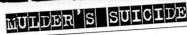

12 MULDER'S SUICIDE

EPISODE: "Gethsemane" (4x24)

WHAT HAPPENS: Mulder dies from a self-inflicted gunshot wound to the head!

WHY IT'S SO COOL: The cliff-hanger of all cliff-hangers! Mulder's apparent suicide is a real shocker. The sight of our hero, tearful, a broken man is almost too much to bear. The wait for Season Five is torturous.

X-TRA: It's not the first time either of the agents has 'died' or come close to death. Check out Mulder in "Colony"/"End Game", plus Scully was close to death following her abduction in Season Two. And they both got blown up repeatedly in "Monday".

AND: If you like this (you sicko!) you'll also like Mulder on the edge in "Ascension", "One Breath", "Demons" and "The Sixth Extinction".

11 THE DEATH OF X

EPISODE: "Herrenvolk" (4x01)

WHAT HAPPENS: Having been set up, X is murdered in cold blood. As he bleeds to death he manages to scrawl the letters SRSG in his own blood.

WHY IT'S SO COOL: X wasn't a particularly likeable guy, but even in death he proved an invaluable ally by leaving Mulder a message which would lead him – and us – another step closer to the truth about his sister. Plus, it was a pretty amazing death scene!

X-TRA: X made his first appearance in "Sleepless", although originally the character was to have been played by a woman. Other informants have included Senator Richard Matheson and Marita Covarrubias.

10 SCULLY LEARNS THAT SHE HAS A DAUGHTER

EPISODE: "Christmas Carol" (5x05)

WHAT HAPPENS: Scully gets a surprising Christmas gift. DNA tests delivered by a courier on Christmas morning confirm that three-year old Emily Sim is her daughter!

WHY IT'S SO COOL: This cliff-hanger really comes out of the blue! After all, Scully is unable to conceive. No wonder she's virtually speechless – and so are we!

X-TRA: Emily was Scully's first child. Not conceived by natural circumstances, but rather a scientific experiment, Emily's young life was cut short when she became ill and slipped into a coma and died. Although she lost Emily physically, it wasn't until "All Souls" that Scully was able to let go of her emotionally.

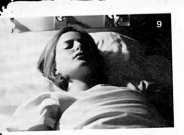

9

09 SCULLY BREAKS TRAGIC NEWS TO MULDER

EPISODE: "Memento Mori" (4x15)

WHAT HAPPENS: Mulder receives shattering news when Scully reveals that she has cancer; an inoperable tumour.

WHY IT'S SO COOL: "Memento Mori" provides us with a hauntingly beautiful insight into a horrifying condition; a condition that's far more terrifying than any 'X'-file could ever be. The bond between Mulder and Scully has never been stronger, and this shocking and surprising plot development is as heart-rending as it is brave.

X-TRA: Scully should be well-accustomed to hospital food by now. She was hospitalized in "One Breath", "Redux II", "The Red and the Black", "Tithonus", "Requiem", "Within" and "Alone".

9

08 SCULLY IS ABDUCTED BY DUANE BARRY

EPISODE: "Duane Barry" (2x05)

WHAT HAPPENS: Former FBI Agent and alien abductee Duane Barry breaks into Scully's apartment, before brutally attacking and abducting her.

WHY IT'S SO COOL: Where did that come from?! Although the Scully-in-peril scenario occurs in many X-Files episodes, her sense of helplessness here is quite simply overwhelming, making this edge-of-your-seat stuff.

X-TRA: Scully's abduction was an ingenious ploy by the writers, working around Gillian Anderson's real-life pregnancy.

AND: If you like this you'll also like Scully in peril in "Irresistible", "Our Town" and "Orison".

7

07 A DEADLY GAME OF RUSSIAN ROULETTE

EPISODE: "Pusher" (3x17)

WHAT HAPPENS: Robert Modell, a man capable of imposing his will on others, engages Agent Mulder in a deadly battle of wits and will.

WHY IT'S SO COOL: Tense and riveting, this dramatic climax is made all the more fascinating due to the relationship cultivated between Mulder and Modell. Plus, Mulder's self-destructive nature has never been more apparent.

X-TRA: Shipper alert! Right at the end of the episode, after all Modell has put them through, Mulder and Scully tenderly hold hands.

6

6

06 SCULLY'S CLOSE ENCOUNTER

EPISODE: "The Red and the Black" (5x14)

WHAT HAPPENS: Scully undergoes hypnosis in an attempt to remember what happened to her and Cassandra Spender.

WHY IT'S SO COOL: Even if she doesn't remember, Scully has seen a UFO! It's an extremely emotional journey for Scully and quite a gut-wrenching moment watching the vulnerable agent clearly very distressed.

X-TRA: Mulder has seen UFO activity more times than he can probably remember – check out "Deep Throat", "Fallen Angel" and "Paper Clip". But he got his closest encounter ever in "Requiem".

SCULLY LEARNS SHE HAS CANCER — 05

EPISODE: "Leonard Betts" (4x14)
WHAT HAPPENS: After her close encounter with cancer-eating Leonard Betts, later that same night Scully wakes up coughing, shocked to discover blood on her pillow and her nose bleeding profusely.
WHY IT'S SO COOL: The look on Scully's face says it all: her worst nightmare is only just beginning. It heralds a major turning point for both Scully and the series. Never have we been left hanging onto such a shocking, disturbing and unresolved ending. Are they really going to do this to Scully?!
X-TRA: Leonard Betts is one of *The X-Files'* most disgusting monsters, ranking up there alongside the likes of Eugene Tooms, Virgil Incanto, and the Flukeman.

5

3

4

4

4

04 — A DEADLY 3-WAY STANDOFF

EPISODE:
"The Blessing Way" (3x01)
WHAT HAPPENS: It's Scully versus Skinner – guns drawn.
WHY IT'S SO COOL: Okay, we've just been shocked by seeing Melissa Scully getting gunned down, and now we've got an even bigger shocker. An unstable Scully; Skinner's allegiance in doubt; it's time to trust no one in another great cliff-hanger.
X-TRA: For the most part, Skinner has always appeared to be Mulder and Scully's only real 'ally' in the bureau. But there's always been an air of doubt about him, no matter how hard you try to shake it. It's almost as if he's got a hidden agenda. You're never quite sure just who is pulling the strings.

03 — CLOSURE FOR MULDER

EPISODE: "Closure" (7x11)
WHAT HAPPENS: Mulder encounters a group of ghostly children playing in the woods, one of whom is his sister, Samantha.
WHY IT'S SO COOL: A powerful scene, both visually and emotionally. This moment is all about death and acceptance; Mulder coming to terms with his loss, and becoming free of his pain. If another X-Files episode had never been made, this would have been a fitting way to conclude the series.
X-TRA: Boasts a cool Moby soundtrack. The track in question is 'My Weakness', which features on Moby's album *Play*. Yet another Moby song, 'The Sky is Broken' appears in the episode "all things".

02 THE DEATH OF DEEP THROAT

EPISODE: "The Erlenmeyer Flask" (1x23)

WHAT HAPPENS: Deep Throat is gunned down by the mysterious Crew-Cut Man. Before dying in Scully's arms, he warns her to "Trust no one".

WHY IT'S SO COOL: The first season finale ends with shocking ramifications; as a result the X-files division is shut down and Mulder and Scully are separated. Even more importantly, the viewers learn that no character – however important they may seem – is indispensable on this show.

X-TRA: Deep Throat first appeared in the titular second episode of the first season. In "E.B.E." he revealed more about his intentions for helping Mulder. Although deceased, the character has turned up occasionally in the likes of "Musings of a Cigarette-Smoking Man", "Talitha Cumi" and "The Sixth Extinction".

01 "BAD BLOOD". THE WHOLE EPISODE. NUFF SAID.

EPISODE: "Bad Blood" (5x12)

WHAT HAPPENS: Mulder and Scully are in big trouble! The FBI faces a $446 million lawsuit following the death of a teenager whom Mulder suspected of being a vampire. In order to get their stories straight, Mulder and Scully go over the events. Their recollections, however, couldn't be more different!

WHY IT'S SO COOL: From the teaser to its closing scene, "Bad Blood" is absolutely hilarious. The 'he said, she said' spin gives maximum comedic effect. Arguably The X-Files' finest hour!

X-TRA: The X-Files has always been great at reinventing itself and challenging our expectations. But who would have thought a show about aliens and monsters would have made comedy such a vital part of its repertoire?

OTHER GREAT TV TIE-IN COMPANIONS FROM TITAN

**Buffy - The Slayer Collection:
Welcome to the Hellmouth**
On sale now
ISBN 9781782763642

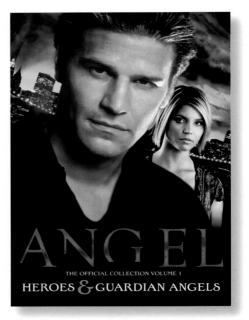

**Angel - The Official Collection Volume 1:
Heroes & Guardian Angels**
On sale now
ISBN 9781782763680

COMING SOON...

**The X-Files - The Official Collection Volume 2:
Little Green Men - Monsters and Villains**
On sale March 2016
ISBN 9781782763727

For more information visit www.titan-comics.com